AF479271

Beyond devolution and decentralisation

Manchester University Press

DEVOLUTION series
series editor Charlie Jeffrey

already published

Devolution has established new political institutions in Scotland, Wales, Northern Ireland, London and the other English regions since 1997. These devolution reforms have far-reaching implications for the politics, policy and society of the UK. Radical institutional change, combined with a fuller capacity to express the UK's distinctive territorial identities, is reshaping the way the UK is governed and opening up new directions of public policy. These are the biggest changes to UK politics for at least 150 years.

The *Devolution* series brings together the best research in the UK on devolution and its implications. It draws together the best analysis from the Economic and Social Research Council's research programme on Devolution and Constitutional Change. The series will have three central themes, each of which are vital components in understanding the changes devolution has set in train.

Between two Unions
Europeanisation and Scottish devolution
Paolo Dardanelli

Territorial politics and health policy
UK health policy in comparative perspective
Scott L. Greer

The English Question
Robert Hazell

Devolution and electoral politics
Dan Hough and Charlie Jeffery (eds)

1 **Delivering public policy after devolution: diverging from Westminster**: Does devolution result in the provision of different standards of public service in health or education, or in widening economic disparities from one part of the UK to another? If so, does it matter?

2 **The political institutions of devolution**: How well do the new devolved institutions work? How effectively are devolved and UK-level matters coordinated? How have political organisations which have traditionally operated UK-wide – political parties, interest groups – responded to multi-level politics?

3 **Public attitudes, devolution and national identity**: How do people in different parts of the UK assess the performance of the new devolved institutions? Do people identify themselves differently as a result of devolution? Does a common sense of Britishness still unite people from different parts of the UK?

Beyond devolution and decentralisation

Building regional capacity in Wales and Brittany

Alistair Cole

Manchester University Press

Manchester and New York

distributed exclusively in the USA by Palgrave

Published by Manchester University Press
Oxford Road, Manchester M13 9NR, UK
and Room 400, 175 Fifth Avenue, New York, NY 10010, USA
www.manchesteruniversitypress.co.uk

Distributed exclusively in the USA by
Palgrave, 175 Fifth Avenue, New York,
NY 10010, USA

Distributed exclusively in Canada by
UBC Press, University of British Columbia, 2029 West Mall,
Vancouver, BC, Canada V6T 1Z2

British Library Cataloguing-in-Publication Data
A catalogue record for this book is available from the British Library

Library of Congress Cataloging-in-Publication Data applied for

ISBN 0 7190 7092 9 *hardback*
EAN 978 0 7190 7092 1

First published 2006

15 14 13 12 11 10 09 08 07 06   10 9 8 7 6 5 4 3 2 1

Typeset by Servis Filmsetting Ltd, Manchester
Printed in Great Britain
by Biddles Ltd, King's Lynn

Contents

List of tables

Preface

Beyond Devolution and Decentralisation has been a long-standing enterprise, conceived in 2000 and begun in earnest in 2001. The research project upon which the book is based was financed by the Economic and Social Research Council under the title of 'Devolution and Decentralisation in Wales and Brittany' (Grant number L 219 25 2007). I thank the council for its support. With assistance from colleagues on the research project, a total of 104 interviews in Wales and 101 interviews in Brittany were conducted from April 2001 to March 2004. These interviews were taped and transcribed, and lasted between thirty minutes and one hour. Thanks are due to all the interviewees in the two countries for their co-operation. Beyond that Market Research Wales and Efficience 3 were commissioned to carry out a comparative public-opinion survey in Wales and Brittany in June and July 2001. A representative sample of around 1000 (1008 in Wales, 1007 in Brittany), selected by quotas of age, gender, socio-economic group and locality, was interviewed in each region.

Beyond Devolution and Decentralisation compares the politics, policies and polity building dynamics of devolution in Wales and decentralisation in the French region of Brittany. Through investigating two historic regions (Wales and Brittany) in two neighbouring European Union states, the aim was to achieve a deeper understanding of processes of comparative regional governance in Europe. Empirically, the book draws conclusions from in-depth fieldwork within the two regions and reports the findings of the comparative opinion survey. Theoretically, the intent was to contribute a fascinating comparative case study to the understanding of the various dimensions comprising regional political capacity.

Comparison of Wales and Brittany plays itself out at a number of levels, each of which has a rather different intellectual rationale and supporting body of literature. This study seeks to establish comparative dynamics in Wales and Brittany. What weight should be given to national institutional traditions in both countries? How important are regionally specific explanations and how can these be conceptualised? Can distinctions be drawn between policy issue-areas (regional languages and training) and, if so, what does this tell about the operation of regional institutions in the two countries? What lessons can policy-makers draw from observing practice elsewhere? How does public opinion view the prospect of greater regional autonomy, and what are the acceptable parameters within which public policy is formulated in the two regions? Throughout the book, empirical answers are sought for these questions of comparative analysis.

In addition to the mass survey, the research endeavoured to uncover the dynamics of devolution in Wales and decentralisation in Brittany through extensive face-to-face interviews. These interviews were semi-structured, combining a small number of routine questions with a range of institutional and policy-specific questions aimed at attaining a maximum of information in areas of great technical complexity and institutional uncertainty. This method was especially pertinent in Wales, due to the new institutional framework put into place by devolution. I sincerely thank everybody who agreed to be interviewed during the 2001–2002 period, a formative stage in the development of the devolved institutions in Wales and a period of expectation in Brittany as well.

I would like to record my sincere gratitude to the following people, all of whom contributed to the development of the project and freely gave up their time: Gaelle Abily, Thierry Acquitter, Martine Allais, Michel André, Olier ar Mogn, Loiag ar Roc, Yannig Baron, Lorraine Barrett, Pierre Baudewyns, Maurice Baylé, Michel Bellion, Graham Benfield, Chris Bettinson, Mark Beynon, Mike Bialyj, Pierre Blanc, Sylvie Blottière, Christian Bonnet, Nick Bourne, Pierre Boyer, Jean Brihault, Fanch Broudig, Paul Bullock, Eleanor Burnham, Henri Bussery, Marcel Calvez, Lauro Capdevila, Daniel Carré, Denis Cassell, Anna Vari Chapalain, Christine Chapman, Geneviève Chignac, Des Clifford, Helen Conway, Jacques Cosquer, Jean-Yves Cozan, Richard Crawshaw, Jean-Jacques Creac'h, Cynog Dafis, Daniel David, Jane Davidson, Byron Davies, Glyn Davies, Jocelyn Davies, Ron Davies, Josselin de Rohan, Marc Debène, Annick Decrop, Patrick Délorme, Christian Demeure-Vallée, Gwendal Denez, Per Denez, Michel Denis, Alasdair Denton, Philippe Desnos, Shelia Drury, Jean Claude du Chalard, Elisabeth Dupoirier, Mel Edwards, Daffyd Elis Thomas, Ieuan Ellis, Delyth Evans, Emyr Evans, Jenny Evans, Phil Evans, Chris Farrow, Francis Favereau, Anne Fayolle, Yvette Folliard, Jo Fontaine, Eve Fouilleux, Yann Fournis, Yves Fréville, Gérard Gauthier, Olivier Geffroy, Mike German, Bernard Gestyn, Yvonnig Gicquel, Russell Goodway, Alain Gourves, John Graystone, John Griffiths, Miriam Griffiths, Ifor Gruffydd, Annick Guillou-Moinard, Christian Guyonvarc'h, Christine Gwyther, Gareth Hall, Tony Harris, Alain Hellard-Goff, Edmond Hervé, Stephen Hutchinson, Mark Isherwood, Glenville Jackson, Yvon Jacob, Philippe Jacq, Charlie Jeffery, David Jenkins, Pippa John-Clarke, Alun Ffred Jones, Barry Jones, Elin Jones, Gareth Jones, John Walter Jones, Sir Harry Jones, Tom Jones, Jean-Louis Jossic, Jacques Kergoat, Marc Kerrien, Riwanon Kervella, Tim Key, Shelaagh Keyse, Milica Kitson, Marie Knox, David Lambert, Alain Lancelot, Jean-Louis Latour, André Lavennant, Peter Law, Ronan le Coadic, Jean-Yves Le Drian, Alain Le Gal, Patrick Le Galès, Bernard le Nail, Ronan Le Prohon, Michèle le Roux, Pierre Le Treut, Marylise Lebranchu, André Legrand, Renaud Lemaire, Jacques Leroy, Huw Lewis, Andrew Lincoln, Lena Louarn, Tangi Louarn, Sean Loughlin, Paul Loveluck, François Madelain, Pierre Malrieu, Gérard Marcou, Anne Marek, John Marek, Jean-Pierre Marholtz, Alan Marin, Joseph Martray, Georges McKechnie, Pierre Méhaignérie, Philippe Merrien, Rozen Milin, Stefan Moal, Jonathan Morgan, Rhodri Morgan, Tom Morgan, Yves Morvan, Paul Murphy, Marie Navarro, Erik Neveu, Peter Normann, Marie-Renée Oget, Jean-Pierre Orhan, James Osborne, John Osmond, François Pannetier, Steve Pantak, Leslie Parfitt, Laurence Park, Simon Pascoe, Isabelle Payoux, Michel Phlipponneau, Mike Pierce, Gilles Pinson, Bernard Pivette, Steven Place, Gerard Poidevin, Steve Pomeroy, Gérard Pourchet, James Price, Helen Prosser, Alun Pugh, François Quéré, Matthew Quinn, Gareth Rees, Terry Rees, Soazig Renault, Llew Rhys, Loic Richard, Nia Richardson, Alain Rissel, Jean-Louis Robert, Henry Roberts,

David Rosser, Bernadette Rouvière, Jan Royall, Meurig Royles, Joseph Salvi, Olivia Schofield, Karen Sinclair, Marie-Pierre Sineau, Anne Stevenson, Alan Storer, Chris Thomas, Mike Thomas, Rhodri Glyn Thomas, Richard Thomas, Jean-Pierre Thomin, Alan Tillotson, Jane Timmins, Bernard Toulemonde, Christian Troadec, Caroline Turner, Jean-Yves Veillard, Luc Vivier, Sir Adrian Webb, Daffyd Whittall, Daffyd Wigley, Colin Williams, John V. Williams, Phil Williams and Rhodri Williams.

Special thanks go to my colleagues on the ESRC project Barry Jones, Sean Loughlin and Colin Williams, as well as to my three research assistants: Alan Storer, who assisted me in interviews across Wales in 2001/2002; Nia Richardson, who efficiently organised the conference on 14 March 2003 which brought the Welsh and Breton regional leaders together; and Yann Fournis, who carried out some fascinating interviews in Brittany. As usual, most thanks go to Caroline, for her unbearing patience. Mind you, she did get something in return . . .

Alistair Cole, Cardiff, 27 January 2005

1

Regional capacity building in Europe

Much of the devolution debate in Wales has centred upon the uniqueness of Welsh constitutional arrangements and political traditions. There has been a strong temptation to resort to a form of Welsh exceptionalism to explain the emergence of the new Welsh quasi-polity. A comparative dimension facilitates a just appreciation of what really is distinctive within Wales and which trends are more generally applicable in similar regions. In *Beyond Devolution and Decentralisation*, the intention has been to deepen the understanding of processes of comparative regional governance by investigating two highly distinctive regions (Wales and Brittany) in two neighbouring European Union states. The term 'region' is used as a generic phrase to facilitate comparison within and beyond France and the United Kingdom, with the acknowledgement that in Wales, and to a lesser extent in Brittany, this term is a contested one. The binary Wales-Brittany comparison does not pretend to exhaust the possibilities of other comparisons. The empirical focus is only on two regions, and generalisation from two cases is hazardous. But there are compensatory advantages with the preferred binary method. Focusing on Wales and Brittany allows a mix of qualitative, quantitative and comparative analysis unavailable to a larger set of cases. From the outset, the position is taken that the comparative case-study method allows for in-depth comparisons which would be unrealistic with a larger number of cases (see Ragin, 1987).

The general context of the study is one of the reconfiguration of European states proclaimed in the abundant academic literature on governance (see Cole and John, 2001 for a summary). Though the state remains a key player, it has everywhere been undergoing a process of restructuring. In contemporary European societies, the classic institutions of government have had to adapt to new types of endogenous and exogenous demand, to the emergence of new stakeholders and changing political agendas (Keating, Loughlin and Deschouwer, 2003; Kooiman, 2003; Le Galès, 2002; Pierre, 2000; Rhodes, 1997). These changes have challenged the authority of central governments, even in traditionally unitary states such as France and the

United Kingdom. All governments have been confronted with a weakening capacity to steer society by proposing solutions to the problems they have identified. Modern states of very different traditions have felt the need to develop new policy instruments and management philosophies to meet these challenges. There is an obvious link between the reform of the state and territorial capacity building. There has been a general tendency for states to institutionalise a meso-level of public administration, usually at first to achieve a more effective implementation of central government objectives. These meso-level public administrations have sometimes provided institutional capacity for the development of more autonomous forms of regional governance.

In this book, interest is primarily (though not exclusively) with the meso-level. Defining levels is, of course, a hazardous exercise, most especially in relation to regions which, more than localities, nation-states or international regimes such as the European Union, have a certain virtual quality (Le Galès and Lequesne, 1998). The identification of a European regional space consistently runs up against operational difficulties. There is no single level of regional government in Europe. For the purposes of the present comparison, 'region' is understood as being a meso-level of (actual or potential) public administration and site for political exchange.

This introductory chapter elucidates the general research question: that of regional capacity building, beginning with a brief overview of the literature on new regionalism, one of the most popular approaches over recent years. Next, a framework for studying regional political capacity is developed, followed by a brief presentation of regionalism elsewhere in Europe, focusing mainly on those countries which Breton and Welsh interlocutors declared to be their main comparators. Finally, there is a definition of the main dimensions of the Wales-Brittany comparison to be developed in subsequent chapters.

The new regionalism

The manner in which the regional question has been conceptualised, and political and public policy approaches to it, have varied quite considerably since the 1960s. In many European countries, regions were initially considered to be backwards, the antithesis of the modern nation-state building project. In the United Kingdom, one of the driving motivations of imperialism in the late nineteenth century was to cement a sense of British identity, over and beyond a feeling of belonging to the component nations of the Empire. Modern French identity was even more systematically founded upon a refusal to accept provincial or regional diversity. The French regions officially created in 1982 were the first new institutions created since the French Revolution of 1789. We observe similar trends in most other European countries. Germany was unified as a federation in 1871, but Prussia was so dominant that other states were cowed into subservience. Regionalism in Italy fell foul of national unification and later of fascism. Post-war Italy contained provisions for regionalisation in the 1946 constitution, but these lay dormant until the late 1990s. In Spain and Portugal, civil war and/or authoritarian political leadership crushed regional diversity. Only after Franco's death did modern Spain reinvent itself as a decentralised, multinational state. Much earlier, west Germany had been resurrected as a semi-sovereign state in 1949 with a federal constitution, designed to check the re-emergence of a powerful central authority. After unification in 1990, Germany's model of co-operative federalism was applied to the five *Länder* of the former East Germany, as well as the 11 remaining in the western part of the country.

New regionalism focuses upon the role of local and regional actors in constructing communities, building institutions and developing capacity. While the rich literature on governance above all emphasises structural change, new regionalism places more emphasis on human agency. Advocates of the new regionalism insist upon the importance of territorial politics in the emerging European polity. Keating, Loughlin and Deschouwer (2003) identify five general trends converging to underpin the new regionalism debate. As thorough an exposition as any other, these will be considered briefly here and referred to throughout the book.

The first trend identified by Keating, Loughlin and Deschouwer (2003) relates to the *crisis of the model of top-down state territorial management*. Almost everywhere, regions first emerged in the 1960s as units of administrative decentralisation. In the area of economic development, the emphasis was on state-led modernisation and planning. The State intervened to create regional development poles and direct industrial investment to regions in difficulty. The regional level was the one considered most appropriate at which to iron out territorial disparities, unacceptable in the context of the Welfare State. The State made few concessions to accommodate the cultural and linguistic specificity of regions. By the 1990s, the 'regional question' came to be formulated quite differently from that during the early 1960s. By this time, the top-down regional policies of the Keynesian state had given way to a new bottom-up model of regional development, based on notions such as the 'innovative' or 'learning' regions, where regions became political actors in their right. Although there was some early interest in the notion of a 'Europe of the Regions', this soon gave way to the more modest proposition that regions (and other sub-national authorities) are now key players in a wider system of European governance. New regionalism signifies first and foremost the development of regional capacity, whether conceived of in terms of stages of development (Loughlin, 2001), development coalitions (Keating, 1998), regional 'regimes' (John 2001) or powerful regional political institutions.

The second theme, introduced above, relates to the effects of *economic globalisation*. The classic nation-state was based on the idea of an all-embracing state national identity rooted in cultural and civic axes. Globalisation, as well as internal change, have corroded such a neat fit between state and nation. Summarising the complex and highly abstract debates about globalisation is not proposed here. Globalisation can be sub-divided into three categories: the 'hyper-globalists' argue that the nation-state is dissolving, faced with the pressures of globalisation (see Clift, 2003); the sceptics see not much difference (Hirst and Thompson, 1999); the transformationalists see globalisation as important, but difficult to predict. There are conflicting opinions between those who argue that globalisation is devoid of any link to territory and those who favour theses of 'glocalisation'. Keating and McGarry (2001) argue that globalisation encourages the expression of new regional identities, as regions offer the most appropriate scale for a collective social consciousness to express itself. The increased importance of territory is not just a debate about distinctiveness, but also one about new forms of interdependence and co-operation within territories.

The type of regional capacity on offer links closely to the third theme: *the rise of regional economic specialisation*. The economic integration of Europe, competition from new regional centres of economic activity and changes in the concentration of multinational firms have all had an impact upon regions and localities. Increased economic interdependence has led to growing competition between and within cities and regions. Economic interdependence has arguably made economic management at the level of the nation-state much more difficult, but it can favour regional or sub-regional cohesion. Cities and regions believe they can influence investment decisions by deliberate strategic actions (Harding 1998). There is, it is argued, a direct link between external challenges and the internal quality of local governing coalitions (John, 2001). Cooke and Morgan (1998) talk of the 'associational economy' characterised by networks, associations, linkages between firms, social groups and government. Putnam (1993) goes furthest, linking local cultures of civic participation, prospects for economic growth and effective democratic performance. Quite apart from their institutional forms, regions are also a principle of organisation in civil society. Regional government works well when civil society is well developed, has a sense of identity, civic traditions, community life and relations of confidence (Putnam, 1993).

The fourth theme of the new regionalism is that of *cultural regionalism*. Everywhere in the old continent there has been a revival of the territorial identities at the local or regional levels (sometimes in competition with each other). Moreno and McEwen (2003) identify the emergence of a 'European cosmopolitan localism', as a new form of territorial mix of traditional and constructed identities. These imagined communities can take variable forms: city-states, regions, small nations. As regions have become socially constructed actors, so there has been a much closer interest in the link between regionalism and various forms of identity, especially culture and languages. In a number of states, minority languages have been revamped and multiple identities have prospered. Compound national identities are now the norm in most EU states. These compound identities can be cohesive or disintegrative, as we illustrate below in the case of Belgium and Spain. At the same time there has been a 'de-ethnicisation' of territory. Ethnic appeals have been de-legitimised, so the territory is presented as involving the experience of those living within it.

The fifth theme identified by Keating, Loughlin and Deschouwer (2003) is that of *top-down functional regionalisation*. There has always been a tension between political decentralisation and state regionalisation. Decentralisation 'entails the exercise of autonomous decision-making concerning a set of political powers by sub-state governments, elected and democratically accountable to the citizens under their jurisdiction' (Moreno and McEwen, 2003: 18). It requires elected Assemblies which can, if necessary, contradict the will of central government in specified domains. State regionalisation, on the other hand, implies no such democratic legitimation and is more concerned with co-ordinating the activities of the state at a local or regional level. Even states traditionally hostile to regional decentralisation (such as France and the UK) have introduced administrative structures to co-ordinate state activities at the meso-level. The Government Offices of the Regions in England correspond neatly to this description, as do the regional prefectures in France. Such efforts of co-ordination are essential if 'regions' are to become eligible for EU funding regimes.

Advocates of the new regionalism and new localism insist upon the importance of territorial politics in the emerging European polity (Keating, 1998; Parkinson *et al.*, 1992). While globalisation and Europeanisation (arguably) challenge national state sovereignties, they might, through the concomitant process of enhancing regional governance systems, strengthen regional identities and vest a new significance to the concept of 'territority' (Loughlin, 2001; Keating, 1998; Cooke and Morgan, 1998). Regional actors assume new roles, functions, challenges and opportunities. The logical consequence of the new regionalism approach is to affirm common purpose through territorial differentiation.

While the governance literature opens interesting avenues of enquiry, new regionalism allows a more precise focus based on regional policy capacity, a theme now to be developed in more detail.

Studying regional political capacity institutions, relationships, identities, constraints

While governance is a useful descriptor for a set of complex processes, we prefer the concept of political capacity as a tool for comparing regions. Political scientists understand capacity in a variety of ways (John, 2001). We use capacity building as a generic term to identify a virtuous circle of resource synergy. Capacity building most obviously comprises regional political institutions, but also involves developing trusting horizontal and vertical relationships. There is a value-added dimension, insofar as good relationships are required to make institutions function effectively and to maximise policy outputs. Insofar as it involves relationships, capacity building is linked with trust and interconnectivity (Brown, Green and Lauder, 2001; Randles, 2001; John, 2001). Capacity is also rooted in identities, which we understand as a compound term for describing historical narratives, representations of community, beliefs and values. Regions are the classic imagined communities in which identities are constructed. Capacity building, finally, takes place within overarching sets of constraints and opportunities, first and foremost that of the relationship with central government.

Thus defined, we understand regional political capacity as an interactive process encompassing institutions and institutional processes, actors and their relationships, socially constructed identities, and forms of overarching regulation (Kooiman, 2003; Le Galès, 2002; Loughlin, 2001; Keating, 1998). Analytically, political capacity can be conceptualised as comprising four closely related but distinct components: institutions, relationships, identities and constraints. Each of these themes is now developed in more detail, a prelude to the in-depth comparative case study.

The study of *political institutions* is arguably the major growth area in contemporary political science. Political scientists have always studied institutions. Old institutionalist frameworks would generally describe organisations in terms of their formal rules and their legal rights and responsibilities (Finer, 1970). There was a sociological variety of old institutionalism, especially well developed in France. In the 1960s, the French Centre for the Study of Organisations (CSO) developed a series of innovative (for the period) 'actor-centred' studies of regionalism and local government. The emphasis of these early studies was upon the strategies adopted by actors within organisations, especially upon how actors were able to bypass formal rules by building networks and developing high-level contacts (Worms, 1966). There was some emphasis on relationships between organisations, but this fell short of what would be understood today as a policy community approach (Jouve, 1995).

What has become known as the 'new institutionalism' was launched by March and Olsen. New institutionalism developed as a reaction to the behaviouralist and rational choice theories that had dominated American political science since the 1960s. It is still running strong in spite of its inherent limitations. There are a number of somewhat contradictory ideas associated with the new institutionalist literature. In various accounts, institutions are understood as organisations, beliefs, historical understandings, incentives for human action or forms of appropriate behaviour (Peters, 1999; March and Olsen, 1989). There is a great deal of elasticity with the concept. Hall and Taylor identified three new institutionalisms in 1996. By 2000, Guy Peters presented six analytically separate versions of new institutionalism. Following Guy Peters (2000), normative institutionalism emphasises the overarching values and prescriptions of appropriate behaviour that provide stability for organisations. Historical institutionalism points to the historical determinants of the life of organisations. Sociological institutionalism stresses actor strategies within and across organisations. Ideational institutionalism emphasises the role of ideas within institutions. Pluralist institutionalism emphasises how groups attempt to occupy positions within institutions. Finally, rational choice institutionalism focuses upon how individuals use organisations in pursuit of their own goals. The value of the new institutionalist debate is to go beyond simply describing institutions in terms of their legal responsibilities. Its main disadvantage is that of concept-stretching: there has been such adjectival inflation that the new institutionalist debate has lost much of its early focus.

However we interpret them, institutions lie at the heart of regional political capacity. The present study draws upon old and new versions of institutionalism. Consistent with old institutionalist traditions lies an interest in the rule-making potential of regional political institutions and their ability to edict norms. From the new institutionalist framework comes an interest in the part played by regional political institutions in the broader development of regional public spheres (especially through their role in embodying collective beliefs and their linkage with popular identities). This approach, then, concerns institutions both as independent and as dependent variables. As independent variables, the intent has been to discover how the selected institutions have made a difference upon policy outcomes and the operation of regional political societies. The chosen institutions are even more interesting when they are seen as dependent variables: has the development of regional political institutions acted as a focus for territorial identities? Have institutions become arenas for the mobilisation of social and economic actors, as argued by Nay (1997) concerning the French region of Aquitaine? How is the operation of institutions shaped by patterns of social capital? These are difficult questions, which can only be investigated by using the comparative case-study approach.

Even with such an expansive definition, institutions do not cover everything. A comparison of regional political capacity must include relationships, identities and constraints, to which attention is now turned.

However far their meaning is stretched, institutions do not explain everything. In terms of building regional political capacity, *relationships* are every bit as important as institutions, perhaps more so. In normative terms, effective regional governance is predicated upon good relationships and shared values, as well as upon powerful institutions. Such presuppositions are present in much (but not all) of the literature on policy networks (Marsh and Smith, 2000; Marin and Mayntz, 1991), on territorial forms of governance (Le Galès, 2002; Keating, 1998; Putnam 1993), as well as in regime analysis (Stone, 1989) and the advocacy coalition framework (Sabatier, 1999). These concepts all involve shared visions and values amongst political, economic and societal decision-makers. Relationships are important since the co-operation of a broad range of actors is required for effective decision-making. Policy stakeholders in complex sectors such as education or economic development are engaged in a series of interdependent relationships. While good horizontal (and vertical) relationships can increase governing capacity, negative-sum inter-organisational rivalries can have a detrimental effect on the quality of policy outputs. If policy networks represent new forms of policy-making to deal with the complexity of modern governance, Richardson (1996) makes good sense in saying that the metaphor of community best captures the close personal linkages between actors involved in relationships in specific policy sectors and/or territories. The early policy-community literature was developed to explain stable interpersonal relationships, as a counterweight to an excessive concentration on formal political institutions such as parliaments (Heclo and Wildavsky, 1974; Richardson and Jordan, 1979). The use of community implies regular personal relationships and shared values.

The classic policy community literature was focused upon vertically organised policy sectors, rather than horizontal territorial communities (Marsh and Rhodes, 1992; Le Galès and Thatcher, 1995). Past research into local and regional policy communities in France and the United Kingdom has emphasised the importance of building trusting relationships across organisations and distinguished between French and British cities on the basis of contrasting patterns of local political leadership (John, 2001; Cole and John 2001). The John-Cole project also drew a distinction between the tightly organised policy sector of education, where territorialisation was complicated by the presence of vertical organisational structures, and the more open, pluralistic networks in economic development. The existence of place-specific influences was in part dependent upon the nature of the policy sector (rooted in places or based on abstract principles), in part upon institutional variables (the provisions for local political leadership) and in part upon the nature of localised relationships. Following from the John-Cole project, Keating and Loughlin (2004) argue that 'a territorial policy community is one where the territorial framework is of primary importance in the construction and frames of reference of that community'. In the use of policy community in Chapter 7, there is comparison of territorial and sectoral policy communities operating in specific issue areas (regional languages, training and lifelong learning) and places (Wales and Brittany).

The third dimension of regional capacity building is that of *identity*, a theme developed in more detail in Chapter 6. From the new-regionalism debate can be drawn a basic distinction between regions as appropriate levels for the delivery of services, and as distinct polities articulating specific territorial identities. Regions can be identified either by differentiation of economic structures, or by specific historical traditions and cultures – or by both. A basic distinction can be drawn between instrumental and identity-based forms of sub-state capacity building. Instrumentalism focuses on the meso-level as the appropriate one for the delivery or co-ordination of a range of services; the identity model looks to regions as historic, cultural and political entities and argues for an institutional focus for identity-based loyalties.

The instrumental approach views the meso-level in functional terms, as the most appropriate one for the strategic co-ordination of lower-level authorities and the provision of middle-range services (in economic development, transport infrastructure, training, sometimes education). The main criterion adopted in the instrumental approach is that of the goodness of fit between levels of public administration and the delivery of particular types of service. The argument is sometimes made that policy fields deemed to be *strategic* – economic planning, regional labour policy, training, the environment, employment – ought to fall within the sphere of responsibility of meso-level authorities. Economic development is usually portrayed as a sphere of regional influence, as are associated strategic activities such as training, the environment and employment. On the other hand, regions rarely have policy responsibilities in the sphere of social solidarity. Welfare-state issues tend to be national, while local social solidarity is municipal. Where *proximity* is the fundamental criterion – in areas such as personal social care, housing, primary education, street cleaning, parks – municipal authorities ought to be vested with responsibility.

Underpinning these arguments is the idea of a goodness of fit between specific issue areas and particular scalar institutional responses. Goodness-of-fit arguments will always be subject to controversy. The overarching characteristic of modern governance lies in its complexity and the refusal of functional problems to respect the boundaries between different levels of public administration. Yet, efficiency arguments have been at the forefront of the most important territorial reforms since the 1980s in the UK, France and elsewhere. The first moves towards regionalism in western Europe in the 1960s were generally of the functional variety, and functional concerns continue to dominate much official thinking in both France and the UK about the justification for regional political institutions.

The identity model starts from a different set of preoccupations. Regions are understood in terms of their historic, cultural or political qualities, rather than those of the functional services they deliver or co-ordinate. The case is made in Chapter 3 for the comparability of the Wales-Brittany pair in part because of the importance of culture and identity. Rather than focusing upon functional services, the identity model views regions as subjects, and investigates the linkage between regionalism and the critical identity markers comprised by culture and language. For Keating (1998) the revival of local and regional cultures is part of a broader process of social change provoked in part by globalisation. Local cultural movements have prospered along with the rediscovery of local and regional production systems and the restructuring of the state. Identity markers can be highly disruptive of existing state formations. In Belgium, the linguistic cleavage has divided society and reshaped political institutions. In Spain, the historic nationalities have contributed to reshaping the party system and creating a powerful dynamic of asymmetrical devolution, which is considered below. In the UK, Welsh and Scottish nationalists combined arguments based on internal colonialism and regional affirmation with those of economic need.

These brief examples demonstrate that there is no single model of regional political capacity. We would reject a straightforward identity-instrumentalist dichotomy. What passes for instrumentalist in one context (for example economic development) might be the founding myth of regional identity in another. The case of Brittany provides some support for this argument. While identity and instrumentalism are not hermetically sealed opposites, they do provide a useful spectrum for comparing different dimensions of regional capacity. The interplay between identity and efficiency is ever present and is combined in varied forms in varying doses in the case studies examined in this book. While some regions are merely administrative creations, others are places of historic identity. There are different configurations of actors and cognitive codes according to region. These cognitive codes influence the ability of regional institutions to make a difference.

The fourth dimension of the framework developed here is that of environmental *constraints* and opportunities. Understanding political capacity building in Wales, Brittany or any other region requires cognisance of the overarching context within which regional institutions operate and the interplay between micro-, meso- and macro-level processes. In the case of Wales and Brittany, there is an identification in subsequent chapters of a number of environmental variables that weigh upon regional political institutions, most notably the legal-constitutional order, financial arrangements, party political ties, the prevalent style of intergovernmental relations and the (limited) opportunities provided by European integration. While these variables can be seen as external constraints, each gives rise to sets of opportunities that can enhance regional political capacity.

This general framework for understanding regional political capacity is relevant beyond the examples of Wales and Brittany. The penultimate section of this introductory chapter considers the case of a number of the regions and small nations in Europe with which interlocutors in Wales and Brittany felt some affinity.

Regions and small nations in Europe

An important part of the new regionalism argument is that local and regional communities are imagined in distinctive ways in different places. Though national paths shape the precise form taken by the new regionalism, the norm in Europe is for an 'asymmetrical configuration of government and a multiplicity of institutional regimes' (Majone, 2003). The structures of regional public administration throughout Europe are highly differentiated. In some states, regions are weak or non-existent, especially where there is a tradition of strong local government, as in the Netherlands, the Scandanavian countries or – for much of its history – the United Kingdom (John, 2001, Keating, 1998). In some of the smaller European Union countries, such as Portugal, Greece or Ireland, there is a tradition of centralisation, which has difficulties in accommodating regions. In the countries of central and eastern Europe, there is no tradition of autonomous regional level administration (Marcou, 2003). During the EU enlargement negotiations, there was much opposition from within these countries to creating new decentralised structures, with the new entrants fearful lest irredentist national minorities try and break away and create their own states.

Though the European Commission started off by advocating decentralisation, it swiftly moved to the idea of centralised 'regional' economic planning. In some countries, regions are principally city regions, based around large cities and their hinterland (Parkinson *et al.*, 1992). Sometimes we refer to provincial regions, as large-scale entities resulting from the division of the state into large units (Le Galès and Lesquesne, 1998). Within the same state, there can be many different regions of varying sizes. In Germany, the three city states – Bremen, Hamburg and Berlin – coexist alongside vast entities such as North Rhine Westphalia, and tiny states such as Saarland. In Spain, there are large regions such as Andalusia and Catalonia, alongside tiny ones such as La Rioja and Cantabria (Keating, 1998). France and the UK also have 'regions' of variable size. Even at the EU level, there are no simple definitions. The EU uses the NUTS criteria, but these are aggregates of national administrative units (Marcou, 2003).

In face-to-face interviews with the representatives of the political and policy communities in Wales and Brittany were uncovered three or four territorial models that attracted particular interest, a theme returned to in Chapter 7. These were Spain, Belgium, Germany and Canada, to which we can add the small Scandinavian nations and Ireland. Depending upon interlocutor, these countries were either models to aspire to or examples to be avoided. In subsequent chapters, regional political capacity in Wales and in Brittany are examined in some detail. As a prelude to this exhaustive investigation, there follows a brief overview of some of the main comparators that focus attention within the policy communities under discussion, beginning this comparative analysis by presenting the cases of Spain, Belgium and Germany – representative respectively of asymmetrical devolution, linguistic polarisation and instrumental federalism – and concluding with a concise summary of viewpoints within both policy communities about Ireland, a star performer and model to emulate.

The *Spanish* model was frequently evoked in interviews in Wales as the ideal solution for enhanced autonomy, including by First Minister Morgan. The Spanish case is attractive for Welsh policy-makers in particular because it appears to hold out the promise of allowing the autonomous development of the 'national region', along the lines of Catalonia or Galicia. The move to democracy in Spain from 1975 onwards was closely linked with accommodating Spain's historic nations and regions and rallying everybody to the democratic cause. The 'State of Autonomies' embodied in the 1978 Constitution represented the most radical regionalisation of any European state at the time. It created 17 Autonomous Communities with far-reaching devolved powers. Catalonia, the Basque Country and Galicia were recognised early on as 'historic nationalities', facilitating their support for the plural Spanish nation.

The Spanish constitution-makers had to square the circle between recognition of historic nationalities and the perspective that, in a decentralised and democratic regime, all regions should be allowed to develop their competencies as and when they felt ready. There is an inherent tension between recognising historic identities and providing the opportunity for all Spanish regions to develop their own institutional capacity within the Union State. In some important respects, the Spanish model does *not* favour the historic nationalities over other regions. The constitution does not establish a hierarchy between the historic communities and the others. In legal terms, any autonomous community can call itself a nation, if it so desires. While during the 1980s, only the three historic nationalities plus Andalusia had proclaimed themselves to be nations, by 1999 there were eight out of 17 autonomous communities recognised as nationalities. Weaker regions have pointedly developed their 'national' identities in order to prevent incorporation by stronger neighbours (the case for Valencia in relation to Catalonia). Devolution in Spain has somewhat artificially provoked a wide range of regionalist demands. Thanks to the devolved institutions, peoples in regions such as Murcia, la Rioja or Extremadura have created their own imagined historical communities. In the case of Spanish devolution, then, can be identified a clear institutional effect. Institutions create a spiral effect and have introduced a race for autonomy, a lesson policy-makers in the UK would be advised to take on board.

In interviews, Spain was identified as a model of asymmetrical devolution, which the UK should aspire to imitate. But asymmetry must be set in context. Apart from one or two exceptions (such as the Basque tax-raising powers) in theory all autonomous communities have the right to exercise the powers of the strongest communities. Since 1995, the weakest communities have caught up with the stronger ones in terms of competencies. The precise list of competencies depends on the organic laws in existence in each of the autonomous communities. In some policy areas, the autonomous community has complete legislative and regulatory powers, not dependent upon the Spanish State. In some areas, there are shared powers, and in still others exclusive Spanish State responsibility. Where there are shared powers, the Spanish State enacts framework legislation and the autonomous communities implement central decisions by their own legislation or regulation. In practice, the autonomous communities determine their own priorities in areas of education, health, culture, territorial management, urban development, tourism and women's affairs. Rather like the devolved authorities in the UK, the autonomous communities have autonomy in managing expenditure, but little autonomy to raise taxes. Spain is still searching for a coherent financial structure and there is bitter opposition by the poorer communities to any measures that would increase regional fiscal autonomy.

Belgium has one of the most distinctive forms of regional governance in Europe. The Belgian regions are highly relevant levels of government (De Rinck, 1998). The three Regions have directly elected parliaments with complete authority in the devolved areas, which encompass almost everything except social security (Baudewyns and Dandoy, 2003). The Belgian case is chiefly of interest for highlighting the disintegrative force of communitarian identities. Belgium was only created as a unitary state in 1830. From the beginning, the Dutch-speaking Flanders and French-speaking Wallonia were differentiated from a linguistic, economic and religious point of view. Flemish regionalism developed out of a sense of Catholic and linguistic identity, as well as a desire for greater social mobility, frustrated because of the traditional French economic and linguistic domination. As early as 1840, the Flemish community began to demand the recognition of religious, socio-economic and linguistic rights. At first, the claim was for Flemish equality with French; this later became a demand for an exclusive use of Flemish in a unilingual Flanders. As Flanders became richer than Wallonia from the 1960s, the Walloons in turn adopted a more autonomous stance.

Faced with the failure of a Dutch 'consociational' model to take root, negotiations engaged in the 1960s eventually in 1993 produced a loose federal state in Belgium. Two parallel models of self-government were created side by side. Since 1963, French, Flemish and German 'language communities' have existed in Belgium; these are institutions vested with control over education, cultural policy and language issues. The basic principle is that the language of the region is the only language for conducting public affairs. In Flanders and Wallonia, Flemish and French are the official languages, while in Brussels both languages have official status. In Flanders (but not in Wallonia), the language community has merged with the regional government to form one institution. For all other issues, separate regional governments (for Flanders, Wallonia and Brussels) deal with most aspects of policy-making. Each of these governments has its own executive, its directly elected parliament and its civil service. The Belgian model, unlike the German, is aimed at giving each level exclusive fields of interest. There is no hierarchy between the levels. The system at best allows for the coexistence of divided communities.

Germany provides a contrast to both Spanish asymmetry and Belgian communitarianism. The Federal Republic of Germany provides the interesting case of a federal system that allows limited room for policy diversity. By imposing federalism upon western Germany in 1949, the occupying Powers sought to reduce the power of central government and ensure a stable democracy. Even after fifty years of operation, there remains something artificial about German federalism. Unlike in a country such as Canada, German federalism does not reflect the organisation of a society with specific minorities. There are no significant ethnic, cultural, social or religious tensions in Germany. Moreover, the 16 state governments (the *Länder*) are artificial units that do not correspond to historic German regions and do not reflect cultural, historic or linguistic differences within Germany. Even after fifty years of institutional existence, Germans feel themselves to be members of a local or a national community rather than a *Land*. Their real attachment to regions is to those based on dialects, customs and culture such as the Rhineland, Palatinate, Badenia or Franconia (Benz, 1998).

All in all, the *Länder* are less autonomous than they appear at first sight. While in the US the institutional architecture promotes institutional competition and a separation of powers, in Germany the emphasis is on sharing power between levels of government. There is a very close interdependency between the federal and the state (*Länder*) governments, the system of 'interlocking politics' described by Scharpf *et al.* (1976). The *Länder* are legally bound into a system of joint decision-making and revenue-sharing, and share a strong normative commitment to policy uniformity. The *Länder* co-operate closely with the federal government in matters of regional economic policy, agriculture and the planning of universities. The *Länder* are closely involved in decision-making at the federal level through the composition of the second chamber, the *Bundesrat*, which has a veto on federal legislation in around 50 per cent of cases. Unlike in Belgium or even in Spain, there is a strict system of fiscal redistribution and most resources for federal governments and the *Länder* come from joint taxes. For all these reasons, there is a greater uniformity of policy in Germany than might be expected in a federal system.

Apart from these examples drawn from EU member states, the most autonomist-minded interlocutors in Wales and Brittany looked to small nation-states within the EU as their preferred models: the small Scandinavian countries (Sweden, Denmark and Norway) and Ireland. The Scandinavian countries were attractive because of their small size, their social-democratic model of society, their socially inclusive mores and their economic success. The case of Ireland above all others exercised a genuine fascination for decision-makers in Wales and Brittany. From an economic-development perspective, politicians in Wales marvelled at the success of the Irish economy since the 1980s, underpinned by Objective One funds, attractive incentives for inward investment and a drive to raise skills. Ireland had succeeded in crafting a successful nation-state with independent membership of the European Union and participation in the Euro. The rise in Irish GDP, to well above the EU average, led decision-makers in Wales and Brittany to pilgrimage to Dublin in search of practical solutions. Apart from these instrumentalist concerns, some autonomists in Wales and Brittany looked to Ireland as a possible model for independent statehood.

These various examples highlight the wide disparities that exist even within states that are considered as models by those favouring enhanced devolution. There are no prescribed parameters for engaging in cross-national comparisons and only loose reference frames can be consistent with the full complexity of case studies.

Studying Wales and Brittany: a roadmap

The ambition of this book is to deepen an understanding of processes of comparative regional governance by investigating two historic regions in two of the European Union's oldest states. The case for the Wales–Brittany comparison is presented in some detail in Chapter 3. Devolution and decentralisation is a comparative work. At various stages throughout the book, the focus of the comparison shifts. At times (especially in Chapter 2), attention is turned to overarching state contexts provided by France and the United Kingdom, two of Europe's oldest states. At others, focus is more squarely upon the internal operation of Wales and Brittany either as quasi-polities, as political arenas or as policy spaces. Rather than limiting analysis to a single dependent variable, mostly an inductive approach emphasising diversity and complexity is adopted (Kooiman, 2003). The various dimensions identified might each be interpreted in a more deductive manner. In Chapter 6, for example, a more explicitly deductive approach is taken when analysing the results of the comparative survey. But, in general terms, the inductive approach is preferred. This methodological choice is consistent with the comparative case-study approach which works best for binary comparisons involving years of fieldwork. In focusing upon two cases, they can be studied in depth. With the choice of Wales and Brittany, two historic regions with complex but strong identities were selected, the comparison thus involving a mix of the 'most similar' and 'most different' methods (Sartori, 1991; Ragin, 1987; Dogan and Pelassy, 1990). Functionally similar regions were selected in order better to elucidate the contextual differences between them.

The Wales–Brittany comparison revolves around three main dimensions of regional political capacity building. The polity-building (institutional) dimension was central to the comparative investigation. The devolved or decentralised political authorities are (relatively) new institutions. How are they viewed by elite groups and by the mass public? Are they perceived as legitimate, effective and accountable? What political dynamics underpin their operation? How have they made a difference? Chapters 4, 5 and 6 seek to provide answers to these linked research questions. The second comparative dimension was that of public policy. Issues of training, education, economic development, agriculture and regional language policy have a high political saliency in Wales and Brittany. They respond to real problems at the forefront of public debate which public-policy-makers have to face in both regions. Chapters 4, 6 and 7 examine similarities and differences in these issue areas. Chapter 7 has a comparison of the political and policy communities in Wales and Brittany, with a special focus on territorial policy communities operating in two distinctive policy sectors (training and lifelong learning and regional languages). The third dimension of the Wales–Brittany comparison is that of the linkage between identities and institutions, a theme addressed in Chapter 6 by means of the comparative survey. The concluding chapter provides an evaluation of devolution and decentralisation in Wales and Brittany, and offers a framework for analysis combining criteria drawn from institutions, relationships, political opportunity structures, identities and regulation.

2
Comparing France and the United Kingdom

Beyond Devolution and Decentralisation is inspired by a long tradition of Franco-British comparison (Lagroye and Wright, 1979; Ashford, 1982; Cole and John, 2001). Whether they are defined in terms of legal frameworks, state traditions or political culture, the UK and France have represented distinctive liberal democratic poles. These two states share sufficient traits in common, however, to make comparison meaningful. In his conceptual map of Europe, Rokkan identified three types of European state: the strong empire-nations of the Atlantic west; the economically weaker states of the eastern plains; and the states of the imperial central Europe, unified only in the nineteenth century (Flora, Kuhnle and Urwin 1999). Both France and the United Kingdom formed part of the Atlantic-seaboard states, with strong central authorities and powerful economic resources.

There were many commonalities, as well as differences, in the process of state consolidation in France and Britain. The idea of citizenship was born in the English Revolution of the seventeenth century, and greatly refined during the American and French Revolutions of the eighteenth century. In both countries, civic identity became transformed into state nationalism in the nineteenth and twentieth centuries. Both France and the UK were long considered as unitary states, with coherent doctrines of undivided political sovereignty that break with the federal tradition (republicanism in France, parliamentary sovereignty in the UK). They are countries of comparable economic and demographic importance with strong senses of their respective historical legacies and continuing world-views. Crucially for our purposes, they are also – historically speaking – centralised states containing within their midst regions with distinctive identities. Today, the UK and France are 'old States' confronted with many similar challenges (of European integration, globalisation and adaptation to post-colonial and post-cold war realities). Most EU states were created through the triumph of one ethnic group over another, and France and Britain are no different from most others in this respect. Nations were built by core hegemonic groups, such as the

Piedmontese in Italy, the English in Britain, the Castilians in Spain, the Franks in France, the Prussians in Germany, the Walloons in Belgium (Moreno and McEwen, 2003). Minority 'nations', such as the Welsh and the Bretons, were assimilated by the dominant group at around the same time (in the early sixteenth century) at the early modern stage of state formation. The contrasting degree of regional autonomy they enjoy today is closely related to the pursuit of opposing models of territorial integration in France and Britain since the eighteenth century.

In comparative European terms, France and Britain are both old states. In both countries, the process of state formation combined military force, constitutional evolution, central affirmation and territorial diversity. In France, the idea of nation was driven from the fifteenth century onward by an ambitious, theoretically absolutist monarchy, which succeeded in imposing its control on a large number of previously independent principalities (in Normandy, Brittany, Aquitaine, Burgundy, Provence, Savoy and so on). In France, the idea of a powerful central authority was deeply embedded in the absolutist monarchy from the seventeenth century onward. In spite of military conquest, diplomatic manoeuvre and civil war, the pre-Revolutionary French monarchy kept the form of a Union state, its constituent parts (such as Brittany) being incorporated by means of treaty and agreement and being guaranteed certain privileges. The convoking of the provincial *parlements* until 1789 embodied these rights, though in practice the power of the *parlements* had waned since the absolutist monarchy of Louis XIV (1648–1715). The French Revolution of 1789 swept away all vestiges of provincial autonomy and created a sophisticated administrative infrastructure whereby the French State penetrated down to the smallest towns and localities. Postrevolutionary France created powerful homogenizing institutions, with an egalitarian institution-focused appeal (the public schools, the army, the Republic). In this way, French nationalism proved highly attractive, including in 'peripheral' regions such as Brittany where state modernization offered the prospect of social mobility (Ford, 1993). In the case of France, the state project was based on transcending archaic, pre-modern identities, and building a modern, unified state-nation, based on respect for universal values. Irrespective of their origins, citizens had a duty to conform to central norms, as they would become peers with equal access to a set of universal rights and obligations. The state-project was deliberately designed to be attractive to provincial elites, for whom ascending to Paris was the height of social achievement.

In the UK, the model of state formation was based on the preservation of traditional elites and respect for regional diversity, rather than the elaboration of a sophisticated state machinery in the provinces. England and Wales were unified in 1532, England and Scotland were only united in 1707 and England and Ireland later still (from 1800 to 1921). The 'glorious revolution' of 1688, which finally destroyed the absolutist monarchy, embedded the dual principles of constitutional monarchy and parliamentary sovereignty. The doctrine of parliamentary sovereignty refers to the sovereignty of the 'Crown in parliament', an arcane formula allowing for strong executive government responsible to a theoretically omnipotent parliamentary assembly. The related doctrines of parliamentary sovereignty and *ultra vires* vest absolute sovereignty on parliament in the abstract, but in practice the British model has been one of limited government. British elites have tolerated social and political differences and, to a degree, territorial variations. Scotland was integrated into the Union in 1707 on the basis of these understandings.

This model became the dual polity, theorised with talent by Bulpitt (1983). For Bulpitt, the dual polity has characterised the British elite's operation and way of thinking since the late 17th century. At the top, the elite was socialised into Parliament and into the civil service, and concerned itself with the core functions of the state. But most day-to-day administration and implementation was left to the localities. Though the centre retained the theoretical oversight of localities and peripheries, it was not worth exercising practical authority over English localities, still less over the peripheral nations. The British model was a function of early modernisation. There was an 'organic interdependence of society and government' (Todd, 2003). Government in the seventeenth and eighteenth centuries did not have the means to transform society, had it wanted to. The model was based on a safeguard of traditional liberties. Moreover, the boundaries of the state were tightly drawn so not to interfere with the free operation of the market and civil society. Regional and institutional exceptions could be accepted without breaching the principle of parliamentary sovereignty. For the peripheries, regional nationalism could coexist alongside political Britishness.

The UK and France are thus shaped by distinctive historical and institutional legacies. The two countries form part of a more general framework for comparing sub-central governments across Europe. Differences in institutions, legal frameworks and political cultures underpin the comparison of British and French local politics (Lagroye and Wright, 1979; Ashford 1982). Writers such as Page (1991) and Sharpe (1993) contrast local government systems across Europe. They distinguish countries with Napoleonic traditions such as France, Spain and Italy, with their strong states and weak local government, from the functionally stronger local governments in states such as Sweden and the UK (Page and Goldsmith, 1987; Page, 1991; Sharpe, 1993; John, 2001). The British and French models have bestowed varying levels of discretion upon local governments (Wunder, 1995). Local government was functionally stronger in the British case than in the Napoleonic French model, but it was less well linked into central government networks. In the British case, the corollary of local autonomy was a separation between the spheres of local and central administration. This was well captured in Bulpitt's metaphor of the 'dual polity', where politicians in the UK centre and the periphery coexisted in two separate policy spheres (Bulpitt, 1983). In the UK, in keeping with its ideology of the limited state, the formal apparatus of the centre was kept small, while service-delivery functions were offloaded onto local government or other public bodies. In France, the state took on a more direct and directive role. Unlike in Britain, the French welfare state was either administered directly by government departments (in education or social welfare) or by social partners (in social security, health and housing), with local authorities reduced to a minor service-delivery function. The counterpart to weak and divided local authorities in France was a pattern of strong peripheral linkage to central government.

The thesis of French and British local divergence was pushed furthest by Ashford (1982) who contrasted centralist and inflexible traditions of policy-making in Britain (dogmatism) with a flexible and negotiated style in France (pragmatism). Ashford's thesis was that the British state was locked into a rigid system of central control: it pushed through dogmatic solutions because it did not have much contact with (and fundamentally distrusted) local government. In contrast, the practice of French central-local relations, revolving around the *cumul des mandats*, was based on the political representation of local interests in central government and resulted in more pragmatic solutions. Ashford's controversial thesis focused attention upon the disdain with which central decision-makers in the UK viewed sub-national administrations. The Ashford model of British dogmatism could be adapted to apply to the Celtic 'periphery'. In the case of Scotland and Wales, the ignorance by central government of territorial interests had dramatic consequences. The Thatcher government (1979–1990) spurned the social consensus upon which the dual polity had rested and sought to construct a Britishness based on commitment to neo-liberal economic modernisation. There was a territorial dimension to this, as southern England appeared to be furthering its interests over the rest of the union. Scottish national identity began decisively to reject the notion of Britishness from the early 1970s onwards. The drive to devolution was given a major boost by the creation of the Scottish constitutional convention in 1988, a cross-partisan forum of political, economic and associative actors advocating a Scottish parliament. Scottish support for independence peaked at around 39 per cent in 1990 – a decisive rejection of Thatcherism. Upon achieving power in 1997, Blair had little choice but to accede to demands for referenda in Scotland and Wales.

Until the early 1960s, neither the UK nor France openly embraced regionalism, considered as either a threat to national unity or an irrelevance. This began to change in the 1960s. The British 'Union State' was never justified with quite the same ideological fervour as the French unitary and indivisible Republic. The deep penetration of the French state into civil society – characteristic of the Napoleonic model of state-society relations – has never had a British equivalent. British empiricism made it easier to engage in forms of functional, then political regionalisation. In the British 'dual polity' tradition, local government traditionally provided and administered services, a role shared with special-purpose agencies, and, in Wales, Scotland and Northern Ireland, with territorial departments. With the exception of the Thatcher period, British responses to territorial pressures involved developing empirical solutions to deal with problems as they arose. Insofar as the Celtic nations of Wales and Scotland were concerned, British governments grudgingly admitted the wisdom of asymmetrical responses. The creation of the Scottish and Welsh offices bore testament to this. There has been no equivalent in the UK to French Republican ideology equating equal treatment with territorial uniformity and hierarchy – though in practice this model prevailed in England. At one level, devolution in Wales can be read as a return to the dual polity tradition of the British State, with the Assembly performing the role of a greatly empowered local authority, vested with strengthened legal, personnel and policy resources, but ultimately dependent for its legal competencies and finance upon the British state.

Even after the 2003 Constitutional reform, which will be briefly considered below, France appears to be the only one of the five major European nations determined to resist a form of polycentric state development on its mainland. Germany, Spain, to a lesser extent the UK and Italy have each undergone developments that can in some senses be labelled as federal, or quasi-federal. In the case of France, though a distinctive form of sub-national governance has evolved, it has been bounded by a powerful coalition of centralising institutions (especially the Council of State), state-centric professional interests (in the teaching unions, for example, or among social workers or tax officers) and widely disseminated ideas equating republican equality with uniformity. For many French citizens, decentralisation is synonymous with social regression, unequal provision, even a return to a pre-republican social order. Upstanding republicans equate territorial uniformity with ideas of progress, equal opportunity and citizenship. The building of France as a modern state-nation provides the key to understanding this equation of territorial identity and political reaction. Almost by definition, regional political formations are suspected, by a certain brand of republican, of anti-republican intent. The French state-building enterprise has, historically speaking, been remarkably successful in inculcating deeply rooted beliefs linking the national territory with social progress. This touches at the core of state sovereignty which, in the French case, is intimately tied in with perceptions of national prestige and territorial hierarchy. French sub-national authorities have traditionally operated within the confines of a highly centralising state tradition, which emphasises the indivisible nature of political legitimacy and the organisational pre-eminence and legitimacy of the state. The revolutionary and Napoleonic periods established the Republican model of territorial integration, which remains important even today.

Devolution in the United Kingdom

The UK model of asymmetrical devolution has produced variable outcomes across the Kingdom: full legislative devolution in Scotland, a (suspended) devolutionary process in Northern Ireland, secondary legislative, or 'executive' devolution in Wales and a commitment to regional referendums in England. From the start, there has been an explicit distinction between the four nations forming the United Kingdom.

The United Kingdom is best described as a Union State, rather than a unitary state. To this extent, James Mitchell (2004) is right in saying that the United Kingdom provides for a curious mix of the Union and Unitary State, the Union State allowing for the development of territorial asymmetry, but the Unitary version, underpinned by a doctrine of parliamentary sovereignty, emphasising the hierarchy of the centre over the periphery. In other words, Scotland, Wales, Northern Ireland and England are subject to rather different rules. Of primary concern here is the case of post-Devolution Wales. Each of the four nations which together comprise the United Kingdom – England, Scotland, Wales and Northern Ireland – has its own distinct histories and political characteristics. Wales was unified with the English Crown as early as 1536 (see Chapter 3), far earlier and more comprehensively than either Scotland or Ireland. When England and Scotland agreed to the Act of Union in 1707, there was an understanding that the Scots would retain their national identity, their Presbyterian Church and their separate education and legal systems. Ireland was united with the British crown in 1800, an unhappy marriage that ended in civil war and partition in 1921. The interested reader will find more details of the Scottish and Irish experiences elsewhere (Todd, 2003). In the 2001 census, the United Kingdom had just under 60 million inhabitants, split unevenly between England (83 per cent of the total population), Scotland (9 per cent), Wales (5 per cent) and Northern Ireland (3 per cent).

Unlike in Ireland during the nineteenth and early twentieth centuries, until the 1960s there was little overt demand for devolved, directly elected political institutions in either Scotland or Wales. Both nations had their own forms of administrative decentralisation (the Scottish and Welsh Offices) which – within limits – allowed for local solutions to be adapted to territorially specific problems. Both nations were dominated politically by a Unionist Labour party which looked to capturing the commanding levers of the British economy, rather than encouraging regional separatism. The political imperatives of Labour at the United Kingdom level (the reliance on the Scots and the Welsh for any Westminister majority) strengthened their natural instinct towards centralisation and their suspicion of devolution. Throughout the nineteenth and early twentieth centuries, the Scots and the Welsh also appeared as beneficiaries of the wider British enterprise, a sense of Britishness being inculcated first by empire, then by economic growth and the welfare state. The Scots (especially) and the Welsh were overrepresented in commerce, the civil service and the imperial army. There was a distinction between Scotland and Wales. In Scotland there was a well-developed sense of dual identity – a Scottish nationality and a British citizenship – along with recognisable national institutions. In Wales, the political sense of dual identity was less strong, as were distinctive Welsh institutions (though these existed). On the other hand, the Welsh language performed a mobilising role that had no equivalent in Scotland.

The complacent unionism of the Labour Party was shaken to the core by the rise of the Scottish National Party (SNP) and Plaid Cymru (PC) in the late 1960s. Scottish nationalism was revived by the discovery of North Sea oil in the 1960s, with the SNP making a strong economic case for independence. Welsh nationalism was originally more focused upon defence of a traditional lifestyle and language which appeared in danger of extinction, a theme developed in the next chapter. In the general context of a nationalist awakening in Wales and Scotland, the Labour governments of 1964–1970 and 1974–79 sought to undermine the nationalists by introducing measures of administrative, then political devolution. The creation of the Secretary of State for Wales and the Welsh Office in 1964 was a major landmark upon the road of distinctive Welsh institutions, a form of administrative decentralisation considered below. In 1967, Labour introduced the first Welsh Language Act. Pressures for devolution (and the victories of Welsh and Scottish nationalists in by-elections in 1969) led to the appointment of the Crowther Commission in 1969, set up to consider devolution in Wales and Scotland. When it finally reported in 1973, the Kilbrandon Commission published a radical report, proposing four options for local self-government. A majority recommended a Parliament for Scotland and an Assembly for Wales, with executive-only powers. A minority went further, arguing for a full legislative Assembly for Wales with its own budget and tax-varying powers and authority over most areas of domestic politics.

Even more dependent upon the Welsh and Scottish nationalists than previously, in 1974 the Labour government produced fresh proposals for Scottish and Welsh devolution. The initial proposals again distinguished between Scotland and Wales. While Scotland would have a full parliament with tax-varying and legislative powers, an elected Welsh Assembly with executive-only powers would be financed by an annual block grant. The bills to create a Scottish Parliament and a Welsh Assembly were given a third reading on 9 May 1978. The referenda took place on 1 March, 1979. In Scotland, a small majority of those voting favoured the proposals, but this fell short of the required 40 per cent of the total electorate. In Wales, only 11.8 per cent of the total electorate supported the Assembly, with 46.5 per cent opposed and the rest abstaining. If the Scottish were, on balance, favourable to devolved political institutions, the Welsh in 1979 remained deeply suspicious, hostile to anything that might hasten independence or threaten the social and economic benefits they already possessed.

Decisively rejected in 1979, devolution in Scotland and Wales re-emerged onto the political agenda in the 1980s in reaction to Conservative policies. Despite being in a small minority in Scotland, the Conservative governments of 1979–1997 were uncompromisingly and provocatively unionist. Under Mrs Thatcher, in particular, Scotland was viewed as experimental territory, a terrain where neo-liberal policy initiatives could be tried and tested. Thus, the community charge (poll tax) was introduced into Scotland one year earlier than in England and Wales. Thatcherism produced mass civic mobilisation within Scotland. The Constitutional Convention, established in 1988, brought together a broad cross-section of actors from Scottish politics and civil society to deliberate upon the future architecture of devolution. The cross-partisan basis of this initiative strengthened its appeal; only the Conservatives were absent. Once elected in 1997, new Labour acknowledged the legitimacy of the Convention, announced a referendum and, shortly afterwards, began the negotiations which would produce the Scotland Act (1998). In the referendum of September 1997, 75 per cent of electors voted Yes to a Scottish parliament, with a slightly lower figure (72 per cent) agreeing that the new Parliament should have tax-varying as well as primary legislative powers. A comfortable majority of the entire Scottish electorate agreed to both proposals. The definition of Scottishness was a civic, rather than an ethnic one: all UK citizens living in Scotland at the time of the referendum had the right to vote (Schlesinger, 1998).

The Scottish parliament is composed of 129 members (MSPs), 73 elected by the first-past-the-post system (along with 73 Scottish seats in the Westminister parliament), with the 56 remaining chosen by a system of proportional representation in eight regions. This mixed system, based on the German model, has made it more difficult for a single party to obtain a majority. In the first elections of May 1999, Labour with 56 seats came in first, ahead of the SNP (35), the Conservatives (18) and the Liberal-Democrats (17). Since May 1997, Scotland has been governed on the basis of a Labour-Liberal Democrat coalition. Devolution in Scotland has produced a multi-party reality and a bargained model of coalition politics, with the reality of coalition having a measureable impact upon Scottish public-policy outputs. Decisions such as free care for the elderly, or the abolition of tuition fees for Scottish students, have been facilitated by the presence of the Liberal-Democrats in the coalition. Though the Labour-Liberal Democrat coalition was severely tested in the May 2003 election, this challenge came about more thorugh the rise of minor parties (the Scottish Socialists and the Greens) than by the resurgence of the SNP.

The devolution settlement in Scotland built upon a large measure of administrative decentralisation. A Scottish Office was created in 1885, headed by a Secretary of State for Scotland, who also represented Scottish interests in the UK Cabinet and negotiated financial transfers with the UK Treasury. The Secretary of State was assisted by several junior ministers. In 1997, the Scottish Office consisted of some 40,000 civil servants, spread across five main bureaucratic divisions. Prior to devolution, the Scottish Office, which directly implemented laws as they applied to Scotland, already had a large measure of autonomy with respect to issue areas such as education, econonmic development, health, agriculture and the environment. Scotland could also count upon a parliamentary commission, the Scottish Grand Committee. Created in 1907, the Scottish Grand Committee brings together all Scottish MPs sitting in Westminister The Secretary of State for Scotland still sits in the Cabinet and still intervenes directly with the Treasury to plead Scotland's case, but the role has lost much of its importance since devolution.

In the Scotland Act, the Scottish parliament was granted primary legislative powers in all areas except those reserved by Parliament for the UK government: namely everything except constitutional affairs, financial relations, foreign policy and defence, the EU, social security and citizenship. Even in the reserved areas, however, the Scottish executive has found ways of influencing UK policy, especially over European Union issues (Carter and Scott, 2003). On the other hand, there have also been overarching binding ties which have limited policy divergence (Mitchell, 2004). Close ties between the Labour leaderships in London and Edinburgh has created a regime of 'no surprises' (Laffin, Shaw and Taylor, forthcoming), an agreement on both sides to forewarn and negotiate. Such a method of behind-closed-doors collaboration is often effective, though there has been some evidence of increased policy divergence with England, in the areas of old-age care and higher education notably. Both sides recognise a large degree of functional and political interdependence. The Scottish executive has relied heavily on the Sewel Convention, whereby Westminister can legislate in areas normally reserved for the Scottish parliament (Trench, 2004). By the end of the first term, almost as many Scottish laws had been passed in Westminster as in Holyrood. The Scottish parliament has not attempted to exercise its tax-varying powers, though complaining of the Barnett formula. Scottish civil servants remain part of the home civil service (Parry, 2001). The calculation made by Blair in 1997 that a large measure of autonomy would weaken the demand for independence has appeared to be sound. Those supporting complete independence from the UK have stabilised at around 25 per cent of the Scottish population and the SNP has been losing ground in elections (McEwen, 2003). A strong case can be made that devolution in Scotland has strengthened the Union State. Strong institutions, well enmeshed into civil society and supported by a cohesive policy community, have embedded Scottish devolution, which has in turn found an acceptable modus vivendi with the UK State.

The Scottish experience is not the only model of devolution. Ulster has had the longest experience of devolved institutions – the Stormont parliament from 1921–1972 – of any part of the United Kingdom (Arthur, 2003). Unlike Scotland or Wales, moreover, Northern Ireland has always had its own civil service (Parry, 2001). Studying devolution in Northern Ireland lies beyond the scope of this study, even in descriptive form. The central *problématique* in Ulster is one of communitarianism rather than that of regional capacity building. The Good Friday agreement of April 1998 and the subsequent majorities in both communities in favour of the agreement were highpoints in Blair's premiership. The 1998 referendum produced a novel form of power-sharing which witnessed real influence being exercised by Sinn Fein and the Catholic community, as well as close collaboration (and co-management of certain issues) between London, Belfast and Dublin. Though power-sharing eventually collapsed in late 2002, the 1998–2002 experience left hope for the revival of an advanced form of devolution at some later date. In the meanwhile, devolution has coincided with a ceasefire and a dramatic scaling down of paramilitary violence.

During the 1997 election campaign, Labour held forth the prospect of creating regional assemblies in England. Once Labour was in power, these proposals were watered down, after strong opposition from Whitehall. Blair's indifference initially appeared to seal the fate of English regions. While in

Scotland and Wales devolution was the political price to pay for the victory, in England new Labour has assiduously courted the new middle classes. There was little overall coherence in the constitutional schema introduced by Blair. In November 1998, the government announced the creation of eight Regional Development Agencies (RDA), indirectly nominated bodies with precise economic-development functions. At the same time, under the pressure of (northern) English devolutionists, the Blair government did not exclude the possibility that these agencies might eventually become directly elected regional assemblies. In 2002, the government's White Paper put into place mechanisms for allowing referendums to take place to determine whether or not to establish regional Assemblies. Yorkshire and Humberside, the North-East and the North-West announced their intention to hold referendums in late 2004. The first of these referendums, in the north-east in November 2004, produced a major setback for English devolutionists, with the proposed elected Assembly being supported by only 22 per cent of voters. The comparisons with Wales in 1979 were obvious.

In the meantime, the RDA are curious hybrid bodies, calibrated more on the model of semi-autonomous agencies than that of directly elected assemblies. Premier Blair was insistent that the English RDA should be led by business interests, that business representatives should occupy at least half of the posts on the governing councils of the RDA, leaving local government, the trade unions and voluntary associations to fight over the remaining places. The RDA are important organisations which have left their mark in the dense meso-level of British public administration. The RDA draw up economic development plans, distribrute grants, promote public-private partnerships, help to negotiate and distribute EU structural funds (where applicable) and advise ministers on enterprise grants and training. Their financial resources are far from negligible (£2B per annum, divided among the 8 RDA). Rather like the Welsh or Scottish offices in the pre-devolution period, however, their legitimacy rests upon their hypothetical transformation into elected regional assemblies.

We might also consider the case of London as a form of devolution to a city region. After the abolition of the Greater London Council in 1985, London became the only major European capital city without political representation. At a fourth constitutional referendum in May 1998 (after those of Scotland, Wales and Northern Ireland), the people of London voted comfortably (72 per cent on a 34.6 per cent turnout) for the creation of a Greater London Authority (GLA) and a directly elected mayor. Ken Livingstone was triumphantly elected as mayor of London in May 2000. The case of London is original insofar as that the London Act (1999) institutionalised a separation of powers between a directly elected mayor and a Greater London Authority composed of 25 councillors (14 returned in new constituencies, 11 elected at the level of London as a whole). The mayor of London alone has the power of proposition in areas of strategic importance, such as urban planning, transport (but not the underground), economic development, the environment. The elected Assembly has the power to block the initiatives of the mayor and has to give its approval for the budget. The explicit separation of leadership and representative functions is novel within the context of English local government. In its first year of operation, the budget of the GLA was more than double that of the National Assembly for Wales, though the functions are far more restrained. The mayor of London cannot impose local income taxes or introduce sales taxes.

From this brief overview can be observed the coexistence of several alternative models of local and regional capacity building within the United Kingdom. These include legislative devolution in Scotland, suspended power-sharing in Northern Ireland, executive devolution in Wales, the strengthening of the city-region in London, the creation of development agencies everywhere else. Most parts of the United Kingdom, however, have shown no particular desire to recreate a meso-level of elected public administration. When voters in the north-east were given the opportunity to choose, they decisively rejected an elected Assembly. This rejection recalls the need for the utmost caution before describing the UK in terms of quasi-federalism or other labels.

Taking the UK as a whole, several distinctive patterns of meso-level administration can be observed. The elected regional Parliaments or Assemblies in Scotland, Wales and Northern Ireland have developed institutional capacity in part because they respond to the identity demands of their populations (or a proportion of them at least). This process is much less complicated in Scotland than elsewhere. The strong sense of national identity observable in Scotland and Wales is obviously a resource for building political institutions. Leaving aside the national cases of Scotland and Wales, it can be noted that territorial identity does not usually produce support for creating regional political institutions. Specifically, the existence of forms of strong urban governance or identification with cities can preclude support for regional Assemblies. Where there is competition between neighbouring cities (Newcastle, Sunderland and Middlesborough in the north-east; Manchester and Liverpool in the north-west; Leeds, Sheffield and Hull in Yorkshire and Humberside), urban concerns prevail over those of rather artificial regions. There is nothing unusual in this. Competition between strong cities and looser but broader political regions is present across the European continent, including that in France, Spain and Italy. As in other comparable countries, regions and cities are in competition with each other. Across England as a whole, there is little support for introducing another level of elected public administration. There is also a serious democratic deficit, however: the low rate of participation in English local elections (around 30 per cent) suggests disillusion with a disempowered local democracy.

This variety of responses is entirely consistent with British empiricism, which has adapted to bottom-up pressures in a pragmatic way. As will be seen later on, such a laissez-faire approach would be much more difficult in France.

Local and regional government in France

French local and regional authorities have traditionally operated within the context of a highly centralising state tradition. In the 'one and indivisible' French Republic, local government units were long considered to be the antennae of central government. The 36,500 municipal councils in the communes and the 96 departmental councils in the *départements* were instruments of central regulation before becoming locally elected authorities. There was a major difference between departments and communes. While the departments replaced the pre-Revolutionary provinces, the communes were based on the parishes of the pre-Revolutionary *Ancien Regime*. The communes remained the foci of local identities and community interests which persisted in spite of the centralising ambition of the Republic. It should also be noted that, during the post-Second-World-War period, the emergence of powerful regional movements – such as the CELIB in Brittany – gradually contested the centralised Jacobin model and the ideology underpinning it.

The pattern of central–local relations known as the French 'system of territorial administration' was a key feature of the traditional French model of policy and politics (Sadran, 1992). It rested upon the principle of administrative uniformity across the nation, and recognised the superiority of central state interests over those of parties, regions, interest groups and localities. It formed part of a hierarchical mode of top-down organisation, whereby public policies originated within government departments or administrative corps, were implemented in localities by state field agencies and local authorities, and were co-ordinated by the prefect, the representative of the French State in the departments. Local influences could be brought to bear in numerous manners. City case studies – such as those of Lagroye (1973) on Bordeaux, Biarez (1989) on Lyons and Lille, Phlipponneau on Rennes (1977) – all emphasised the importance of local actors in mitigating the effects of national policies. There was an incentive for ambitious politicians to accumulate elective offices (*cumul des mandats*) as office gave access to higher levels of authority and consolidated local power bases. But local authorities existed in a state of dependency on central government and genuinely local public policies were rare. The regional layer was non-existent until the 1950s.

Regionalisation in France dates back to the late 1950s, when the French State first established administrative structures in the regions to assist in the strategic functions of economic development, transport and territorial planning. Created as public corporations in 1972, the regional councils have been fully operational, democratically elected authorities only since 1986. They have modest budgets and have been beset by problems of a political nature, themes to be developed in the next chapter. The regions have had neither the organisational heritage nor the political or bureaucratic resources available to the departmental councils. But they have gradually made their institutional presence felt and they have steadily accumulated precise legal responsibilities in economic development, secondary education, training, transport and several other fields. They have used their powers ambitiously and are actively seeking and obtaining new powers. The real problem with the French regions is that they are institutions without a clear link to territory. The process of regionalisation in France bears the hallmarks of the centralising French republican tradition. French regions were created in a standardised form throughout the French territory, including in areas where no regional tradition existed. The Region of the Centre thus enjoys exactly the same prerogatives as Brittany. To institutionalise France's historic regions would be tantamount to admitting the posthumous existence of a union state of the UK variety, rather than the French unitary version. French decentralisation was intended to produce more effective decision-making, not to give rise to regionalist identities.

The regions have not replaced the French State, which has never abandoned its territorial ambitions. Since 1802, the prefect has been the direct representative of the French State in the 96 departments and, since 1964, in the 22 French regions. The creation of the regional prefectures in 1964 was an important staging post in the regionalisation of state structures. Rather like the regions later, the regional prefectures were to be fairly light, strategic bodies which could co-ordinate the activities of the much weightier departmental prefectures. Though the regional prefectures cover, by definition, a much broader geographical area than those based on the department, the latter are more consequential administrative structures. The significance of the regional level, however, cannot be measured merely by quantatitive criteria such as budgets or numbers of staff. The regional prefectures have been the privileged site for co-ordinating bids for EU structural funds (which until recently escaped from direct control by the regions). The regional prefectures are also the main arena for the negotiation of the five-yearly State-Region planning contracts with the regional councils, which are considered in Chapter 5. Insofar as the State-Region plans involve formal negotiations between the French State and the regional councils, they have the capacity to confer leadership on the regional council, over and above the other sub-national authorities. The State-Region plans help to legitimise the idea of a regional public sphere within which numerous organisations interact in a relationship of 'competitive interdependency' (Cole, 2001; Breuillard and Cole, 2003). None of this would have been possible without the decentralisation reforms enacted since 1982, discussed next.

Decentralisation in France, 1982–2004

The French Socialist government's ambitious decentralisation reforms of 1982–83 represented a major challenge to the republican model of territorial administration. The decentralisation reforms of 1982–83 were highly complex. Amongst the numerous laws and decrees, the most prominent decisions involved the creation of directly elected regional authorities as a separate tier of sub-national government; the transfer of executive authority from the prefect to the elected heads of the 96 Departmental councils and 36,500 communes; the right of communes and Departmental councils to set their budgets without prior prefectoral oversight, and the transfer of some staff from the prefectures and the ministerial field services to the Departmental councils. The decentralisation reforms did not, however, alter the basic structure of French local government. This remains a highly fragmented system. Policy-making responsibilities were henceforth divided among three tiers of sub-national authority as well as a varied array of ad hoc and inter-communal bodies. In contrast to the pattern of ongoing change in the United Kingdom, there has been no root-and-branch structural reform of local government in France. Rather, a process of incremental accretion has taken place. New structures have been added to existing ones, without a fundamental overhaul of the territorial system as a whole.

There remains much confusion about the division of policy-making and administrative tasks between central and sub-national units and amongst the local authorities themselves. While decentralising major areas of responsibility, the 1982 laws did not specify clearly which body was responsible for what activity. Education, for instance, is divided between three levels of sub-national administration. The communes manage the primary schools, the departmental councils the *collèges* (11–15-year-olds), and the regional councils the *lycées*. Until 2004 at least, matters of curriculum and staff management remained the policy preserve of the Education ministry, either in the regions (the rectorates and Academic Inspectorates) or in Paris (the central divisions of the Education ministry). There is an ongoing dispute about the extent of the regional councils' authority in matters of substantive educational content, and certain ambitious regions have laid a claim to influence classroom content. The situation in the sphere of training and lifelong learning is even more complicated, as will be developed in Chapter 7. The regional councils are in charge of post-16 training and adult education, but they must contend with the powerful influence of companies, of the social partners (employers and trade unions), of the French state in its regional and central manifestations, and of the employment service. While the Regions have been steadily increasing their influence and control over the whole of training supply, the system is inherently complex.

The various sub-national authorities have overlapping territorial jurisdictions and loosely defined spheres of competence. Even when responsibilities are clear, they are not respected. Communes, departments and regions compete openly with each other and adopt policies designed to appeal to their electorates. Moreover, there is no formal hierarchy between them. In theory, no single authority can impose its will on any other, or prevent a rival authority from adopting policies in competition with its own. Unlike in genuinely federal systems, the French regions do not exercise leadership over other local authorities. If anything, the French regions are dependent upon the co-operation of lower-level authorities – the departments in particular – for the successful implementation of their own policies.

In interviews there was a large consensus that there are too many layers of sub-national administration in France, but it has proved difficult to reform the complex and confusing structure described in Table 2.1. Each reform has added a new layer, but is incapable of dispensing with the old. Recent reforms – the Voynet and Chevènement laws of 1999 and the Raffarin reform of 2002–4 – have been consistent to form. They have introduced new structures (communities of communes, city communities) without fundamentally overhauling the pattern of territorial administration. No French government has genuinely confronted the problem of the relationship between the 96 departmental and 22 regional councils, let alone the various inter-communal and ad hoc structures that exist. Central governments are loath to challenge the role of the departments, because the organisation of the state's own field services – especially the prefectures – remains predicated upon those of the departments. There is, in many respects, an objective alliance of the departmental councils, the prefectures and the central ministries, whose field services operate generally at a departmental, not at a regional level. The state can rely on the departments to be relatively compliant with its own interests – unlike some regions and the communes in larger cities. The departments remain a force of conservation, institutionally if not always politically.

Table 2.1 Sub-national authorities in France in 2002

Type	*Number*	*Functions*
Communes	36,500	Varying services, including local plans (POS), building permits, building and maintenance of primary schools, waste disposal, some welfare services
Voluntary Intercommunal syndicates*	not available	Groups of communes with a single function (SIVU), or delivering multiple services (SIVOM)
Tax-raising inter-communal public corporations (EPCI)* Includes: urban communities; city-wide communities and communities of communes	2174	Permanent organisations in charge of intercommunal services such as firefighting, waste disposal, transport, economic development, housing.
Departmental Councils	96	Social affairs, some secondary education (*collèges*), road building and maintenance
Regional Councils	22	Economic development, transport, infrastructure, state-Region plans, some secondary education (*lycées*)

Source: INSEE 2003–2004 *Tableaux de l'Économie Française* (Paris: INSEE, 2004)
Note: *These organisations are legally considered as local public establishments, rather than fully fledged local authorities

After President Chirac's re-election in 2002, France entered into another period of major institutional reform. Chirac had rallied to the idea of a new stage in decentralisation in a speech in Brittany in 1998. With the Jospin government also undertaking reforms aimed at strengthening local and regional authorities (the 1999 Chevènement law, the 2002 law on Corsica) political circumstances were favourable for a renewed phase of reform. Decentralisation had never left the political agenda, as demonstrated by the ongoing process of incremental reform throughout the 1990s. Surveys such as the one we carried out in 2001 suggested broad support for more decentralisation, but also that further reform was not a high public priority.

Once named Prime Minister, Jean-Pierre Raffarin announced there would be a massive public consultation on the future of decentralisation. In preparation, public meetings (the *Assises des libertés locales*) were organised in all French regions, bringing together over 40,000 people drawn from politics, the voluntary sector, the chambers of commerce, firms and trade unions. These meetings came up with some unexpected results (Reynié, 2004). In total, there were 603 separate submissions by local and regional authorities calling for a transfer of competencies. Most of these concerned education and training (28 per cent), followed by social affairs (24 per cent), infrastructure (20 per cent), economic development (17 per cent) and the environment (11 per cent). On the other hand, the *Assises* also revealed a number of fears: notably that decentralisation would be followed by local tax rises, and that there would be an increased inequality between local areas. Local mayors expressed some concern that a 'regional Jacobinism' would replace the national version: strong regional councils might be less respectful of communal rights than the central state or the departments. Surveys carried out to coincide with the *Assises* were strongly suggestive of public support for the regional level. The *Observatoire Interrégional du Politique* (OIP) carried out a major survey in September 2003, with the largest representative sample ever (13,000 people). The main finding was that the French were very favourable to the transfer of functions to the regional councils: 56 per cent thought health care should be a regional responsibility; 60 per cent thought education should be transferred to the regions and even 48 per cent thought that control over educational diplomas should be a regional priority (Reynié, 2004).

There were four main principles to the constitutional reform adopted in March 2003. It embeds the regions in the Constitution and refers to the decentralised organisation of the Republic. It contains provisions for special statute authorities. It refers to the experimental transfer of functions. It sets out that a 'preponderant proportion' of local government expenditure must be raised by local resources. The original version of the constitutional text, proposed by Premier Raffarin, had proclaimed that 'France is an undivided, lay, democratic, social and decentralised Republic'. On the insistence of President Chirac, the new Article 1 of the constitution now reads: ' France is an undivided, lay, democratic, social Republic. Its organisation is decentralised'. This weaker formulation does not challenge the hierarchical control of the state over its constituent regions and France remains very much a unitary state. Explicitly rejecting federalism, the constitution reaffirms that all territories must be treated according to the principle of equality. The French constitution now recognises four levels of local authority within the constitution: the commune, the department, the region (new) and those with a 'special statute' (new).

The 'special statute' clause covers the various inter-communal bodies that were greatly strengthened in the 1990s (the city communities and the other inter-communal public corporations). It also refers to the eventual merging of existing sub-national authorities into larger units, potentially a radical break with the past. Following adoption of the constitutional amendment, there were calls to merge separate regions into single authorities in Normandy, Savoie, the Rhine, Corsica and Brittany. In Brittany, traditional regionalists called for the Brittany region to recover the 'lost' Loire-Atlantique department and to restore Brittany in its historic boundaries. These demands were counterbalanced, however, by those calling for the creation of a vast western region by joining together the existing Brittany, Normandy and Pays de la Loire regions. The momentum toward institutional engineering was stopped short in July 2003, when voters in Corsica narrowly rejected in a referendum the proposition that a single regional authority should replace the existing Haut-Corse and Corse-Sud departments. A further reverse occurred in December 2003, when voters in Guadeloupe and Martinique rejected plans for more autonomy.

The constitutional reform introduces the possibility for the experimental transfer of functions to sub-national authorities. In the 2003 constitutional reform (and the law voted in July 2004) there is a provision that any sub-national authority can bid to exercise policy responsibilities lying within the policy domain of the central state or other public authorities such as the chambers of commerce. The initial expectation was that the regions would impose a form of leadership over other authorities, even that they alone could bid to run new services. The reformed Article 72 of the Constitution refers to an experimental transfer law designating one or other local or regional authority as being the lead authority for the policy concerned. But it does not explicitly designate the regions in this role. The departments and the communes (and EPCI) can also bid to run services and, where appropriate, can be recognised by the legislator as the lead authority. As in 1982–83, the competition between regionalists and departmentalists has prevented a clarification of responsibilities. A strong rearguard action in the Senate (where most senators favour departments over regions) ensured that the interests of the departments were defended. Against the hopes of many, the 2004 law did not enshrine the leadership of the regional councils over the other sub-national authorities.

The 'experimental transfer of functions' was given legal status in the decentralisation law of July 2004. Experimentation can either be seen as very radical within the French context or as a timid measure controlled by existing institutions. Experimentation needs to be understood on two levels: as an internal process of state reform and as an empowering of local and regional authorities. In terms of the organisation of the French State, the reform allows for more administrative decentralisation. The new Article 37.1 of the French constitution allows central ministries to transfer new functions to their territorial field services. In conjunction with the new financial regulations introduced by the 2001 Finance Law (which favour global rather than item-specific budgets) this measure ought to enhance the development of the territorial field services of government departments. Chavrier (2004) argues that these measures have created a form of subsidiarity as a principle of the organisation of the State: matters should be dealt with by agencies operating as closely as possible to the people.

In relation to local and regional authorities, Article 72 creates a local power of initiative and derogation (*pouvoir normatif local*). It enables central government competencies to be transferred on an experimental basis to regions, departments or communes (including inter-communal structures). Not only can local and regional authorities bid to run new functions, they can also derogate themselves from providing services on a case-by-case basis. Article 72 stipulates that experimental functions/derogations can remain in force for up to eight years, before any definitive decisions are made. Eventually, however, the French parliament will have to decide whether the transfer of functions should be made permanent. If so, the new policy responsibility will be transferred to all cognate sub-national authorities throughout France, thereby ensuring equal treatment.

The 2003 constitutional reform and the 2004 Decentralisation Act introduce new ways in which outcomes can vary across the country. Governments can attempt to transfer responsibilities to regions or other local authorities on an experimental basis. If such transfers succeed, they will be generalised to all authorities. If they fail, they can be abandoned. If they succeed in one region, but are not considered transferable to other regions, then a special statute can be arranged for particular authorities. There remain many divergences between the French model and those of France's principal neighbours. There are no provisions to provide legislative powers for regions, unlike in Germany, Spain or Italy. On the other hand French governments are slowly moving towards the obvious truth that a modern complex democracy cannot be administered in exactly the same way across all of its territory: solutions need to be locally adapted. Article 72 creates a degree of asymmetry within the French State, and there is a strong possibility that at the end of this transitional eight-year period there will be a new law, to ratify these asymmetrical arrangements.

Quite apart from experimental transfers, the 2004 law on local responsibilities identifies a range of areas where functions are transferred to local or regional authorities. As a general rule, the regions were strengthened in matters deemed to be strategic: economic development, education, training and the management of European Union structural funds. They were given responsibilities in some new areas, such as health, from which they were previously excluded. But the most significant transfers, involving large-scale service-delivery responsibilities, were to the departments, which took over roads and increased their responsibilities in social welfare and intermediate education. The departments obtained 70 per cent of transferred funds, as against 20 per cent for the regions and 10 per cent for the communes/EPCI (Fréville, 2004). This 'victory' of the departments could only in part be explained by political choices. The basic institutional architecture of French sub-national governance, whereby the departments have a much more sophisticated administrative infrastructure than either the regions or communes, accounted in practice for the decision to transfer new responsibilities to the departmental councils. For their part, the regional councils are not major service deliverers or personnel managers. The presidents of the regional councils were deeply ambivalent about assuming new responsibilities. Taking over the management of school technical and maintenance workers was headache enough, with the regions having to create new personnel departments.

Conclusion

There are important differences between France and the United Kingdom, in terms of both their inherent characteristics and their overarching state environments. While in France the regional layer covers the entire national territory, the pattern is more asymmetrical within the UK, where three of the four historic nations (Northern Ireland, Scotland and Wales) have their own political institutions and/or administrative machinery that set them apart from England. On the other hand, if the regions in France are more consistently present throughout the national territory, their formal powers are weaker than those of the devolved territories in the UK, including those of the National Assembly for Wales.

In addition to the obvious contrasts, there are also many similarities between France and the United Kingdom. In both France and the United Kingdom, there has traditionally been little demand in most areas for regional political institutions. In both states, regional institutions, where they exist, are newcomers. They have had to establish their credentials and demonstrate their authority in relation to existing institutional players and public opinion. The ability of regional authorities to develop good relationships is complicated by the survival of pre-existing forms of local government and, in the case of France, by the penetration of the French State down to the lowest levels. The challenges are not only organisational. Existing institutions, such as the communes in France or the counties in England, are the recipients of diffuse favourable images from public opinion. In both of these traditionally centralised states, identities have been localist and national, rather than regional. On this most basic measure, France and the UK share much more in common than usually acknowledged. The challenge for regional political institutions in both countries is to develop capacity in an institutionally crowded space. Chapter 3 now explores these issues in more depth, presenting the Wales-Brittany comparison in some detail.

3
Wales and Brittany: history, politics, society

The choice of Wales and Brittany to form the core of a comparative case study presents two historic regions with complex but strong identities. Insofar as their quality as regions is concerned, the mix of similarity and difference makes the Wales-Brittany pair a good one for comparative analysis, fulfilling the criteria of comparability in terms of spatial location, population size, economic activity, linguistic specificity and common historical ties. The Wales-Brittany comparison was designed to elucidate similar political and policy challenges in specific regional and national contexts. As outlined in Chapter 1, the overarching research question was that of building regional political capacity. The study adopts an inductive approach, emphasising the interplay of institutions, relationships, identities and overarching environments. Evaluating regional political capacity in Wales and Brittany involves calibration against this comparative framework of reference, an exercise to be carried out in Chapter 8. In the present chapter, the main dimensions of the Wales and Brittany comparison are introduced: regional political institutions; identity and values; regional public policies and policy communities, external constraints and opportunities.

In terms of regional institutions, important differences between Wales and Brittany are observed. The powers of all French regions are weaker than those of National Assembly for Wales, a theme which will be developed in Chapters 4 and 5. But there is a foresight dimension to this. Brittany is the birthplace and driving force of regional political identity and institutions in France and, if UK-style devolution ever comes to France, it will probably prosper in Brittany more than anywhere else. The history of regional institutions is testament to contrasting opportunity structures. Though for most of its history there was little to distinguish Wales from England, state-approved institution building in Wales took root in the late nineteenth century. In Brittany, autonomous institutions arose during the post-war period in spite of initial state opposition. The strongest argument in favour of Wales-Brittany comparison is that both regions possess distinctive institutions and strong political and/or cultural identities, features setting them apart from most regions within their respective nation-states.

The case for the Wales–Brittany comparison is made even more pertinent in terms of identity and values. Wales and Brittany are both located on the far Western Atlantic seaboard of Europe, on the geographical margins of traditionally highly-centralised states (Le Bourdennec, 1996; Le Coadic, 1998). Both regions have strong cultural, linguistic and political identities. A brief tracing of the role of political parties, cultural and linguistic movements follows below. Closely-related Celtic languages, Breton and Welsh, are spoken in both regions, which provides a direct object of comparison (Favereau, 1993). Religion has been important in shaping regional identities. Catholicism in Brittany, one of France's most pious regions, for long performed a critical role in defining acceptable political and societal choices. Nonconformism in Wales had at least as strong an influence. Though Catholicism and nonconformity have both declined as identity markers, in each case they have an important political and cultural heritage (Lagrée, 1988). Unlike in many other regions in both states, in Wales and Brittany there is a strong 'communitarian' tradition in politics and civil society that makes both regions distinctive within their larger state settings (Monnier, 1994; Morvan, 1997).

Issues of identity spill over into concerns of public policy and policy communities. Throughout the book, there is a concentration on policy issue areas having an obvious regional dimension, such as education and training, regional languages, and to a lesser extent economic development and spatial planning. Consistent with the most similar comparative research design, focusing on cognate policy issue areas allows interesting contrasts to be drawn between Wales and Brittany and, further afield, between France and the United Kingdom. The focus on regional political institutions and cognate policy areas also invites broader international comparisons, a theme addressed briefly in Chapter 7.

These two regions are broadly comparable in terms of the challenges they face. In historical terms, both Wales and Brittany correspond to those regions identified by Rokkan and Urwin (1982), in which the development of regional consciousness is a function of economic dependency and the persistence of a strong cultural identity. Wales and Brittany share many similar features. Traditionally, both regions were poor, peripheral, economically underdeveloped regions. As measured in terms of GDP, Brittany was France's poorest region in 1945, and Wales has always been one of the poorest parts of the United Kingdom (with GDP hovering around 80 per cent of the national average). Brittany has recovered impressively in the post-war period and is now in the average of French regions, with a GDP just below the national French average. Wales remains the UK's poorest region, a status that allowed most of the country to qualify for Objective One status for the 2000–6 period. Both regions share problems of economic underdevelopment or adjustment. In the case of Brittany, recent years have produced a farm crisis, a process of painful industrial restructuring, environmental catastrophe and attempts to overcome the physical distance from markets. Compared with Wales, however, which has lagged behind the UK and EU average, Brittany has been a post-war success story. There are some striking similarities between the two regions. In both Wales and Brittany, there is a large preponderance of small and medium-sized companies and sole traders. Both Wales and Brittany have attracted state firms and agencies as a deliberate measure of post-war territorial planning. Both regions have been favoured destinations for foreign direct investment, though mainly for opposing reasons (cheap labour in Wales, a well-educated workforce in Brittany).

There are also obvious contrasts between the two regions. While Wales was a major industrial force in the nineteenth century, Brittany's industrial take-off is much more recent. There are signs, however, that Brittany is now suffering from an over-concentration on foreign direct investment and over-reliance on a few industrial sectors (agro-alimentary, defence, telecommunications), as well as upon agriculture and fisheries. Wales suffers from a poor economic and transport infrastructure that hinders trade. Brittany, on the other hand, has an excellent transport infrastructure that facilitates trade. If Breton policy-makers appear overly focused on issues of transport infrastructure, it is in the knowledge that transport investments have opened up Brittany to the outside world. Though it defines itself as a maritime power, the existence of good road and rail links is even more important.

Wales and Brittany have many similar cultural and linguistic characteristics. As regions with closely related minority Celtic languages, Wales and Brittany face directly comparable problems of regional language policy. While a fragile consensus has emerged over the role of Welsh in Wales, in Brittany the language issue remains highly divisive. A cumulative history of tackling language issues has given Wales a wealth of experience as regards language policy, a policy responsibility of the National Assembly since May 1999. In the case of Brittany, the state of the language is even worse than in Wales. Survey findings for this study demonstrate a very widespread support for promoting the symbols of the Breton language and culture, with public opinion much more evenly divided over the wisdom of introducing a more interventionist language policy of the type existing in Wales.

Both regions operate within overarching national and EU environments. Neither Wales nor Brittany can escape from the legacy of its past. The contrasting prospects for Wales and Brittany of autonomous forms of regional governance today are to some extent tied into their different experiences of nation-state building. The French State building enterprise has, historically speaking, been remarkably successful in inculcating deeply rooted beliefs linking the national territory with social progress. The UK Union State was far more permissive and inclined to take into account territorial differences. The UK was less inclined than France to link state structures and the enjoyment of civil and political rights. In Brittany, regional autonomists face ideological as well as institutional challenges going beyond those in the UK. Though there is a difference of degree, Wales and Brittany are good comparators, insofar as their comparison informs us a good deal about the evolution of democracy in France and the United Kingdom, the two key non-federal European Union states. In both states, the degree of autonomy enjoyed by these distinctive peripheral regions has been defined by central government, rather than by the regions themselves.

Finally, the comparison is enhanced by the strong links existing between the two regions, be they economic (the Atlantic Arc), cultural (the Inter-Celtique festival) or political (the Memorandum of Understanding of 2003 between the Welsh Assembly Government and the Brittany Regional Council). These themes are developed in more detail throughout the course of the book. When Wales and Brittany are compared, there is not just comparison of two regions, but also an invitation to policy-makers in Wales to consider French experience in general, especially as it manifests itself in a region with historic ties to Wales. The two regions are now introduced in more detail, focusing in turn on their historical and political development and their party systems.

History, politics and society in Wales

Wales boasts a proud history sharing much in common with, but also distinctive from, that of its powerful English neighbour. The Norman Conquest of Wales was drawn out over two centuries, and finally complete only in 1282. Full unification with the English crown had to await two further centuries. In 1485, the Tudor family, originating from Anglesea, ascended to the English throne (Williams, 1961). Under the influence of the Tudor King Henry VIII, the Act of Union in 1536 consolidated English influence, consistent with the new model of strong central monarchy taking root throughout Europe at this time. The government of Wales became identical to that of England. The English system of local government was introduced everywhere in Wales, which was divided into 10 shires with equal legal status. The Welsh shires now

Table 3.1 Comparing political and policy contexts

	Wales	*Brittany*	*Commentary*
Population	3,000,000	3,000,000 (4,000,000 with Loire Atlantique)	Good fit
History	Tudor Act, 1536, Wales attached to English Crown	Independent Duchy until 1532, then part of France.	Breton 'state', 848–1532.
Geography	West Atlantic Seaboard. Atlantic Arc	West Atlantic Seaboard. Atlantic Arc	Good fit
Political governance	Devolved Assembly in 'Union State'. Model of Executive devolution. Devolution a process of uncertain dimensions	Limited administrative, then political decentralisation since 1960s. Brittany birthplace of regional political institutions. Bretons regarding Wales with interest	This asymmetrical comparison makes sense in an overarching Franco-British comparative context.
	Wide-ranging regulatory and secondary legislative powers; no tax-varying powers.	Some tax-varying powers, but no equivalent legislative/ regulatory powers. 2003 constitutional reform allows regions to bid to exercise new functions of an experimental basis. Regions are major actors in economic development, training, culture, transport. Influence over education	British Union State more flexible than the French unitary one.
Economy	Tourism, Aerospace, Automotive, Electronics, Steel, low-skilled service sector (call centres)	Food Processing, Shipbuilding, Defence, Tele-communications, Automotive, Farming, Fishing, Tourism.	Wales and Brittany share many similar features: farm crisis, industrial restructuring, physical distance from markets

Table 3.1 (*continued*)

	Wales	*Brittany*	*Commentary*
	Mostly SMEs, but a strong old manufacturing base. FDI important.	Some large firms – Citroen, France-Telecom, DCN – mostly SMEs. FDI more important than elsewhere.	
	Poor infrastructure hinders trade. Political Networks run from North to South; Economic networks from East to West	Good infrastructure facilitates trade	
	GDP *c.*80 per cent of national average	Brittany poorest French region in 1945, now 14th out of 22. GDP just below average	
Language	17 per cent fluent/ fairly fluent Welsh (MRW poll, July 2001).	12 per cent fluent/ fairly fluent Breton (Efficience 3 poll, July 2001).	

all sent representatives (knights) to the English parliament. The 'England and Wales' legal tradition was consolidated by the Act of Union. Wales was given the same land-tenure and inheritance laws as in England. The Act determined that the English language alone could be used in law courts (a provision finally repealed in 1942) and that all public servants had to be able to speak English.

Writing of the 1880s, Kenneth O. Morgan concluded that the idea of Wales was 'a singularly ill-defined one' (Morgan, 1982). Wales had many attributes of a distinctive national identity: the widely spoken Welsh language kept alive the sense of distinctiveness, and there was a rich collection of national myths. Resistance to Anglo-Norman centralisation, the most powerful of these, has a pedigree going back to the thirteenth century. Periodic outbursts of rebellion, such as the Owain Glyndwr uprising of the fourteenth century, gave expression to this Welshness. By comparison to the Irish or the Scots, however, the Welsh did not possess an articulate view of nationalism. Unlike the Duchy in Brittany, or the Kingdom of Scotland, the principality had never possessed its own unity. In the Middle Ages, Wales was a fragmented collection of princedoms, finally conquered and subdued by Edward

I in 1282. Since 1536, Wales had been largely assimilated into the central and local government structure of England, offering no resistance comparable to that of the Irish people. In the case of Wales, the national idea did not emerge spontaneously out of empire, as was the case for so much nineteenth-century nationalism (including in Ireland). Rather, the idea of Wales emerged relatively late on as a social construction, drawing its inspiration from nonconformist religion, the Welsh language, a specific model of economic development and the emergence of political radicalism coinciding with the advent of democracy.

Welshness was defined first and foremost by religion and language. Originally a loyal Catholic territory, from the eighteenth century Wales developed a form of indigenous nonconformist Protestantism which drew its inspiration from a rejection of Anglicanism, the Church of England and the Anglicised gentry class which owned much of Wales. With its origins in the Reformation and the English Civil War, nonconformity lay at the heart of the Welsh national consciousness from the eighteenth century onwards. The Reformation succeeded so well that Wales came to reject the high-church values of the Anglican Church. The chapel movement crafted a distinctive Welsh identity. The chapels spread puritan values such as temperance, but also called for social justice and political reform. Nonconformists campaigned for the disestablishment of the Anglican Church in Wales, as had occurred in Ireland in 1867, a political demand finally granted after the First World War. With the development of industrialisation, nonconformist influence spread into the mining valleys, becoming a truly all-Welsh movement in the process. Nonconformism, which was partially proscribed until the nineteenth century, was also linked with the development of political rights. During the nineteenth century, the causes of full religious emancipation and disenfranchisement of the Anglican Church became intertwined with that of the extension of the suffrage. From the first mass elections in Wales in 1868, a majority of electors supported the cause of political radicalism, in the form first of the Liberal Party, later on that of Labour.

Even more than nonconformism, the Welsh language was the critical identity marker of Welshness. During the nineteenth century, Welsh was spoken by 75 per cent of the population, and by virtually everybody outside of the border country. The language was closely associated with dominant institutions of the land: the *eisteddfod*, the chapels and the press. The dominant nonconformist religion expressed itself through the medium of Welsh, and most nineteenth-century literature was written in Welsh. The Welsh language remained vigorous as the medium of daily conversation, especially in the north, west and central parts of the country. In the 1891 census, 54.4 per cent were recorded as speaking Welsh. In 1901 and 1911, the proportion of Welsh speakers was, for the first time, recorded as falling, declining to just under 50 per cent in 1901 and 43.5 per cent in 1911. In 1921, Welsh-speakers represented only 37.1 per cent of the population and in 1931, only 36.8 per cent spoke Welsh (Williams 2000). With the decline of Welsh, the structure of the Welsh-language community became geographically more distinctive. Welsh remained strong in the rural counties of the north, west and central Wales. In the new growth areas of south-east Wales, however, English was the language of communication. In Glamorgan in 1921, 68 per cent spoke English, a figure reaching 90 per cent in Monmouthshire. The decline of the Welsh language continued after 1945. From 1951 to 1991, the proportion of Welsh speakers regularly declined: 28.9 per cent in 1951, 26 per cent in 1961, 20.8 per cent in 1971, 18.9 per cent in 1981, 18.7 per cent in 1991 (Williams, 2000). All in all, Welsh has held up much better than either Gaelic, Scots Gaelic or Breton. By 1971, the rate of decline had slowed and by 2001 it had been it reversed (21.3 per cent of Welsh speakers) thanks mainly to the influence of the education system and the bilingual policy adopted under the Welsh Language Act of 1993 (Cole and Williams, 2004).

The social structure of Wales remained static for centuries after the Tudor dynasty. At the beginning of the nineteenth century, Wales was still a country of small rural hamlets, rather than towns (Morgan, 1982). Rural Wales was dominated by the landed gentry and by a quasi-feudal social organisation. The English-speaking gentry had little in common with the vast mass of the population. Wales did not have a developed social leadership. There was no parallel with the Scottish land-owning class which sided with the nationalist cause, nor with the sophisticated middle class which had allowed Scotland to play an important role in the enlightenment. Most Welsh farmers were small tenant farmers and agriculture was in a primitive state.

Demographic trends demonstrate very clearly the shifting contours of Welsh society. In 1801, Wales and Monmouthshire had a combined population of 588,000. In the 1801 census, the largest town was Merthyr (7,700), in the Valleys, the centre of the burgeoning mining industry. Swansea (6,800) had also expanded. Cardiff (1,870) was a small market town (Williams, 1961). By the 1880s, there had been a major transformation since the beginning of the century. In the 1881 census, the population of Wales had increased to 1,577,000. Most of the new population settled in the new industrialising areas: in the county of Glamorgan and in the burgeoning cities of Swansea (93,001) and Cardiff (106,164). By the end of the nineteenth century, the south-Wales Valleys were in full expansion. In contrast, there was a move of population away from the rural areas of north, central and west Wales. Industrialisation produced greater difference between the expanding south and the rural north and west. The growth axes of Wales were along the south-eastern and north-eastern border areas: namely Cardiff, Newport and Deeside, areas whose futures were closely tied to those of England. The role of Cardiff has been deeply controversial. Cardiff has been recognised as capital of Wales only since 1951. Though concentrating most national institutions within its midst, the capital city voted against devolution in 1979 and 1997 and remains a largely anglicised city. Cardiff city fathers look to creating Cardiff as a dynamic city-region more than anything else.

For most of the twentieth century, the twin poles of the Welsh economy were small-scale agriculture and large-scale heavy industry. Wales began to develop industrially as early as the seventeenth century. The principality was important because of its iron, copper, lead and coal deposits. The growth of mining in South Wales in the nineteenth century transformed the Welsh economy. The cities of Cardiff, Newport and Barry developed so rapidly that by 1913 Cardiff had become the largest coal-exporting port in the world. This prosperity was not to last. Traditional Welsh smokestack industries – Iron, Steel, Coal – had already begun to decline by the 1920s and the situation became chronic after 1950. Throughout the postwar period, the Welsh model of economic development has relied heavily on external investment. Central governments in London, highly politically sensitive to the principality, directed important state investments to Wales, such as the Ordnance factory in Bridgend, the passport office in Newport, the Vehicle Licensing Authority in Swansea, the Royal Mint in Llantrisant (Morgan, 1982). Low-level service employment expanded rapidly, so much so that by 1968 it had doubled from 1945. Massive state investment and direct government grants began to attract private industry, in steel, plastics, rubber and automobiles. The arrival of Ford in 1965 provided a major boost to this strategy. In 1976, the Welsh Development Agency (WDA) was set up, initially as a Welsh version of the National Enterprise Board. The WDA was given real powers and finance, with responsibility for administering regional grants, managing low-rate loans, overseeing government-owned factories and providing training. The WDA became the principal instrument for seeking out foreign direct investment (FDI), much of which flowed into Wales in the 1980s and 1990s.

By comparison to territories elsewhere in the UK, Wales has continued to employ more people in heavy industry. In spite of large-scale state-directed investment in Wales aimed at diversifying the economy, and in spite of vigorous efforts to attract FDI, much Welsh manufacturing has suffered from low productivity, managerial inefficiency and a low rate of capital investment. Industrial restructuring in the 1970s and 1980s hit Wales especially hard, with the running down, then closure of the coal industry and the loss of major capacity in steel. Such trends did not stop with devolution. One of the major tests for the Assembly Government was how to deal with the lay-offs in the

Corus steel factory in Port Talbot in 2001 (Storer and Parsons, 2003). Wales has consistently had a higher unemployment rate and a lower standard of living than elsewhere in the UK. How to raise Welsh GDP and how to train an underskilled workforce have been permanent policy dilemmas.

Political forces and the party system in pre-devolution Wales

A brief overview of the party system in Wales since the nineteenth century demonstrates the pull of the idea of the United Kingdom on Welsh politicians. It also reveals the slow emergence of a political Welshness, which is distinctive from Britishness and has come to focus upon the devolved institutions. For most of the twentieth century, the attraction of the United Kingdom as a Union-State was much more important than the support for devolved or autonomous political institutions. UK governments sought to accommodate Welsh cultural and, to a lesser extent, political demands as the best way of safeguarding the Union. Most Welsh politicians were convinced that Welsh interests were best safeguarded through the UK, rather than by a hypothetical Welsh state, or even devolved political institutions. The hostility of the Labour Party to devolution for most of the period from the 1920s to the 1970s bore witness to the political opportunity structure provided by the United Kingdom, as well as to a belief in class solidarity above territorial identity. The breakthrough of Plaid Cymru in the 1970s forced the hitherto dominant Labour Party to modify its traditional unionism and develop a more distinctive Welsh message.

Throughout the history of democratic institutions in Wales, there has been a tendency for single-party hegemony. The Liberals were dominant from 1868 to 1922, testament to the force of a new democratic agenda and the emergence of new groups into the political forefront. David Lloyd George was the tribune and voice of this new Wales. Lloyd George dominated national politics from 1910 to 1916. With the Welsh economy booming and Wales playing an important part in the British Empire, Welsh home rule did not have much appeal. After flirting with home rule in 1896, the Liberals evolved into a centralising party thereafter. Liberal Wales left an important legacy: the University of Wales, the county schools and the disestablishment of the Anglican Church, all achieved within the framework of the UK as a Union State.

The Labour ascendancy was even more complete than that of the Liberals, and Labour's commitment to a London-centric model even more thoroughgoing. Labour's domination of Welsh Politics throughout most of the twentieth century built on a tradition of working-class radicalism, trade-union organisation and class solidarity. From 1945 to 1970, Labour never fell below 50 per cent of the Welsh vote and it has always been the largest party in Westminster and Assembly elections. In addition to holding a majority of seats in parliamentary elections since 1924, Labour controlled nearly all local councils from the early 1920s onwards. Labour completely dominated the Welsh political scene at all levels of public administration, as well as in the outlying educational and cultural spheres. The symbols of post-war identification were mainly Labour symbols, such as the National Health Service, social housing or social security. Unlike that of the Liberals, the Labour elite in Wales was a working-class one. Welsh Labour councils adopted innovative policies and provided local services well beyond their statutory duties. They also sought to implement local development policies and to improve social and housing conditions.

Imbued with a belief in class solidarity and struggle, traditional Labour was suspicious of any talk of administrative or political devolution. Wales was treated as part of England. The objective was equality for Wales within the UK, rather than differentiation within the Union, or, even worse, separation from the UK. Consistent with the prevailing beliefs amongst socialist parties at the time, Labour supported state centralisation and the capture of the commanding heights of the economy as the best guarantors of equality and progress. The party was divided over the prospect of devolution. There were distinctive viewpoints within the party, ranging from the pro-devolution stance of James Griffiths to the Unionism of Nye Bevan, the founder of the NHS, or, later on, of Neil Kinnock, leader of the Labour Party from 1985 to 1992. The anti-devolutionists were convinced that the UK State offered the appropriate framework for the pursuit of equality. Economic revival, conceived as a UK-wide process, was given far more emphasis than was respect for Welsh culture. Apart from Labour, the Liberal Democrats were lukewarm about devolution and the Conservatives resolutely hostile. There was no equivalent in Wales to the social and civic mobilisation in favour of devolution that occurred in Scotland.

Rather as in the case of Brittany considered below, for most of the period political nationalist movements in Wales were of marginal importance. The first influential movement calling for self-government, *Cymru Fydd* (1886), was a league rather than a party. It set out to influence the behaviour of Welsh politicians within the Liberal Party and to call for home rule for Wales. The next movement, *Plaid Cymru* (1925) was a marginal political force throughout the inter-war period, polling between 1 and 3 per cent in elections. The historic leader of Plaid Cymru, Saunders-Lewis, held a romantic vision of nationalism, which looked to creating an independent Wales in a medieval style of European federation. Saunders-Lewis' Roman Catholicism sat uneasily with the Protestant nation; his looking to continental 'fascist' experiences for inspiration proved highly unpopular. From 1914 to around 1960, there was no social demand for developing political institutions to acknowledge Welsh nationhood. Most Welsh citizens looked to the UK State to preserve their interests, rather than developing a separate nation-state as in Ireland. In part as a result of Labour hegemony, the idea of Wales was rooted in one of the social-democratic, collectivist ethos of its people, rather than a romantic attachment to the land, a belief in ethnic separation or a demand for autonomous political institutions. At the same time, there was growing anxiety about the decline of the language, which eventually gave birth to a powerful cultural movement and sowed the seeds of political nationalism.

By the late 1960s, the Plaid Cymru brand of nationalism had shifted from being a rural, conservative, reactionary movement, to becoming a broader one concerned with the distinctive social, economic, political and cultural development of Wales. Welsh nationalism was noticeably more socially progressive than that of the SNP in Scotland. The breakthrough of Plaid Cymru from the late 1960s reflected concerns beyond those of the language or the preservation of rural communities, though these remained important (Christiansen, 1998). In the early 1960s, there was a division of labour within the Welsh nationalist movement. The creation of the Welsh Language Society, at the 1962 party conference, allowed Plaid Cymru to focus more on the aims of political nationalism. Plaid Cymru now linked issues of language and identity with those of economic development, environmental preservation and social justice. The issue which underpinned the rise of Plaid Cymru in the late 1960s – the Tryweryn affair – illustrated the broadening of concerns, in this instance the argument that Welsh water should be preserved for local Welsh communities, rather than exported to England. The election of three Plaid Cymru MPs in October 1974 had a major impact. Holding the balance of power, the Welsh and Scottish nationalists were able to ensure that the Labour government forwarded proposals for devolution. The pivotal position of the Welsh and Scottish nationalists placed devolution firmly on the political agenda. Though proposals for Welsh devolution were decisively rejected in 1979, the pro-devolutionists' case was greatly strengthened during the Conservative years, when, as in Scotland, there was no majority for the neoliberal policies associated with the English Right. The second referendum on Welsh devolution, won on a wafer-thin majority in September 1997, finally vested Wales with devolved political institutions, the functioning of which is the theme of Chapter 4.

A number of themes can be identified from the above survey. Welsh distinctiveness was embodied in a tradition of radical politics that developed in the nineteenth century, linked first to Welsh nonconformity and the Liberals, later on to Labour and the industrial working class. For most of the twentieth century, the socio-economic issues were the ones that really mattered, not those based explicitly on region or nation. Many Welsh people continue to define contemporary Welshness in terms of class identity. One recent survey of Welsh attitudes towards identity revealed that a majority of the Welsh identified themselves as being working-class, strong testimony to the importance of Wales' industrial past (Wyn Jones and Scully, 2004). Wales also appears as a society that is divided on geographical, linguistic and political grounds. Divisions within Wales were well captured by Balsom's metaphor of the three Waleses (Balsom and Burch, 1980). According to Balsom, Welsh Wales, in the northern and western Welsh-speaking areas, was a self-sufficient society with a strong sense of its own identity, broadly nationalist in political terms and committed to the indigenous language. English Wales also had a deep sense of Welshness, which it defined in terms of class solidarity and collective beliefs, rather than a cultural attachment to the language. British Wales occupied the border country. It had no sense of Welsh identity and some hostility to it. The results of the 1999 Welsh referendum on devolution gave some substance to these territorial divisions within Wales, as the eleven counties bordering England all voted against an Assembly, while the 11 counties of western Wales all supported it.

In spite of these divisions, by the late twentieth century Wales had a much more distinctive sense of its own identity and history than one hundred years previously. Late twentieth-century Welsh identity was built upon a reaction to Thatcherism, the influence of new political forces (Plaid Cymru) on political agendas, and a widely diffused, if vague, belief in Wales as a land with a more egalitarian, social-democratic and collective ethos than its large English neighbour. At the same time, the symbols of Welshness underwent major change during the twentieth century. The nonconformist chapels lost their dominant place in society. The *eisteddfod* became less central in people's lives. After 1945, a far more homogeneous, Anglicized and secular society emerged. In a rather paradox manner, the consciousness of being Welsh developed during the twentieth century, at the same time as the traditional markers of identity (such as language and religion) were becoming diluted. The challenge for the National Assembly is to unify these distinctive and divisive representations of Welshness and to link the image of the new Wales with the devolved institutions themselves.

History, politics and society in Brittany

In the opinion of one Breton autonomist interviewed in the summer of 2001, the French nation-state was imposed by 'blood, sweat and tears'. One of the most distinctive regions of France, Brittany has a strong sense of its specific position within French society (Favereau, 1993; Flatres, 1986; McDonald, 1989; Le Bourdennec, 1996; Le Coadic, 1998). First an independent monarchy (845–938), then a Duchy (from 938 to 1532), then a French province with special prerogatives (1532–1789), reduced for long to being a collection of disparate *départements* before becoming an administrative (1972) then political region (1982), modern Brittany is a French region with a difference. Unlike many other French regions, Brittany can look to its past existence as an independent duchy, with its own institutions and founding myths. Though the symbols of statehood have long been suppressed, the region retains many distinctive characteristics. The Breton language is the European continent's only Celtic language. The enduring symbolic importance of the Catholic religion is ever present physically in the architecture of Breton villages, as well in higher than average rates of religious practice. The spectacular growth of Breton cultural movements (music, dance, theatre, costume) is testament to a revival of Breton values and self-consciousness. At a more abstract level, observers have noted the capacity of Breton actors to join forces to promote their common interests and to defend Brittany against attacks from the outside world (Pasquier, 2004). Breton solidarity can also be gauged more intuitively by the effectiveness of Breton elite-level networks in Paris and Brussels, and by the importance of the Breton diaspora in retaining a sense of distinctiveness.

Brittany is sometimes taken as a litmus test for the health of regional identity within France. Bretons speak with pride of their nation as a prosperous maritime power from the fifteenth to eighteenth centuries, an outward-looking region/nation with an important position along the Atlantic trading routes. The prosperity of Breton ports was testimony to its maritime vocation. Brittany also had a thriving business culture, centred around textiles and commerce (Pasquier, 2004). The decline of Brittany from the eighteenth century onwards is sometimes linked to its political and economic union with France. Brittany was integrated into the French tariff system under Louis XIV in the late seventeenth century. As a result of integration into French markets and French protectionist economic policies, Brittany was cut off from its main trading partners, notably the British Isles and the Caribbean. By the end of the nineteenth century, Brittany was the poorest mainland French region, and also the one with the highest level of emigration. With few natural resources, Brittany missed out on the industrial revolution. It was forced back into subsistence agriculture, notwithstanding the poor quality of most arable land. There were no large cities and only a few medium-sized towns. There was a weak indigenous bourgeoisie, with no financial or human capital concentration. Brittany became a reservoir of labour for the more industrialised regions.

The ideology of republicanism itself favoured emigration away from peripheral areas such as Brittany and drained the most productive forces to Paris.

The First World War represented a major turning point in Breton history. Bretons were mobilised en masse to fight in the war. With the loss of 150,000 lives, twice as many as the average for the rest of France, Bretons suffered incomparable human losses (Lebesque, 1970). The First World War also socialised the young Breton generation into the French national community and inculcated a daily use of the French language. In 1918, Brittany emerged emotionally and physically exhausted by the First World War (Le Coadic, 1998), its economy structurally damaged and economically underdeveloped, and its future compromised by the massive emigration of its young people. During the inter-war period, there was a strengthening both of the Breton cultural movement and of political nationalism. Cultural groups centred around defence of the language. More explicitly political movements developed also, strongly influenced by the Irish uprising of 1920–21 and the conception of the Irish Free State. Breizh Atao ('Bretagne toujours'), created in 1920, presented a platform for Breton autonomists from across the political spectrum, an ideological and political precursor to the Breton Autonomist Party (Parti Autonomiste Breton – PAB), formed in 1927. The PAB was increasingly split between a pro-European federalist left, and a hard-line nationalistic right, which eventually won out. Dissolved in 1939, the PAB reappeared as the Breton National Party (Parti national de Bretagne – PNB) in 1940 under the Occupation. A number of leaders of this nationalist party collaborated with the Germans. Around 100 of the most committed nationalists formed the Breton brigade – the bezenn Perrot – which fought as part of the German army. The war had a devastating, probably fatal effect on the Breton autonomist movement. Though Breton nationalists had also been very active in the resistance, the activities of the pro-Nazi minority discredited the Breton movement for a generation and precluded the emergence of a powerful regionalist/nationalist party, a theme developed below.

The rapid demographic and economic expansion of Brittany during the post-war period has been all the more remarkable given its poverty in 1939. From being the poorest French region in 1945, Brittany had climbed much closer to the national average by 2003 (INSEE, 2003). The post-war period has been marked by heavy inward investment into the region, first from the French State in the 1950s and 1960s and, more recently, from foreign direct investment. Brittany has enjoyed strong rates of economic growth, testament to the modernisation of its agricultural sector, external investment in high-technology sectors such as telecommunications, defence and health and a specific pattern of multipolar spatial development. These developments have been facilitated by the reputation for seriousness of a well-trained workforce and by the Brittany region regularly boasting the highest educational standards in France at age 18. External stimuli have combined with an original model of indigenous economic development, in part based upon the co-operative mode of governance identified below.

At the core of this spatial network is the city of Rennes, the capital of the administrative region of Brittany. Rennes has expanded very rapidly during the post-war period, with its population doubling from 100,000 to 200,000 inhabitants between 1950 and 1980. Rennes is an important centre of public-sector employment as a result of the city's university and research institutes, its large hospital serving the Brittany region and its status as a regional capital. Rennes has a modest industrial sector (the car manufacturer Citroën and the publisher Ouest-France are the two main private employers), offset by a large and diversified small and medium business culture, with particular strengths in transport, food-processing industries and telecommunications. Even after continuous post-war growth, Rennes remains only one of several medium-sized Breton towns, operating within a larger regional and national context. According to Phlipponneau (1993) the specificity of the Breton industrial model lay in its multipolar nature. Post-war economic development in Brittany involved a dense network of medium-sized towns, alongside the growth of the capital Rennes. These small and medium-sized towns included Redon, Vitré, Lannion, Brest, Morlaix, Vannes, Quimper, Lorient and several smaller towns. Much of the more dynamic growth was concentrated in towns smaller than Rennes, of which Lannion provided the model (Phlipponneau, 1993).

Rather like Cardiff, Rennes is also a contested regional capital. Breton autonomists are dismissive of Rennes as the 'first station on the Paris metro', and argue strongly that the historic capital Nantes should be recognised as the Breton capital. The competition between Rennes and Nantes clouds somewhat the issue of whether Brittany should recover the Loire-Atlantique and its capital Nantes: many, perhaps most, Bretons do not simply identify their region with the geographical boundaries of the current regional institution, but see it also as including the fifth 'lost' département of Loire-Atlantique (removed from Brittany by Marshall Pétain in June 1941). The June 2001 survey revealed powerful public support for the reunification of historic Brittany (over 62 per cent strongly in favour or in favour), a sentiment shared across the political and geographical spectrum, with only minor variations according to département, partisan allegiance or other variables (Cole and Loughlin, 2003).

One of the most remarkable features of post-war Brittany has been the transformation of the Catholic Church. While the Church had been closely associated with anti-republicanism, in the post-1945 period there was a major shift. As part of the reconciliation with republican democracy and modern society culminating in Vatican 2 in 1964, the Church created a dense network of youth organisations which had a massive impact in Catholic Brittany. The Young Christian Farmers association (*Jeunesse agricole chrétienne* – JAC) in particular had a major influence in Brittany and became one of the channels through which farm leaders became convinced of the importance of modernisation and technical progress. In the appreciation of one interviewee: 'everything is linked to the transformation of Catholicism. The silent revolution in farming is at the heart of post-war economic development. The leaders of the young Christian organisations (JEC/ JOC/JAC) played a very important role here, not least in creating the FNSEA as a modern farming union and in convincing Breton peasants to espouse modern farming techniques. In turn, Brittany produced its own very powerful agri-business sector'. Brittany is today one of France's principal farm-export regions and a leader in the agribusiness sector.

As noted above, in Wales the language has been a critical identity marker. In Brittany, the situation is far more complex. In the absence of formal census data, the figures are less viable than those in Wales. In 1900, there were well over 1 million native Breton speakers (Le Coadic, 1998). The survey conducted in 2001 found that around 200,000 people claimed to speak Breton fluently, to which can be added 100,000 who are able to speak and understand it quite well. This represents 10 per cent, at most, with any sort of Breton-language competency. These figures would appear to be broadly consistent with other recent surveys (Gemie, 2002). More than the total number of speakers, their age and geographical profile are deeply pessimistic for the future of the language. The average Breton speaker is 68 years old and lives in a narrow triangle in the western-most part of Brittany (in-land Finistère and the western half of the Côtes d'Armor). Almost no one under 40 today was born and brought up in a Breton-speaking household. At this rate, there will be no first-language Breton speakers left in two or three decades. The only finding offsetting this rather sombre picture lies in the somewhat broader geographical spread of Breton, along with evidence that there may be some revival of Breton amongst the younger age groups. In the 2001 survey, the number of Breton speakers in Rennes was on the increase, testament probably to the influence of the DIWAN school movement and to the impact of bilingual education, as well as to the vigour of the Breton cultural movement creating renewed interest in the language.

If interest in Breton culture and language has revived in the past two decades, the Breton economic miracle has turned a little sour since the mid-1990s. Heavy investments in telecommunications or defence have produced excess capacity. Medium-sized towns such as Lannion have paid the price for the dot-com collapse in 2000–1, while defence cutbacks from the early 1990s onwards have hit Brest and Lorient hard. The core farming communities in central and west Brittany have suffered from reforms to the Common Agricultural Policy and the drying up of EU subsidies. The fishing fleet has been damaged by reforms to the common fisheries policy. And yet, the picture presented by Brittany in 2005 is starkly different from that in the 1950s: the legendary Breton pessimism has given way to a sense of achievement and regional pride.

Attention is now turned to how the party system in Brittany has facilitated the construction of a regional belief system based upon the value of cross-partisan consensus and the advocacy of the Breton cause in higher arenas.

Political forces and the party system in Brittany

If all main political tendencies have been well represented in post-war Brittany (except the Front National), the prevalent post-war political tradition is best described as one of political centrism. In the immediate post-war period, Brittany was the birthplace and one of the bastions of French Christian democracy and, though in decline, powerful vestiges remain. With the creation of the Fifth Republic, Brittany could not resist the national pull of Gaullism. Brittany also contributed markedly to the rise of the new Socialist Party (PS) from the 1970s onwards, with the Socialist Party in Brittany subtly imbued with values representative of the underlying Breton political culture, notably left Catholicism and social partnership (Hanley, 1984; Sawicki, 1993). The French Communist Party (PCF) also established its own strongholds in the 'red triangle' of north-west and central Brittany and was supportive from an early date of many of the Breton movement's 'anti-colonial' demands (Lebesque, 1970). Long resistant to national trends, the decline of the PCF in Brittany has threatened the survival of an original model of rural communism, largely to the benefit of the PS. Only the far-right Front National has failed to establish solid bases in Brittany, outside of one or two pockets of support (notably in La Trinité sur Mer, birthplace of Jean-Marie Le Pen). The case of the FN illustrates well the innate cohesion of Breton political culture. Having been spared the ravages of excessive urbanisation, industrial decline and unemployment, Brittany's social networks have remained largely intact, providing a barrier to the breakthrough of the far-right movement. In the 2004 regional election, the FN obtained less support in Brittany than anywhere else in France, less than the UDB/Green list (though more than the far left).

Political traditions in Brittany have been deeply influenced by Catholicism, the Catholic Church and by Christian-democratic ideas. A local branch of the Catholic union, the CFTC, was created in Rennes as early as 1925 (Le Galès, 1993). The city became one of the citadels of Christian-democracy; in 1945, 4 out of 7 Ille-et-Vilaine deputies belonged to the Christian-democratic Popular Republican Movement (MRP). The decline of French Christian democracy since the 1960s has favoured both the Gaullists and most especially the Socialists. In the 1970s, the Socialists made considerable local inroads, with the PS winning a string of town halls in 1977 (in Rennes, Brest, Lorient, Saint Brieuc and many other towns), most of which have remained with the party ever since. The Socialist Party in Brittany in the 1970s appeared as the inheritor to the reformist tradition that had been alive in the left wing of the MRP. The PS was renovated in Brittany by forces from outside of the old Socialist Party, the SFIO: these included former PSU activists, members of regionalist political clubs and associative movements, left-Catholic groups and new party members influenced by the ideals of May 1968. Many local Socialists were (and remain) active in the Breton regionalist movement, which had an important influence on the local political community.

In post-war Brittany, there has been a strong political consensus among the regional elites in favour of enhanced regionalisation. The prevailing post-war model of political activism has been one of territorial solidarity aimed at procuring material advantages for Brittany, namely through raising living standards in what had been France's poorest region in 1945. From 1950 onwards, Breton actors of all political persuasions co-operated closely in the CELIB – *Comité d'étude et de liaison des intérêts bretons* – the archetype of a post-war regional coalition (Cressard, 2000). The CELIB brought together politicians from all parties, along with professional and economic interests to promote the interests of the region. Under the impetus of CELIB, Brittany was the first French region to publish a regional plan (in 1953), calling for industrialisation and improved transport facilities. The CELIB served as a model for post-war French planning. The activities of CELIB inspired the French State to launch its first regional plan in 1956. The lobbying activity was crowned with success, as the French State poured massive resources into Brittany in the 1950s and 1960s. The CELIB could certainly claim the credit for many of the improvements in transport infrastructure conceded to the Brittany region in the 1960s and 1970s and remains a powerful reference point today.

Interviews with surviving actors and published historical accounts demonstrate that instrumentalist ends coexisted within the CELIB with a high degree of regional consciousness and a desire for powerful regional political institutions. How to affirm Breton identity continues to be a source of division. The mainstream view has been to lobby for increased state and EU resources to rescue Brittany from its isolated geographical position and to assure its integration with the rest of France (and Europe). Looking to the State – whether for industrial investment or for support for a fledgling intensive agriculture – has been a favoured position, one pursued on a cross-partisan basis. This regional advocacy position has always been contested by an autonomist minority, more concerned to safeguard and strengthen Breton identity than to promote the integration of Brittany within the French nation. This dichotomy was illustrated in interviews by the case of the fast-speed train (TGV). Most interlocutors favoured extending the fast-speed train from Paris to Brest, in the far west of Brittany. MM. de Rohan (President of the Brittany Regional Council from 1998 to 2004) and Le Drian (President since April 2004) combined their efforts to plead Brittany's case in Paris, on this and several other dossiers. A minority of cultural activists was opposed, however, in the name of defending Breton identity. This example demonstrates why most regionally minded politicians have distanced themselves from the Breton movement. The regional cause has been much more effectively pursued by Christian Democrats, Socialists, and even Gaullists, than by the Breton regionalist or nationalist parties.

Breton nationalist and regionalist groups are tiny, apart arguably from the centre-left UDB considered below. Breton nationalist or regionalist movements are scattered across the political spectrum, from extreme left (EMGANN), through centre-left (UDB), to centre right (POBL, Frankiz Breizh, Parti Breton) and extreme right (ADSAV, MRB). Some of these groups operate in conditions of semi-clandestinity. EMGANN, for example, which advocates complete independence for a Socialist Brittany, is the best structured of the extreme-left movements. EMGANN is believed by police to be the political wing of the Revolutionary Breton Army (Armée révolutionnaire bretonne – ARB), assumed to be behind a murderous bomb attack on a McDonald's in the town of Quévert in April 2000. Several traits characterise all of these movements. First, they are extremely small. The best organised, the UDB, counts at best 3,000 activists, and most of the others have fewer than 100. Second, attempts to create a pan-Breton, cross-partisan party have failed, leaving the Breton movement to exhaust its meagre forces in an astonishing array of minor causes. Some of these groups have adopted verbally violent stances, which sit uneasily with the prevailing legitimist representations of Breton political culture. Only the UDB has any sizeable presence.

There are two main explanations for the weakness of the regionalist movements. First, Bretons have refused to support in meaningful numbers any movement that calls into question Brittany's belonging to the French

Republic. One expert explains the weakness of the indigenous Breton political movement as a consequence of the deeply rooted legitimist strand within Breton public opinion (Le Coadic, 1998). Imbued by a Catholic, conformist ethic, the Breton public is not prepared to support pro-independence or pro-Autonomist parties. This conformist sentiment is reflected in the modest scores obtained in elections by the Breton Democratic Union (UDB) and the smaller Breton regional or autonomist parties. Second, the political opportunity structure in the French Fifth Republic is so resolutely Paris-centric that Breton forces have adapted accordingly. There is an underlying consensus amongst the 'French' parties to defend Breton interests to the outside world and limit political conflict. This consensual model is broadly shared within Breton public opinion, where there is a high degree of trust in the regional council, a belief that the region defends Brittany's interest well in other arenas and a preference for the region over other arenas in many important areas of public policy (Cole and Loughlin, 2003). The annual surveys on Brittany carried out by the Paris-based OIP confirms these findings, as docs comparative work with other French regions (Nicolas, 2004; Dargent, 2001). The idea of region has a strong moral authority in the case of Brittany, the birthplace of regional consciousness and identity in France, but it is defined as being complementary to that of the wider nation.

Conclusion

From a political-science perspective, devolution, decentralisation and other forms of regional political capacity building provide a laboratory for comparative analysis. This chapter has set out to make a good case for the functional equivalence of the Wales–Brittany comparison. While firmly rooted in comparative methodology, this comparison of Wales and Brittany goes beyond the preoccupations of traditional comparison. Comparative political studies usually focus on similarities, differences and methods of agreement and equivalence (Sartori, 1991; Collier, 1991; Van Deth, 1998). Comparative public-policy research is driven either by the structural qualities of policy sectors or by the dynamic qualities of the policy process. Policy analysis aims to investigate why some policies are more successful than others, using techniques of policy evaluation (Patton, 1990). The research described in this book lies at the intersection of these approaches: investigating cognate comparisons, uncovering political and policy dynamics and drawing lessons. Its interest is as much in the interactions between Wales and Brittany as in the contrasts between them, a theme implicit in each chapter but resurfacing fully in Chapter 7. In the next chapters comes the investigation into the politics, policics and polity-building potential of devolution in Wales and decentralisation in Brittany. The overarching research question, as established above, is that of regional political capacity building. To gauge regional political capacity in Wales and Brittany (the 'dependent variable'), several levels of analysis are explained. Variables include the operation of, and popular support for, regional political institutions in Wales and Brittany; the role of dual and multiple identities in underpinning moves to regional autonomy; regional public policies and the operation of policy communities; the weight of the external environment. Within this broad framework, the aim is to establish comparative dynamics in Wales and Brittany. What weight should be given to national institutional and administrative traditions in both countries? How important are regionally specific explanations and how can these be conceptualised? Can distinctions be drawn between the policy issue areas and, if so, what does this tell about the operation of regional institutions in the two countries? How does public opinion view the prospect of greater regional autonomy, and what are the acceptable parameters within which public policy is formulated in the two regions? Each of these variables contributes towards refining an overall understanding of how political capacity is developed in these two distinctive regions in neighbouring European Union states.

4
Devolution and polity building in Wales

Much of the devolution debate in Wales has centred upon the uniqueness of Welsh constitutional arrangements and political traditions. Several features set the Wales case apart from those in Scotland, Northern Ireland and the English Regions. Wales had a history of limited administrative devolution from 1964 to 1999. While Scotland retained its separate legal and educational systems, Wales was routinely considered, for legislative and political purposes, either as part of England or as the junior partner in an indissoluble couple. Neither Scotland nor Wales is comparable to Northern Ireland, where the historical experience of devolved institutions runs much deeper, but where underlying communitarian tensions shape and prescribe the nature of the devolved institutions. While many of the challenges facing devolution in Wales and Scotland in particular are similar or identical, the devolutionary path in Wales has been distinctive, shaped by the hybrid nature of the 1998 devolution 'settlement' and the dynamic process thereby unleashed. The main body of this chapter presents findings drawn from about seventy interviews carried out within and around the National Assembly for Wales. Most of these interviews took place at the mid-term point of the first Assembly, from October 2001 to March 2002, supplemented by a smaller number of follow-up interviews in early 2004. Interviews took place with Assembly members, ministers and top officials, as well as within the broader policy community. The chapter presents a general overview of devolution in Wales, with a special emphasis on building a new institution from an actor-focused perspective. Venturing inside the National Assembly we discover members' frustration with the operation of the institution. The evolution of Welsh devolution away from 'all-inclusive politics' to polity building is charted, and the different ways in which the Assembly can make a difference in policy terms are explored, with discussion of relationships between the National Assembly and its semi-autonomous public bodies. The role of the civil service is investigated, as are the party system and financial arrangements in post-devolution Wales. The chapter concludes with a comment on the improbability of an incoming UK Conservative government seeking to turn back the devolutionary tide.

From the Government of Wales Act to the Richard Commission

The Government of Wales Act (1998) created a National Assembly with secondary legislative and regulatory powers, rather than with primary legislative and tax-varying powers as in Scotland. The model of executive devolution implemented in the Government of Wales Act (GWA) of 1998 was heavily imbued with the legacy of the Welsh office, from the precise functions transferred to the key civil-service personnel involved in assuring the transition. The Assembly inherited 'the exact powers of the Secretary of State', though the Secretary of State had been part of central government with a voice in cabinet. Critics argued that powers were transferred solely for reasons of administrative and political convenience rather than on evidence-based criteria, resulting in a patchwork of powers, not a well-thought-out approach. The powers transferred were largely those of the Welsh Office. But the reasons for the transfer of powers had been pragmatic rather than principled in the first place. They had evolved in an arbitrary and haphazard matter, usually reflecting different traditions within Whitehall departments.

Rawlings (2003) diagnoses four basic principles underpinning the Welsh model of executive devolution enshrined in the 1998 Government of Wales Act. These are the vertical division of law-making powers; the horizontal division between secondary and primary law-making powers; the overlapping of powers with central government and the evolutionary character of the devolution process.

Through the vertical division of law-making powers, devolution presupposes a dual polity. There is an implicit division of labour between the devolved and central governments. The core functions of the state remain with central government. These are defence, taxation, social security, immigration and nationality laws. The Government of Wales Act transfers seventeen 'fields', namely agriculture, ancient monuments and historic buildings, culture, economic development, education and training, the environment, health and health services, highways, housing, industry, local government, social services, sport and leisure, tourism, town and country planning, transport and roads and the Welsh language. There is no precise, constitutionally based division as in a genuine federal system. Consistent with the doctrine of parliamentary sovereignty, and the principle of secondary legislative powers, Westminster retains (theoretical) legislative pre-eminence even in transferred areas. Conforming to the traditional local-government model, moreover, the

Assembly can only act where it has precise statutory responsibilities. It cannot raise additional sources of finance. It can, however, make primary legislation within secondary legislation (through statutory instruments and circulars), which vests it with an important policy-formulation role. For the main architect of devolution, the only advantage of this hybrid and obfuscated system was that it helped to deliver devolution to Wales. The Welsh public, apathetic when not antipathetic, would not have accepted a bolder scheme.

The horizontal division between secondary and primary law-making powers is Rawlings' second principle. The amount of power transferred depends on the rules governing a particular statute; powers are literally enumerated statute by statute (Lambert and Navarro, 2004). There is no general administrative competency. The Government of Wales Act explicitly set out few functions; most were transferred by statutory orders by the Secretary of State. The Assembly obtained nearly all of the Secretary of State's previous functions, dispersed across 300 laws and statutes. Altogether, some 3,000 statutory instruments were inherited from the Welsh office – many of which are contradictory. Though creating a form of hybrid partial devolution, the Government of Wales Act empowered the Assembly in several ways. Through its control of statutory instruments, the Assembly can make its own delegated legislation in the seventeen transferred fields. The precise rules vary according to the terms of each Act. In some cases the margins of manoeuvre are very narrow and the Assembly has little possibility to modify rules formulated in Westminster. In other cases, framework legislation can leave much more discretion with the devolved Assembly. The Government of Wales Act also enabled specific functions to be transferred to the Assembly through the Transfer of Functions Order (TFO) mechanism. The number of TFOs has gathered pace as the ground rules of the relationship between London and Cardiff have become established and accepted by the main players. In the early years of devolution, there were few TFOs and upon average only one Wales-only bill in Westminister per annum. After five years of devolution, Transfer of Functions Orders had become a more regular occurrence, with student fees, the fire service and emergency planning transferred in 2004 alone. London has become more devolution friendly, attributed by one insider to the closer relationship between Rhodri Morgan and Prime Minister Blair.

Devolution in Wales is characterised by an overlapping of powers and a policy interdependency inherent in the devolution settlement and the lack of clearly defined generic principles. There is no general legislative competence for the Assembly in the devolved areas: the Assembly can only act where it has a statutory basis for action. Even in the Assembly's areas of decision-making responsibility, it is often unable to act alone. This political dependency produces a form of interdependent policy-making observed in operation elsewhere in the field of education and training, economic development, agriculture and employment policy (Cole and Storer, 2002).

A final principle of devolution in Wales is that of an ongoing allocation of powers. As Rawlings rightly argues, 'this alone ensures that the devolution of today is not the devolution of tomorrow' (Rawlings, 1998). While change can strengthen the Assembly through Transfer of Functions Orders, it does not always have this effect. Westminster can also take powers away from the Assembly. Since devolution several new laws have repealed older ones where Wales had special dispositions. Many Westminster bills do not take devolution into account at all. New bills can take powers away from the Assembly quite simply because they fail to mention the former arrangements. Once this has occurred it is very difficult to override the new Acts, except by a new Transfer of Functions Order, a complicated and timely affair.

The view from Assembly Members

In the interviews with Assembly members during 2001 and 2002, the existing system found few supporters. Assembly Members were generally preoccupied with their uncertain powers and with procedural complexity. Most interviewees were confused about what they could and could not do, with one describing the devolution settlement as 'bizarre, useless and complicated'. One member close to the centre of the Assembly's operations admitted that 'I do not know what the powers are that we have. When Westminster passes a new Act it may repeal previous Acts. If these contained devolved powers, then they vanish, unless they are re-enacted in a subsequent Act. Not many people would know exactly what the powers are.'

Lack of knowledge about what the Assembly could or could not do was a major concern. This produced a form of non-transparent governance. The Assembly could not make coherent policies because it had neither the legislative means nor informational resources to do so. To exercise its available powers, the Assembly needed to know what is going on elsewhere, especially in London and Brussels. It should be able to influence primary legislation enacted in Westminster in a much more consistent manner. There were too few 'Wales-only' bills at Westminster, and UK government departments did not go out of their way to accommodate the Welsh interest. Interviewees from all parties lamented the lack of Assembly resources dedicated to tracking future legislation in Westminster. One Assembly member spoke for many when she described the hybrid devolution system, where the Assembly can only act on the basis of precise statutes, as 'hugely irritating'. Another member expressed the view held by many that 'administrative convenience should not guide democracy in Wales'.

The backbench Assembly members interviewed in 2001 and 2002 clearly were politically inexperienced and bewildered by the complexity of the governing arrangements. Only seven of the sixty Assembly Members elected in 1999 had previously held Westminster mandates, and most had a background in local government. In most interviews with Assembly members from all parties, strong demands were formulated for new powers. A majority of members interviewed favoured moving to a more transparent system based on full legislative and tax-varying powers. As it stood, the consensus view was that, deprived of full legislative powers in the transferred domains, the National Assembly lacked the legal and political means for its policy ambitions. Even the Conservative group accepted that a clarification of the Assembly's powers was essential.

The views expressed above were not unanimous. Some Assembly members took a different view on each of the above themes. To take one example, the demand for new powers was not universally acknowledged. One devolution-sceptic Labour member believed that the Assembly had not fully exhausted its secondary powers and could ill-afford to raise taxes even if given the legal power to do so. The majority view encountered amongst Assembly members is that the system created in the 1998 Government of Wales Act suffered from a lack of clarity and a confused and unworkable attribution of functions.

In a series of follow-up interviews in 2004, opinions were rather more nuanced, though still favourable to the ultimate goal of a Welsh parliament. The existing devolution settlement was demonstrating its ability to innovate, as demonstrated above with the increased number of Transfer of Functions Orders. By 2004, moreover, a recognisable Welsh political leadership had emerged, with many of the same ministers in post for many years (Jane Davidson at Education, Jane Hutt at Health or Carwyn Jones at Agriculture) some of whom had become household names. Even executive devolution had made a difference and had established itself as an object of identification with public opinion.

In summary, the in-depth interviews demonstrated dissatisfaction with the devolution scheme introduced by the Government of Wales Act and a desire to move towards primary legislative and tax-varying powers, the Scottish solution. The opaque character of the current system fuelled demands for future clarification. The arrival in power of Rhodri Morgan proved a watershed in this respect, as in others. Two important initiatives have been undertaken since September 2000. The first of these was the Assembly Review of Procedure, set up by the Assembly in 2000 and operational throughout 2001. The Assembly's Procedural Review was given a precise brief: to evaluate the Government of Wales Act and to clarify the role of the Assembly on the basis of the rules it had inherited. It was a limited exercise, followed by only super-ficial changes. The Labour-Liberal-Democrat Partnership Agreement also contained a provision to establish an independent Commission to deliberate on how the powers of the Assembly could be improved. The Richard Commission, appointed in the first quarter of 2002, reported in Spring 2004.

In its terms of reference, the Richard Commission was guided by the dual criteria of efficiency and democracy, echoing the instrumentalist/identity debate uncovered in Chapter 1. Efficiency questions were foremost in the minds of the Secretary of State for Wales. Peter Hain advocated a 'practical delivery benchmark test', arguing that changes should only be proposed when they would produce a demonstrable improvement in policy outputs. This util-itarian appreciation was far removed from the polity-building logic of the weight of evidence presented to the Commission.

When it finally reported in March 2004, the Richard Commission made a number of key recommendations. It proposed the transformation of the National Assembly into a fully fledged Parliament, with primary powers for all matters not explicitly reserved for Westminster. Legislative devolution on the Scottish model would bring about a more transparent and systematic divi-sion of powers between Westminster and the Assembly. It would endorse the momentum for a distinctive Welsh policy agenda. Logically, the Commission proposed abandoning the doctrine of the Corporate Body in favour of a clearer separation of powers between government and legislature. The Commission proposed an increase in the size of the Assembly from sixty to eighty members, justified in order to meet the new workload of primary leg-islation. The Scottish solution was only partly endorsed; tax-varying powers were deemed to be 'desirable, but not essential'. Finally, Richard proposed replacing the additional member system with the single transferable vote (STV).

The most innovative aspects of the Richard Commission's work lay in its methodology (the evidence-based approach that was reflected in its recommen-dations) and the critical appreciation it offered of the operation of devolution thus far. For Richard, the Assembly has demonstrated that it can be entrusted with developing full policies for Wales. The Assembly has evolved distinctive Welsh policy agendas under the current arrangements, considerable difficulties notwithstanding. The original conception of secondary legislation has been considerably widened, so that Wales 'already has some of the features of legis-lative devolution'. Full legislative authority for Wales was justified with two main arguments. First, the institutional patchwork of the Government of Wales Act does not favour transparent or effective governance and has produced hap-hazard, inconsistent decision-making. Second, experience has shown that Wales is a very low priority for Westminster (primary) legislation.

Under the current arrangements, there are no guarantees that the Assembly will continue to benefit from a benign environment in London. In the event of different political majorities in Cardiff and London, scenarios are difficult to predict. No part of the British constitution sets out what is to be deemed primary and what secondary legislation. At present, there are no guaranteed powers for the Assembly. Rawlings (2001, 2003) points out that a future hostile government could 'cheat the Assembly of its powers' by minimising the range of statutory instruments agreed in future laws. De facto, this would concentrate powers in London. The Richard Commission concluded that Assembly powers needed to be on a firm legal footing in order to secure them for the future. The Commission also set out a tentative timetable for moving to full legislative powers by 2011 at the latest.

From all-inclusive politics to polity building?

For Patchett (2000: 229): 'The National Assembly for Wales is an institution without constitutional precedent'. The Assembly was established as a corporate body, combining rather than separating executive and legislative functions. As with the traditional local government model (and awaiting the implementation of the Richard Commission recommendations) there is no separation in law between the various parts of the Assembly and no obvious distinction between the executive and legislative branches. Osmond (2001) has argued that the smooth running of the Assembly as designed by the Act depends upon the development of a consensus and an inclusive political culture between the Administration (Cabinet and civil service) and the legislature (the sixty Assembly members, acting in plenary session and through committees). As events have unfolded, however, the Assembly has come to resemble in important respects the Westminster model it was set up to supersede. There has been a governing party (Labour since May 2003) or coalition (Labour-Liberal Democrat from October 2000 to April 2003), a recognisable opposition (led by Plaid Cymru, the nationalist party), the development of Welsh Assembly Government as the executive branch and the strengthening of the 'legislature', in the form of the sixty Assembly members and the Presiding Office, the 300–strong administrative support service for the National Assembly.

McAllister (2000) has highlighted the desire of the architects of the Welsh devolution process to move away from the confrontational and adversarial politics of the Westminster model in favour of a more inclusive form of politics. All-inclusive politics implied new forms of cross-party dialogue and the involvement of non-governing parties in policy-making decisions. All-inclusive politics was in part imposed by electoral realities, as the Welsh Labour Party failed to win an overall majority in the first Assembly elections of 1999. The founding fathers were also faced with the need to heal the wounds of the devolution debate which had divided the country into two. The wafer-thin majority (50.3 per cent) in the 1997 referendum raised questions about the commitment of the Welsh voters to devolution. The departure of the father of devolution (and the announced First Minister) Ron Davies in 1999, before the institutions of devolution had had the chance to take root, was a blow to the young Assembly. Many supporters of devolution, including within the Labour Party, resented the appointment of Alun Michael as First Minister in May 1999. Michael, generally regarded as having been imposed by UK Prime Minister Blair, adopted a strictly minimal conception of the Assembly's powers and role. By February 2000 Michael had been forced to resign, ousted by a vote of no-confidence over his handling of the Objective One negotiations with the Treasury.

During the period May 1999 to October 2000, all-inclusive politics was the practical outcome of a minority Labour administration. During the early phase, 'all-inclusive politics' played itself out above all in the Assembly's Subject Committees. The National Assembly has eighteen parliamentary committees, which can be split into three categories: Standing, Regional and Subject Committees, of which the latter are by far the most significant (Sandford and Maer, 2003). Subject Committees have the greatest potential to affect public policy in Wales. According to the 1998 Act, they perform dual roles: those of executive scrutiny and of policy development. All members are allocated to at least one committee. Their executive-scrutiny role is innovative in certain respects. Ministers are also members of committees. In their capacity as Ministers, members of the Assembly Government can be called to account by the subject committees. But in their capacity as committee members, they contribute to formulating policy. This dual role has produced variable situations, best exemplified by the Agriculture and Rural Affairs Committee during the first term. For the first half of its meetings, Carwyn Jones appeared as Minister and was subject to scrutiny, while for the second half he became a normal committee member. Civil servants are also called to appear before committees.

The 'policy-development' role of the subject committees was most in evidence during the early unstable years of Welsh devolution. One of the few instances of successful policy development by a subject committee was the Post-16 Education Committee's review of the Education and Training Action Plan (ETAP) (Osmond 2001). ETAP presented options for the reorganisation of post-16 training in Wales. It was drafted by Welsh Office civil servants in the period immediately prior to the launch of the Assembly. The proposals were first put to the post-16 committee in June 1999, with the Administration anxious to push the plan through quickly to avoid reopening the debate. Cynog Dafis, the Plaid Cymru chair of the post-16 committee, determined otherwise. During the following six months, the committee took evidence from a wide range of bodies. The exercise culminated in a report in December 1999 that added a number of significant amendments to the original report. These substantial policy amendments were all incorporated into the primary legislation put before the House of Lords early in 2000.

This well-documented example of policy development is not unique. There are several other examples where subject committees affected policy outcomes, notably the Culture Committee's review of the Welsh language in 2002. On balance, committee efficacy has correlated negatively with party cohesion, as it usually does in most legislatures. The subject committees were most effective during the operation of the minority Labour administration during 1999 and 2000. From September 2000 until the end of the first Assembly, the partnership agreement provided for more traditional party discipline. Not only did the coalition have a majority in plenary, but it also had a majority on the subject committees. During the second term, the subject committees have performed an even less important role, with the Welsh Assembly Government insisting on reducing the regularity of their meetings (now once every three weeks instead of every two) and being less open to their findings. The constitutional responsibility and the legislative initiative for developing policy now rest clearly with the Assembly Minister and not the subject committees.

The political style of the Assembly has gradually become more confrontational, more akin to a genuine parliamentary democracy. All-party inclusive policy-making began to wither as soon as Rhodri Morgan took over from Alun Michael as Labour First Minister in February 2000. Morgan's victory marked an important watershed in the history of Welsh politics, symbolising the coming of age of a specifically Welsh Labour party, cognisant above all of its core territorial interests. Head of a minority Labour administration from February to September 2000, Morgan was forced to accept a Labour/Liberal Democrat coalition from October 2000 to April 2003, the 'partnership agreement'. But he never concealed his preference for a single-party administration. This wish was granted after the 2003 elections, when Labour formed a single-party administration after the second Assembly elections. All-inclusivity has given way to a more ambitious political discourse based on polity development, articulated most clearly by Carwyn Jones, the Agriculture minister. There has been much less talk of the Assembly as a corporate body, much more emphasis on building a political system based on a Welsh Government accountable to a Welsh parliament. Though the rhetoric of all-inclusivity is associated with the early period of devolution, all Welsh parties have moved closer together in some important respects. There is general agreement across all parties that the Assembly's powers need to be revised, though institutional preferences differ greatly. For the UK-based parties there is awareness that devolution encourages a territorial adjustment of their core political message. Even the Welsh Conservatives have learned this lesson.

How the Assembly has made a difference

Though the Government of Wales Act did not vest the Assembly with tax-varying or primary legislative powers, in practice the devolved institutions in Wales have demonstrated much policy innovation. There have been an impressive number of independent policy initiatives in Wales since Devolution. Some of the better known include the creation of the UK's first Children's Commissioner, free bus passes for the over-60s or the important structural and substantive reforms in health, in education and training and in economic development (Jeffery, 2004a). Rather than enumerating a list, it is useful to classify these policy initiatives in terms of a policy spectrum. These initiatives can be conceptualised in terms of incremental changes, institutional capacity building, identity markers, interdependency and policy inflation.

The Assembly has introduced incremental changes that contribute to the image of Wales as a small country committed to social justice and equality. The decision to introduce free bus travel for pensioners is a case in point, as is free school milk for the under-7s. These small incremental measures have undoubtedly captured the public imagination. In some important respects, the Assembly has been acting as a large local authority, the 'glorified county council' much decried by opponents of devolution in 1997. Though the twenty-two unitary authorities in Wales have responsibility for most service delivery, some of the best-publicised actions of the Assembly Government have been rather akin to those of a County Council in pre-Thatcher Britain.

The Assembly has introduced far-reaching structural reforms forming part of a wider exercise of institutional capacity building. In health and education, the two main priorities of the Welsh public, the Assembly has used the full scope of its regulatory authority to reshape the structures of service delivery and the goals of public policy. In healthcare, policy initiatives have ranged from introducing free medical prescriptions for the under-25s and over-60s, to abolishing NHS trusts, to setting up twenty-two Health Boards to replace the seven Area Health Authorities and to work alongside Wales's twenty-two local authorities (Sullivan, 2002). Inspired by the Scottish Parliament's introduction of free care for the elderly, the Welsh Assembly has pledged itself to providing six weeks' free home care for the elderly after discharge from hospital. These reforms have been overshadowed by the controversy over waiting lists and unfavourable benchmark reports into the standard of healthcare in Wales. Health professionals complain of reorganisation fatigue, with at least three major reforms of the NHS since 1999.

Education and training is another field where far-reaching reforms have been introduced (Cole and Storer, 2002; Reynolds, 2002; Rees, 2002). In the field of pre-16 education, the Assembly has rejected Prime Minister Blair's specialist schools, retained comprehensives, ended testing for 7-year-olds and rejected all Private Finance initiatives in education. In the sphere of post-16 adult training, education and lifelong learning, the Assembly has abolished the Training and Enterprise Councils (TECs), piloted a Welsh Baccalaureat, suspended (and then reintroduced) Individual Learning Accounts, undertaken a wide-ranging review of higher education and overhauled post-16 provision. In place of the TECs, the Assembly established and created a new complex new institutional structure co-ordinated by the Council for Education and Learning Wales (ELWa). In its short existence (2001–06) ELWa had strategic responsibility for post-16 education, training and lifelong learning in Wales. The case of education and training is considered in some more detail in Chapter 7.

Third, the Assembly has used its regulatory and legislative authority to promote Welsh identity markers, most notably with respect to the Welsh language, as well as in the sphere of culture and sport.

Fourth, and notwithstanding the overwhelming desire to be different, the Assembly has had to manage a set of interdependent relations that restrict the possibilities for autonomous action. Education, for example, is an area of interdependent policy-making, as well as a field for policy innovation. The Assembly does not exercise control over all secondary legislation concerning education in Wales. For instance, teacher pay and conditions are still decided by London. One interviewee lamented the fact that 'since devolution, more secondary legislation affecting Wales on education has been passed through the Westminster parliament than [through] the Assembly'. In higher education, on the other hand, the Assembly has been gaining ground, most recently with the devolution of student fees and the commitment not to raise fees until 2008.

Agriculture is another interdependent policy field. There is a real difficulty in identifying the locus of decision-making in agricultural affairs, a field which is subject to a high degree of European and UK regulation. Most agricultural matters are subject to EU law and are shaped by European directives. As the EU member-state, the UK central government can ensure that the National Assembly is fulfilling its requirements in relation to implementation of EU laws in this field.

A couple of examples demonstrate the constraints on the Assembly's action. The Government of Wales Act states that the Assembly has no powers to act in a way countervening EU law. There has been at least one occasion when the Assembly stood out against the European Commission. In 2001, the Assembly Government declared itself in favour of a 'GM-free territory', a position supported by all Welsh parties. But the European Commission opposed this and threatened to take the UK government to the Court of Justice for non-compliance (Rawlings, 2003). Though the Assembly delayed implementation for 18 months, it eventually backed down, faced with the prospect of having to pay any fines imposed on the UK government. The 2001 foot-and-mouth crisis also demonstrated the limits to the Assembly's command of agriculture. Its lack of control over animal-health issues rendered its formal powers in the sphere of agriculture virtually meaningless for the duration of the foot-and-mouth crisis. On the other hand, the foot-and-mouth crisis also demonstrated that those at Assembly level were closer to the ground and had better information than officials in London or Brussels. One by-product of the crisis was to strengthen the Assembly's role in the eyes of Welsh farmers.

The management of European Union issues represents another area of shared decision-making. As Carter and Scott (2003) affirm, 'under devolution around 80% of the policies assigned to the devolved institutions were also policies for which the EU has a competence: notably agriculture, fisheries, environment, economic development'. Wherever powers are shared with the European Union, Westminster is able to exercise close supervision over the activities of the devolved governments. Herein lies the creative tension in the British version of multi-level governance. Insofar as they impact upon the European Union, the UK government (as the member-state) retains close control over areas of public policy that have in theory been decentralised to devolved institutions. The UK government (which usually, but not always, signifies central government ministers) negotiates in the Council of Ministers and the European Council – including in those areas devolved to the regional institutions. The UK can insist on adopting secondary legislation at Westminster to implement EU directives. The post-devolution UK model of managing European Union affairs is innovative in several respects, however (Burch and Gomez, 2003; Carter and Scott, 2002). Alone amongst member-states, the UK has allowed ministers from the devolved authorities to represent the UK government in European Council meetings. Officials from the devolved authorities, moreover, are given full diplomatic status within UKREP and have access to more information than is the case for sub-national authorities in other countries.

The Assembly has begun to shape a distinctive European policy. The

Welsh Assembly Government has developed its own pan-European networks and begun to co-ordinate its activity with other 'legislative regions'. The most ambitious recent example of Welsh paradiplomacy is the Memorandum of Understanding signed with Latvia, a full member state of the EU since May 2004. Closer to home, the Assembly is responsible for administering EU Structural funds (including Objective One for the period 2000–6), which are managed on its behalf by the Wales European Funding Office (WEFO). WEFO is an Assembly-sponsored public body (ASPB) using the Assembly's cross-cutting criteria (social inclusion, environmental sustainability and equal opportunities) as a yardstick against which to measure funding bids.

Fifth, the Assembly has engaged in policy inflation. The Assembly Administration has sought to exercise influence where it has no statutory competence. This is the case in employment policy. UK Employment policy is determined by Job Centre Plus, a central-government agency, but this has not prevented the Assembly from setting its own ambitious growth and employment targets. In successive documents – *Plan for Wales*, *Better Wales.com* and *A Winning Wales* – the Assembly Government has identified the need to increase employment in Wales by 135,000 over ten years. By their own recruiting activities, the Assembly Government and its ASPBs have greatly increased public-sector employment since 1999 (Cooke, 2003). Though the Assembly does not have competence over employment policy, it is charged with piloting economic development and has been highly active in this field, as illustrated by its reforms of the Welsh Development Agency and Finance Wales and its ambitious spatial development plan. On the other hand, the reluctance of the Assembly to engage with non-devolved institutions could cause resentment from representatives of central-government agencies such as Employment Services and the Equal Opportunities Commission.

The counterpart to policy inflation is a general process of experimentation and imitation. There are also several examples of where devolved policies have had a knock-on effect in the UK. The Children's Commissioner, first introduced in Wales, was subsequently copied by the other parts of the UK. The Learning and Skills Councils in England were modelled on ELWa in Wales. Issues such as free long-term care in Scotland have established the terms of the policy debate elsewhere. In this way, devolution has facilitated the emergence of policy laboratories, has reduced the transaction costs of formulating new policies and has intensified the search for trans-regional or trans-national policy solutions.

What should be concluded from this brief overview? Taking account of the context within which it operates (one of policy interdependency and a limited capacity for policy innovation), the National Assembly for Wales has definitely left its mark. While it is logically impossible to predict what would have happened had the Assembly never existed, there is room for conjecture. Several interviewees were convinced that Wales would never have obtained Objective One match funding under the old Welsh Office regime. The opportunity to use statutory instruments to adapt Westminster primary legislation has produced variable policy outcomes in a range of fields: education, training, health care, agriculture and others. There is some evidence that Wales has set a number of policy trends, as in the case of opening up and advertising public appointments for some Assembly-sponsored public bodies. Finally, the National Assembly now controls its own agenda in a more forthright manner than was the case in the pre-devolution period. The National Assembly is nowhere near as constrained by the rules of collective cabinet responsibility as was the Secretary of State for Wales before devolution.

Team Wales? The National Assembly, its public agencies and civil society

It was argued above that the efficacy of the Welsh Office depended to some extent upon whether it operated at the centre of a territorial network. Strong links between Welsh Office civil servants and representatives of Welsh local government provided one example of fruitful co-operation allowing Welsh actors to modify Conservative government policies (Jones, 1986). Much more than the Welsh Office, the National Assembly for Wales will be judged on its ability to position itself at the centre of all-Wales networks. At an elite level, at least, actors believe in a 'Wales effect'. In the opinion of one interlocutor, 'We've got better structures in Wales than in England. We've got Team Wales, we're small and we work closely together'. All the main players know each other personally and there are close linkages not only between civil servants and ministers but also between politicians, officials and representatives of Welsh civil society. In its first term, devolution in Wales created several new all-Wales organisations, such as Careers Wales and Education and Learning Wales (ELWa) and reformed old ones such as the Welsh Development Agency (WDA). The Assembly transformed the myriad of agencies (quangos) inherited from pre-devolution days into Assembly-sponsored public bodies (ASPBs) and introduced mechanisms to make them more accountable.

There are now much closer relationships across public-sector organisations within Wales. The transformation of quangos into Assembly-sponsored public bodies made a big difference. In the opinion of one senior official in the Welsh Development Agency, devolution totally transformed the relationship between Cathays Park and the main economic-development agency within Wales. Previously distant, relations have become much more regular, though barely more trusting. Similar views were expressed within Education and Learning Wales (ELWa), the Welsh Tourist Board and the Welsh Language Board. The National Assembly knew that it would be held responsible for the success or otherwise of the WDA, ELWa and the other main Assembly-sponsored public bodies. In interviews, officials within the Assembly government and in the main ASPBs regularly referred to 'Team Wales', the common sense of belonging to a territory with a strong identity. By common consent, 'Team Wales' plays in favour of developing closer relationships across organisations and encouraging personal contacts between the main organisational stakeholders. That the Assembly now names the top officials in the ASPBs has ensured that these agencies are more representative of the Welsh society they are supposed to serve. Even before First Minister Morgan's June 2004 announcement, the Welsh Assembly Government exercised much closer control over the ASPBs than it ever could over a quango during Welsh Office days. The main ASPBs receive annual 'remit letters' from their minister, setting out in precise detail what they are expected to achieve over the coming year. These remit letters have to be incorporated into ongoing strategic documents (such as the ELWa Corporate Strategy, for example). The main ASPBs have to present an annual report to the Assembly, setting out how their objectives have been achieved. On the other hand, as many functions escape the Assembly, many UK agencies over which the Assembly has no direct control continue to operate within Wales (in the area of social security and employment policy notably).

Arguably the most significant development since 1999 is that the Assembly has encouraged the development of a specifically Welsh civil society. The existence of the Assembly has incited leading professional and voluntary associations to organise themselves on a pan-Wales basis. In the case of housing, for example, various professional organisations have reorganised their structures since devolution. Welsh branches of the Chartered Housing Association, of the Valuers' Association or of the Architects' Association have all been created to deal with the devolved institutions. The Assembly itself has made a determined effort to build a Welsh civic society and has created a series of semi-formal networks (the three 'Partnership Councils' for business, the voluntary sector and local government) to associate public, private and voluntary sectors with policy formulation. Opinion from within the policy community regarding the effectiveness of these partnership councils was mixed. If the Voluntary Sector Partnership was considered on both sides as central to the Assembly's aim of promoting social cohesion, there was much less consensus regarding the utility of the Business Partnership Council. The main economic organisations – the CBI and the TUC – were rather sceptical about the usefulness of the Business Partnership Council, complaining of tokenism and of being overburdened with (unpaid) meetings. For its part, the Local

Government Partnership Council has become established as a useful channel of communication between the National Assembly and the twenty-two unitary authorities in Wales. According to one of the participants, the first meetings of the Local Government Partnership Council were 'very tense'. Local authorities feared they would lose powers with devolution. After 18 months, one key player believed that 'we had a very good relationship with local government', as the Assembly and councils got used to working together, a view not really endorsed from the local government side. In spite of its institutional activism, the Assembly has a relatively weak interconnectedness with other significant players, especially in local government and the business community.

In June 2004, First Minister Morgan announced the Assembly Government's intention to take over direct control (in 2006) of the Welsh Development Agency (WDA), the Wales Tourist Board (WTB) and the National Council for Education and Learning in Wales (ELWa). The communiqué evoked problems of political accountability and the desire to give a more democratic steer to policy-making in the areas covered by these semi-autonomous bodies. Undoubtedly, the Assembly Government had become frustrated by the repeated failings of ELWa and jealous of the semi-autonomy of the WDA. There was a political logic also: the WDA and WTB were inherited from older quangos established by the Conservatives. Organisations such as the WDA had demonstrated a high degree of operational independence that First Minister Morgan deemed incompatible with his understanding of democratic accountability. If ELWa was an Assembly creation, the balance of opinion was that it had failed in its mission to provide strategic leadership in the field of post-16 education and learning. The decision to wind up ELWa only five years after its creation was accepted as inevitable by many. The decision to merge the WDA and the WTB into the Assembly government civil service, on the other hand, caused deep resentment amongst officers of these semi-autonomous organisations. Morgan's announcement was followed by the immediate resignation of Graham Hawker, chief executive of the WDA. The decision to absorb the quangos appeared to run counter to trends in international public management, whereby agency independence is seen as a gauge of neutrality, public service and efficiency. On the other hand, we can interpret this decision as being consistent with the polity-building logic of devolution in Wales. Recovering control of the quangos was a political statement that devolution matters and that democratic institutions should control public policy. This decision coincided with First Minister Morgan's strong hint that the findings of the Richard Commission would not be implemented as they stood. Something else was needed to convince a sceptical Welsh public that the institutions of devolution matter. If the logic of institution building arguably explained this move, this was at the expense of maintaining good territorial relationships. Metaphors of Team Wales rang hollow after June 2004.

The ties that bind: intergovernmental relations and the post-devolution State

Devolution is subject to many countervailing pressures. It promises the development of more autonomous forms of political capacity, yet it also requires the invention of new forms of policy and political co-ordination (or at least the adaptation of older forms). In the expression of Charlie Jeffery (2004a), 'no other decentralised system has been conceived and operated with such little conscious attention to state-wide co-ordination of governmental activity'. There are several distinct dimensions to intergovernmental relations in the post-devolution UK State. Devolution in the United Kingdom has been incremental and piecemeal, driven by political and party pressures and founded upon informal relationships, ambiguous legal statutes and unwritten rules. This concluding section considers the ties that bind in the post-devolution state, focusing in turn upon the role of the civil service, formal and informal mechanisms of IGR, financial arrangements and the role of party politics.

Civil-service co-ordination

The National Assembly for Wales inherited the administrative infrastructure of the Welsh Office. All Assembly staff are members of the Home (i.e. UK) civil service. They report to the Permanent Secretary, Jon Shortridge, who was appointed by Prime Minister Blair. Those officials explicitly serving the Assembly (rather than the Assembly government) are organised separately in the Presiding Office, but they are subject to the same home civil service rules. At the very summit of the civil-service, the message is one of business as usual (Parry, 2001). There is regular interaction with Whitehall. The permanent secretaries of Scotland and Wales meet with other departmental permanent secretaries once a week in London. They sit on the civil-service management board charged with overall co-ordination of the home civil service. Lower down the scale, however, evidence suggests that contacts have diminished since devolution, due in equal measure to the tendency for Whitehall departments to ignore Wales and for civil servants working for the National Assembly to prioritise new post-devolution policy agendas.

All interviewees complained of their increased workload. For example, officials now have to prepare for and occasionally appear in front of Assembly committees, something for which most of them had previously had no experience. The biggest difference from Welsh Office days was qualitative. There is 'a lot of pressure from ministers to be different', especially from experience in England. In the devolved areas they 'are very interested in producing Made in Wales policies'. Civil servants are now involved in policy development, an evolution with which not all felt comfortable. Gaining policy development did not mean divesting officials of routine administrative tasks. Some officials complained about the unrealistic expectations held by ministers. There had been a seachange in expectations: 'During the Welsh Office days, we were staffed as an offshoot of Whitehall, relying on the lead department of Whitehall to do the bulk of the legwork. We tuned government policy to the Welsh perspective. We are now being asked to act as a free-standing government!' If the Assembly administration was not given more resources, Welsh civil servants would once again look to Whitehall departments for examples of best practice, going against the injunction to produce Made in Wales solutions. On the other hand, the pressure to produce Made in Wales policies placed Assembly officials at the centre of a network of organisations with a deeper reach than ever before into Welsh society.

One consequence of this increased activity is that there is 'a lot less thinking time', while ministers are constantly demanding higher levels of expertise and imposing a set of procedures that build extensive co-operation into the organisational mores of the Assembly. The Equality Opportunity and Environmental Sustainability agendas meant that every policy had to be viewed through these lenses, whether appropriate or not. The main reason explaining this increased activity was the determination of ministers to make a difference. Whereas the Secretary of State had been hands-off, with a very broad and general brief, the Assembly is much more interventionist. There are nine Cabinet Ministers and seven Assembly subject committees, each of which focuses on particular areas of public policy. In the past regime, Ministers rarely engaged with civil servants. The briefs of ministers were inter-ministerial, and communications tended to be by written documents, rather than face-to-face contact. As there were only three ministers – a Secretary of State and two junior ministers – they were heavily reliant for their information on the Welsh Office civil servants. Since 1999, there has been much closer contact with the minister. In most departments there is now a policy board, where the minister meets with senior and mid-ranking civil servants once a month to discuss forthcoming proposals and identify priorities. Informally, heads of departments are in contact with ministers on a daily basis. For mid-ranking officials, contact ranges from supporting the minister in committee to organising internal meetings to assisting the minister in outside meetings. Much work occurs in liaison with the special advisors, another new development civil servants have had to get used to.

When asked who were their new masters, Welsh civil servants were unanimous: they worked for the National Assembly (and principally the Welsh Assembly government). In the unlikely event of conflict between the devolved administration and the UK government, their principal duty would be to the National Assembly. Their status as civil servants serving the National Assembly was much more important than their status as members of the home civil service.

Interviews with top officials also uncovered the changing nature of their relationships with Whitehall departments. According to one official 'for the first two years of devolution, we had an awful lot of run-ins . . . These were turf wars; there were a range of disputes about what constituted primary legislation and what did not'. There remains amongst Welsh civil servants a feeling that Whitehall 'does not know how to deal with an institution which is not part of collective responsibility'. It goes against the Whitehall spirit of norm- and rule-based consensus between civil servants throughout the United Kingdom. These conflicts formed part of a learning process, as Whitehall and the National Assembly gradually came to terms with devolution.

Though there were good professional working relationships between officers, there was a general belief that contacts with Whitehall had sharply diminished since devolution. In most cases, Whitehall departments simply ignored Wales, Scotland and Northern Ireland. There were two variants on this, the first being to assume that the devolved territories would fall into line, and the second considering that Wales, Scotland and Northern Ireland no longer belonged to the UK. As one official said in sorrow rather than anger: 'One gets the impression we are now regarded as a foreign country, almost. They think we are a 'banana Republic'. But Whitehall ignored the devolved territories at its peril, in the opinion of one insider, since 'joined-up government' could only work if all parts of the United Kingdom consulted with each other. For this official, there needed to be far more explicit criteria upon which to base inter-territorial relations, a charter that would replace the existing civil-service code.

These insights from officials were backed up, from a different perspective, in the interviews in Cardiff Bay. Assembly members of all parties were critical of the lack of consistent principles steering relations between London and Cardiff. One prominent former Secretary of State criticised Whitehall departmental traditions for the lack of a consistent approach to Wales. Different Whitehall Ministers took opposite stances on Transfer of Function Orders, for example, and there was little inter-ministerial co-ordination. Some departments 'have been better than others' at understanding what devolution is about. In the words of one Assembly Member interviewed in 2001, the attitude of the then Department of Transport, Local Government and the Regions had been 'absolutely awful. It wouldn't even allow us to nominate the Welsh representative of the Strategic Rail Authority'. The Department of Environment, Food and Rural Affairs (DEFRA) was the next worst culprit. During the 2001 foot-and-mouth crisis, the Assembly's Rural Affairs Minister Carwyn Jones had to get clearance from London for 'just about anything he wanted to do'. Other departments had integrated devolution more squarely into their thinking. The Department for Education and Skills and the Department for Health have both been more flexible, anticipating developments in Wales, as well as incorporating Welsh-inspired ideas into primary legislation. Such contrasting attitudes of Whitehall departments produced distinctive and varying policy outputs. While the Transport Act of 2000 made almost no reference to Wales, the Learning and Skills Act of 2000 contained a large measure of devolved secondary powers. Though personal relations and departmental traditions made some difference, how the devolved/non-devolved split runs through a Whitehall department was the most important variable accounting for variation. In the case of health, for example, some policy areas remained with central government – such as the regulation of the medical profession, or abortion – but everything else (90 per cent of all health areas) has been devolved. In this case, the relationship is mainly about benchmarking. The relationship was more complicated in Education because important areas such as teachers' pay had not been devolved.

Inter-institutional relations

Co-ordination between London and the devolved authorities is marked by the prevalence of informal mechanisms, especially ad hoc meetings, personal and party contacts. Carter and Scott (2003) emphasise the importance of the rules of the game as informal norms 'based much more on ongoing working relationships rather than on formal rules and procedures'. Informal rules of the game have been very important. Two key general principles are those of 'no surprises' in relations between the devolved authorities, and the solidarity of the 'UK family' in EU affairs. In a situation where there is no longer collective cabinet responsibility, the principle of 'no surprises' aims 'to extend past norms of governance to a new situation' (Carter and Scott, 2003). By their very nature, it is difficult to evaluate such understandings. We observe, however, that rules are there to be broken. The norm of 'no surprises' is not always respected. In the case for free care for the elderly or university fees in Scotland, for instance, decisions taken by the Scottish executive were frowned upon by No. 10 (Laffin, Shaw and Taylor, forthcoming). Raising tuition fees in England (without consultation) placed the Welsh Assembly Government and Scottish Executive in a difficult position. More importantly, perhaps, the Assembly qua legislature is not a party to these interactions. The mode of intergovernmental relations in post-devolution Britain is one of informality, secrecy and incremental adjustments. It is played out at the executive level.

Formal, explicit bargaining has been weak. As was observed above in relation to the civil service, relations between Cardiff and London have lessened in intensity since devolution. The budgetary process is formula-based, rather than involving complex negotiations as in a genuine federal system. Collective cabinet responsibility no longer operates, and there has been little reflection on what should replace it. Formal intergovernmental relations in post-devolution Britain are assured formally by the system of Joint Ministerial Committees (JMCs), by intergovernmental agreements known as 'concordats' and by inter-departmental agreements (such as the Departmental Guidance Notes). The JMC exists in summit and sectoral formats. The summit version brings together the Prime Minister and Deputy Prime Minister, the First Ministers and Deputies of the devolved governments, and the territorial Secretaries of State. The composition of the sectoral version of the JMC varies according to Whitehall department. The JMC performs a role of benchmarking and exchanging ideas, rather than explicit bargaining. Insiders considered that most interaction between London and Cardiff took place outside of these committees, in informal contacts at civil-servant, ministerial or party levels. The one area of genuine innovation has been in relation to European policy, where the JMC operates as an informal mechanism for negotiating the UK-wide position in advance of European summits. Several interviewees were sceptical of the value of these concordats and guidance notes, which do not have a constraining character. These various mechanisms form a new corpus of soft law, based more on mutual understanding and benchmarking than upon hard legal requirements. The JMC and the concordats are both inter-executive devices. Members of the Welsh Assembly Government and of the UK government have insisted upon confidentiality in their dealings, a sine qua non for Welsh interests being considered in Westminster primary legislation.

When the JMC takes on a European format (JMC-E) it is used to co-ordinate policy on the eve of European Summits and Council meetings. There is some evidence of the JMC-E being a site for innovation. In advance of the Laeken summit (December 2001) Morgan, McLeish and Trimble (the First Ministers of Wales, Scotland and Northern Ireland respectively) attempted to co-ordinate their activities and present a united front to Blair, arguing that the devolved governments should be closely involved in the European Convention. A more recent example, from March 2004, saw Blair, Morgan and McConnell using the JMC-E to discuss the UK response to the European Court of Justice's decision on the working-time directive.

Finance

Without tax-varying powers, the Assembly depends almost entirely for its finance on transfers from the UK central government. These transfers are assured under the Barnett formula. Barnett was introduced in 1978, at the time the first devolution legislation was on the books. Under the Barnett formula, the Welsh Assembly (like the Scottish parliament) is given an annual block grant that is based on a complex population formula derived from English expenditure totals. Expenditure totals are increased annually in line with comparable increases in England. Barnett is a formula for distributing resources – not for determining how the devolved authorities spend these resources. For the Devolved administrations, there are two advantages of such a system: they can switch expenditure and back this up with political arguments; they are isolated from Treasury control. Though the 'Barnett squeeze' will eventually produce a convergence in per capita expenditure throughout the UK, at present the Scots obtain 130 per cent of the UK average and the Welsh 115 per cent (Heald and McCleod, 2002). There are two ways of reading Barnett, which, in the expression of Laffin, Shaw and Taylor (forthcoming) 'has a decentralising and a centralising potential'. Its decentralising potential is very important. It allocates a block grant, which is not hypothecated and can be used to pursue the political priorities of the devolved governments. This degree of financial flexibility is rather rare in quasi-federal systems, though financial globalisation is becoming the norm in comparative local government finance. The Barnett formula is centralising, on the other hand, insofar as it determines the spending totals of regional governments by calculations of the evolution of expenditure at the centre. As the formula uses expenditure in England as the basis on which to calculate allocations to the devolved authorities, Barnett wounds the amour-propre of the Welsh and Scottish. Not only does this minimise the Assembly as an institution, but also it refuses to recognise specific Welsh needs different from those in England. In interviews, Barnett was not universally appreciated. When the Assembly receives its annual block grant from the Treasury, it 'can only shuffle the cards in the pack – or arrange the deckchairs on the Titanic', in the colourful expression of one Assembly Member. At the same time, there is no formal system of fiscal equalisation . . . unlike in genuinely federal countries such as Germany, Canada and Australia. This sets the UK apart from the pure federal model: in federal systems, the federal and state governments are in close contact, as they need to agree the federal contribution to the states, as well as the attribution of conditional and specific grants. Both of these require complex inter-governmental machinery absent in the UK.

Party politics

The Labour Party has performed a vital role in co-ordination. Party solidarity has been invoked to smooth out differences between the centre and the devolved territories. There is a sense of shared party identity and solidarity, making the formulation of more explicit co-ordinating mechanisms unnecessary. Political advisors have played an important role in liaison between levels of government. Where possible, the Labour-led administrations will attempt to present a common front, as in the case of the firefighters' strike of 2003. Co-operation is especially important in the case of Wales. Wales has to bargain to get its primary legislation passed in Westminster Acts. The Secretary of State negotiates for time in the parliamentary timetable on the same basis as other Ministers. Government departments have preferred to integrate Welsh demands into England and Wales bills, rather than allowing for separate Wales-only bills (due to the scarcity of parliamentary time). Assembly Ministers generally get their requests agreed in Whitehall. In an interview in November 2001, First Minister Morgan declared that he was 'knocking against an open door' at No. 10, suggesting that Welsh demands were accommodated in 90 per cent of cases. Welsh ministers remain as 'petititioners', however, and they depend upon the goodwill of the centre. The relationship would change power in the event of a hostile majority in Westminster.

The Scottish and Welsh Labour parties have developed their own sense of autonomy since the advent of devolution. There was no role for the centre in the election of any of the leaders: such as Dewar and McConnell in Scotland or Morgan in Wales. In Scotland, there have been higher-profile divergences: over free personal care for the elderly, and education top-up fees. These issues 'appear to challenge the principle that the UK government should determine the key principles of the Welfare State'. Blair saw these measures as threats to his overall strategy. But the key driver was the domestic Scottish situation: that of coalition government with the Liberal Democrats and the reality of multi-party politics. Labour has learnt that it has to recognise the emergence of centrifigual forces after devolution. It has adopted a policy of 'benign indifference' to the Scottish and Welsh Labour party leaderships. The governance of the UK and of England has led central government not to intervene in the policy details of public-service delivery in the devolved territories.

The current piecemeal approach is a source of fragility. In the event of different political majorities in Cardiff and London, scenarios are extremely difficult to predict. No part of the British constitution sets out what is to be deemed primary and what secondary legislation. At present, there are no guaranteed powers for the Assembly. Even without formally challenging the devolution settlements, Rawlings (2001) points out that a future hostile government could 'cheat the Assembly of its powers' by minimising the range of statutory instruments agreed in future laws. Each of the measures of co-ordination evoked in this section are fundamentally unstable. Party ties are, by their nature, contingent on circumstances. A change of government in London would undermine existing patterns of co-ordination.

Conclusion

Though the institutions are still relatively young, the achievements of devolution in Wales are very real, in terms of both political process and public policy. First and foremost, the Assembly has survived. Though the jury is still out (in 2003, the election turn-out declined from 46 per cent to 37 per cent), there is some evidence that the first term of devolution provided the mobilising project necessary to embed the Welsh polity and to build Welsh civil society, in the long run potentially overcoming an important social capital deficit. There is a more cohesive party system, the equilibrium of which is favourable to making the devolved institutions work. There is the 'Team Wales' approach, whatever its limitations in practice. There are much closer contacts between Welsh Assembly government officials and Assembly-sponsored public bodies than in the pre-devolution era. Welsh civil servants have integrated the logic of the new institutional arrangements into their own thinking. There is the appearance, finally, of all-Wales organisations within civil society and the gradual recognition by professional organisations (the CBI and TUC notably) of the need to take devolution into account in their own organisation. Here, the emphasis on the temporal dimension is vital; relationships need to be developed over time, a scarce resource for new institutions such as the National Assembly for Wales.

Any judgement on Devolution and the National Assembly in Wales can only be partial, as devolution is an ongoing process. Though the Assembly is gradually gaining more policy responsibilities and establishing its authority amongst the policy community, it remains caught in a semi-sovereign logic. The implementation of the Richard Commission's main recommendations would do much to end the state of limbo. At the Welsh Labour Party conference in September 2004, the First Minister appeared to downplay any prospect of implementing Richard in the short term. Morgan called for all new legislation to include 'Henry VIII' clauses, allowing the Assembly to fill out the details of framework legislation. That left answered what would happen to the 3,000 laws inherited by the Assembly each of which contains specific provisions. The 'bonfire of the quangos' announced in June 2004 could be interpreted as a sign a weakness, an initiative to bring semi-autonomous agencies under political control. The episode demonstrates that the party ties of UK Labour continue to bind; moving to full Parliament status without a referendum was too much for the London leadership of the Labour Party. The episode also confirms that the forty Welsh members of the Westminster parliament have emerged as a powerful lobby determined to preserve their existence (threatened by Richard).

In the expression of one interviewee, a 'Welsh parliament is at least two terms off'. On the other hand, it seems inconceivable that an incoming Conservative government in the UK would seek to turn back the devolutionary tide.

5
Decentralisation and political capacity building in Brittany

This chapter addresses the theme of decentralisation and political capacity building in Brittany. Venturing inside the Brittany regional council provides an opportunity to investigate the functioning of the region as a political institution, and to explore the theme of public policy-making within Brittany. It will be argued that the influence of the French regions (and Brittany in particular) is tied up with interdependent policy-making and the quality of horizontal and vertical relationships. The chapter's conclusion will focus upon the regional political space and the constraints and opportunities faced by governors in Brittany.

Inside the Brittany regional council

There are a number of institutional features common to the organisation of all regional councils, together with distinctive traits that are dependent upon political variables such as the role of parties and personalities, coalition dynamics and territorial context. The ensuing section will address a number of aspects of the internal governance of French regions, adapting general themes to specific evidence from Brittany. Next will be considered in turn the internal organisation of the regional councils, their political leadership, their committee structures and their permanent administration.

The organisation of the regional council

There is no template set in iron for the internal organisation of a regional council and each region organises itself according to its own internal regulations (*règlement intérieur*). There is usually a similar pattern, however, based on a clear distinction between executive and deliberative functions. The President is the fount of executive authority of the regional council. He prepares the policy decisions that are submitted to the votes of the regional councillors, leads debates in the Assembly and the Standing Committee (*Commission Permanente*) and is responsible for policy implementation, a task in which he is assisted by the regional civil service. Only the President has executive authority, though this can be delegated for most issues to his executive officers (the Vice-Presidents). The President and his Vice-Presidents meet regularly in the bureau, the executive office, to co-ordinate their activity. The number of Vice-Presidents varies according to region. In the new PS-led regional executive elected in Brittany in March 2004, there were fifteen Vice-Presidents – seven Socialists (PS), three Communists (PCF), two Greens, one Breton Democratic Union representative (UDB), one leftist radical (MRG) and one independent left – all of whom participated in the bureau. The distribution of portfolios reflects the results of the regional election and the coalition dynamics surrounding the election of the President. In 1998, for example, the Gaullist de Rohan, narrowly elected to the presidency thanks to the support of an autonomist-minded independent, had to agree to establish a post of Vice-President for Breton Identity. In 2004, the composition of the bureau reflected the broad-based second-ballot coalition, uniting Socialists, Communists, Greens, Autonomists, left-Radicals and independent-left councillors.

The full Assembly of the council meets rarely. Most of the business of the regional council is the preserve of the Standing Committee (*Commission Permanente*), a body representing all political groups in relation to their size, and of the thematic Committees. The Standing Committee can be mandated for all matters except the budget. There are vast differences between regional councils in the composition of the Standing Committee. In 1992–98, the proportion of regional councillors forming part of the Standing Committee varied from 14 per cent to 71 per cent (Muret, 1994). In the case of Brittany, there are thirty-five members of the Standing Committee, out of a total of eighty-three councillors. Representation is determined on the basis of the proportional strength of the political groups (seats, not votes). As a minimum, the full Assembly of the regional council votes the annual budget.

The leadership of the regional council

That the President of the regional council is the sole fount of executive authority is consistent with the strong presidentialist/personalist traditions of French political leadership, from the Elysée palace down to the mayors of small rural communes. While mayors generally dominate their municipal councils, however, the Presidents of regional councils have found it difficult to exercise powerful leadership, on account of the fragile political context within which most regions have operated for most of the time. The prospects for strong presidential-style leadership have been limited by endemic political instability and by the dynamics of electoral and coalition politics.

Most experienced politicians initially avoided the regional councils. The first regional presidents elected in 1986 were secondary figures, with only a few exceptions. In the late 1980s, regional political leadership was no real match for that of the large cities or departments, but it has been gaining ground ever since. In 1992, several leading politicians were elected to head regional councils (including former President of the Republic Valéry Giscard d'Estaing and former Prime Minister Laurent Fabius), a pattern repeated in 1998 and 2004. In 2002, Jean-Pierre Raffarin was the first regional President (of Poitou-Charentes) to be appointed as Prime Minister. As leading politicians have begun to interest themselves in the regional layer, the office of President of the regional council has grown in stature. The President is elected for a period of six years at the beginning of the mandate. An absolute majority is required for election on the first two ballots; a relative majority suffices for the third round. Except in cases of resignation (of which there have been some) the President of the regional council stays in post for six years. As the sole source of executive authority within the region, the President presents proposals for approval to the regional assembly and draws up the budget. He heads the permanent administration that serves the regional council. The President decides how to organise the regional administration. Shortly after his election in April 2004, for example, President Le Drian announced a major administrative reform regrouping the existing policy divisions under three overarching directorates. The President decides when to call a meeting of the regional council. The Breton President de Rohan was criticised for failing to call enough sessions during the 1998–2004 mandate. The President must call full meetings of the regional council at least four times a year and the full Assembly has to debate and approve the budget. An annual debate is held on the budget, getting the budget through being one of the major tasks of the President. In March 1998, the plural-left Jospin government changed the law in an attempt to strengthen regional executives (*Les Echos*, 2003). Henceforth, the regional budget is adopted unless an absolute majority of councillors vote against it and propose an alternative text. During the period 1998–2004, this change prevented the institutional paralysis which had threatened to overwhelm the regional councils.

In the case of Brittany, unlike in most other regions, there has been a tradition of prestigious politicians heading the regional institution. The Regional Public Authority, created in 1972, was presided over by the historic Breton politician, René Pleven, a former premier, a leading light in the CELIB and a close collaborator of de Gaulle. There then followed a string of presidents with reputations as leading national politicians. These were Raymond

Marcellin, the Interior Minister during the events of May 1968; Yvon Bourges, former Gaullist Army minister and Josselin de Rohan, head of the RPR group in the French Senate. All of these Presidents practised *cumul des mandats*; each of them relied heavily on the permanent administration to steer the regional ship and each of them spent more time in Paris than in Brittany. The first Socialist President, Jean-Yves Le Drian, was much closer to Breton cultural networks. Even Le Drian practised *cumul des mandats*, however, combining the presdiency of the regional council with being mayor of Lorient.

Vice-Presidents and policy sectoralisation

The first meeting of the regional council elects the President's executive officers, the Vice-Presidents. In practice, most Presidents delegate powers to their Vice-Presidents to operate in their policy fields. Rather than having a concerted central leadership, regions in France have facilitated the rise of sectoral governance, marked by the influence of the Vice-Presidents as de facto executive officers. In Brittany there is a tradition of powerful Vice-Presidents. Examples have included Pierre le Treut, the delegate Vice-President who ran the regional council for most of the Marcellin period; Gérard Pourchet, who occupied the Education and Training brief from 1986 to 1998; or Jean-Yves Cozan, the Vice-President for Breton Identity from 1998 to 2004. The influence of specific individuals is more dependent on coalition and party dynamics and political circumstances than on formal written rules. The presence of strong individuals in politically sensitive posts renders difficult any straightforward institutionally based descriptions of modes of regional governance. The three Vice-Presidents identified above performed different roles, but each demonstrated the opportunities open to political entrepreneurs.

The first of these – Pierre Le Treut – performed an important role because President Marcellin rarely ventured into Brittany. In his own words 'Marcellin was never here and relied on me to manage current affairs'. Le Treut substituted for the regional President in one-to-one meetings and even in public appearances. There was a functional division of labour. If the regional President were due to announce good news, M. Marcellin would sign the letter. In the case of refusals to agree to demands by the Council, letters would be signed by Le Treut. If Le Treut adopted a self-effacing role, the other two examples are of Vice-Presidents acting as powerful policy entrepreneurs. First Vice-President of training and lifelong learning (1986–98), Gérard Pourchet crafted a highly distinctive and original regional policy towards youth training and lifelong learning. Members of the policy community converged in their belief that Pourchet had made a difference and that there was a sense of drift after his departure in 1998. The case of Jean-Yves Cozan is even more spectacular. Cozan was elected as Vice-President for Breton Identity in 1998, a post he held until 2004. As President de Rohan depended upon Cozan for his majority, the autonomist-minded independent occupied a powerful pivotal position. Cozan was associated with initiatives such as the creation of the Breton language office and increased regional support for Breton-language classes. Under the influence of Cozan, the cultural budget of the Brittany region rose to 5 per cent, though the Region has no statutory responsibility for culture.

All-inclusive policy-making or democratic deficits?

The counterpart to this pattern of executive initiative in French regions is a sharp distinction between executive and deliberative functions. The presidency decides; the Assembly deliberates. If the Assembly refuses to pass the budget, the threat looms that the regional prefect will take over management of the council. The spectre of this nuclear option is sometimes raised, but behind the scenes bargaining usually ensures minimal agreement. The leader of the Socialists (now regional President) put it thus in 2001:

> In principle, we ought to vote against the President's budget. The problem is that, if we vote against, then M. de Rohan will no longer have a majority and Brittany will grind to a halt. We do not consider this to be in the superior interest of Brittany. We will never side with the National Front.

The opportunities for democratic input and political influence between elections thus depend upon the configuration of political forces in presence. In the case of Brittany, as almost everywhere else, small pivotal formations have exercised disproportionate weight. After the 1998 election there was no overall majority. Left and Right had almost the same number of seats. Alongside the recognisable left (PS, PCF) and right (UDF, RPR) coalitions, there were six FN councillors, along with one extreme left, one CNPT and four independents. As all the mainstream parties excluded an agreement with the far-right FN, the pivotal 'party' in 1998 was the Independent list led by the autonomist-minded politician from Finistère, Jean-Yves Cozan. Holding the balance of power between PS and RPR/UDF, Cozan negotiated pride of place (and three vice-presidencies) in a reconfigured RPR-led majority under Josselin de Rohan. This manoeuvre deprived the Socialist Le Drian from capturing the regional majority. When Le Drian finally became President in 2004, the autonomist UDB performed the role of pivotal party. With 9.7 per cent on the first round of the 2004 election, the UDB/Green list obtained eleven councillors and three posts of Vice-President in the new regional executive.

The absence of party majorities has produced informal bargaining between political groups, largely taking place behind closed doors. What democratic scrutiny there is comes from the committee system. There are variable numbers of committees in French regions. While in Brittany the Education and Training committee brings together all issues of training and lifelong learning, apprenticeships and secondary education, in some other regions there are separate committees for Education and Training. In all regions, policy committees are established on a representative basis of the political groups. In Brittany, since the 2004 alteration in power, there have been six committees (Environment and Quality of Life; Education and Training; Culture and Sport; Social Solidarity; Planning and Finance; Economic Development and Research). Committees perform a scrutiny role, rather than a policy-making one. They can suggest amendments to the executive, but these can only be passed in the full Assembly. Committee chairs have emerged as powerful players in some regions, but their influence tends to depend upon the relationship they maintain with the Vice-President. The committee chair/Vice-President relationship is complicated by the fact that the committees are broad in their membership and do not usually mirror the policy responsibilities of the main administrative divisions. Moreover, when questioned on the subject, members of the administrative staff are very clear that they are there to serve the regional executive, not the Assembly itself or its committees.

The result is a rather critical perspective on the operation of committees, especially from opposition members. One participant in the Education and Training Committee in the Brittany region complained that policy sectoralisation and the role of the administration prevented joined-up policy-making: 'The Education and Training committee does not function well. It is nowhere near as effective as in Nord/Pas-de-Calais, for example. Working groups are set up when everything has already been decided. There is little contact with the Economic Development committee, though its concerns are central for issues of training'.

There are other manifest democratic deficits. The sessions of the regional council are infrequent and dominated by the agenda of the executive. There is a lack of accountability for decisions. Political instability and the absence of working majorities has led to a strong influence of small pivotal parties. Above all, the practice of multiple office-holding (*cumul des mandats*) has worked against the emergence of a coherent Breton political class. In the words of one: '*cumul des mandats* is disastrous. It prevents the emergence of a Breton political class organised around the Breton political institutions'. The practice of multiple office-holding worked against the emergence of coherent regional structures, according to one critical interlocutor, because leading politicians took their orders from the Paris-based headquarters of the main parties. They spent most of the week away from the region. *Cumul* affected all levels of the regional council, from former-President de Rohan (head of the UMP group in the French Senate) to run-of-the-mill regional councillors, who often combined regional and departmental mandates. From the perspective of those occupying multiple offices, such criticisms were naive. While awaiting the development of more autonomous forms of regional governance, it was imperative to maintain a presence in Paris and to be well connected with local authorities across Brittany.

L'administration au pouvoir?

A strong theme emerging from interviews within the Brittany regional council was that of the pervasive influence of the permanent administration. Such a perception appears, at first sight, rather surprising. At their inception, the regions had neither the organisational past, nor the bureaucratic resources available to the departmental councils. For the first ten years following their creation, there were fewer than 100 salaried staff in most regions. The 1982 law gave the regions the right to recruit permanent staff. From 1985 onwards, the new territorial public-service statute covered permanent staff working for the regions (the more senior of whom are often on sabbatical from their main corps). The regions are free to determine their own recruitment procedures, on condition that they respect the territorial public-service code.

In the case of Brittany, one or two examples demonstrate the rapid development of regional expertise. The Brittany Region's education division, the DEE, initially consisted of two former officials of the regional state education service and three part-timers (Fontaine, 1992). The DEE gradually expanded and developed in competence, however, and by 2000 the division consisted of more than twenty people in total. In his acceptance speech in 2004, President Le Drian announced that the 400 permanent staff working for the council were woefully inadequate in number and that there would have to be an expansion. In 2006, the Brittany region was due to take over direct control of some 3,000 Education ancillary workers, one of the key planks of the 2004 decentralisation law. In addition to expanding permanent staff, the regions have been in the forefront of contracting out services to non-statutory expertise bodies and using private sector techniques (*concessions* or METP to build schools) to finance public-sector infrastructure projects. The Brittany Region has been an active participant in the main mixed-economy society (SEMAEB) and has performed an important role in the regional investment bank (SDR). Less embedded in traditional structures than the other local authorities, French regions have turned to semi-autonomous agencies and public-private partnerships to carry out many of their new functions. The Regions have developed sophisticated marketing teams and their own regional economic development structures considered briefly below.

In spite of evidence of innovation, the theme of bureaucratic power came out strongly in interviews carried out in 2001 and 2002. For some, the presence since the origins of the same individuals in key administrative posts in the region was a question of concern. In the area of cultural policy, for example, the same official had adopted a critical stance towards issues of Breton language and culture. Some believed bureaucratic power to be the logical consequence of the practice of multiple office-holding. In the words of one, 'the bureaucracy exercises a very strong influence because the regional councillors are rarely present'. Though highly competent, the 'bureaucracy cannot stand listening to people who are not of the same opinion. They consider themselves alone to be vested with the appropriate expertise'. That the official mentioned above did not appear in the new executive's organisational chart demonstrated the limits of such arguments. By January 2005, most key administrative officials in the new regions conquered by the Left had either resigned, been moved sideways or found alternative jobs in other public administrations.

Public policy-making and the Brittany regional council

In a major comparative study of regionalism in France and Spain, Pasquier (2004) summarises the Breton framework of policy beliefs ('*répertoire d'action*') in the following terms. The regional space is a legitimate one, not an artificial construct. Breton political actors seek to build regional consensus, over and above departmental and local rivalries. There are shared views on the regional interest and a shared belief in the necessity of focusing demands on the state (in an equal-to-equal negotiation). The regional policy community seeks a collaborative mode of governance and to build a measure of trust in relations with central government (using direct-action tactics when necessary to back this up). The Breton mode of operation builds upon regional capacity, but is focused upon lobbying the central state.

Reference was made above to the contradictory principles underpinning the 1982 decentralisation laws. While according a general administrative responsibility to the three layers of sub-national administration (communes, *départements* and regions), the law also referred to *blocs de compétence*, policy spheres which would best be exercised at a particular level. The 1982 law identified four broad areas of public-policy intervention for the regions: economic and social development; scientific, cultural and health policy; regional planning and the 'preservation of regional identity'. To these core areas were added responsibilities in education (1983, 1985) in apprenticeships (1983, 1987), in training (1993, 2004), in transport (2002, 2004) and in health (2004). The type of authority exercised by French regions is much more one of networked governance than of strategic command and control. Formal legal competencies are virtually never exercised alone. Building political capacity in the case of a French region involves developing trusting relationships and engaging with other major players to ensure positive-sum outcomes. The ensuing section considers the balance of opportunities and constraints in several important areas of regional intervention: economic development, education and training, language and culture. These are all interdependent policy domains. In their own ways, they all demonstrate the complexity of regional policy-making.

Economic development

Regional economic development in Brittany has been the subject of a number of fairly exhaustive studies in which the interested reader may seek further information (for example Keating, Loughlin and Deschouwer, 2003; Pasquier, 2004). All start with the legacy of the CELIB, briefly referred to in Chapter 3. The Breton Liaison Committee (*Comité d'études et de liaison des intérêts bretons* – CELIB) brought together a broad range of regional interests in a common cause: that of the economic development of Brittany (Martray, 1983; Cressard, 2000). At its height in the 1950s, CELIB was supported by Breton deputies from all parties, local councillors, the farming unions, the workers' unions, the employers' organisations, the chambers of commerce, the universities and associations defending Breton language and culture (Pasquier, 2004). The strength of CELIB lay in its cross-partisan status and its linkage with civil society. The Breton parliamentary group in the Chamber of Deputies in the Fourth Republic – wherein the key players were the Christian-democratic Popular Republican Movement (MRP) and Socialists – was the first of its type in France. Under the influence of CELIB, there was a psychological revolution amongst the Breton elites. There was unanimity about the causes of Brittany's problems (under-investment, the region's peripheral location and under-industrialisation) and the solutions required to redress these (industrial decentralisation, planning and the opening up of the regional economy). At the end of its life in the late 1960s, the CELIB had a considerable number of achievements to its credit, the Roads Plan of 1969 being first and foremost amongst them. Insofar as economic development has become a prominent feature of Breton identity, the legacy of CELIB has been a lasting one, as witnessed by the following quotation from a prominent actor: 'In this region, people are always fighting, but once a project has been decided everybody rallies behind the Breton cause. In every project you find, systematically, the Region, the départements, the main cities . . . all co-operating, even on occasions allying against the state'.

The regions were formally established as public agencies with strategic planning and investment powers in 1972. The 1982 law conferred specific responsibilities on the twenty-two regional councils in the area of economic development; regional economic planning, training and the distribution of state aids. The law also allowed the regions to participate in financial institutions (*Sociétés du développement régional* – SDR) to raise capital and to invest in regional businesses. For its Director of Economic Development, the Brittany region's economic-development strategy was formulated with broader territorial planning objectives in mind. The priority of regional-council policy was to promote economic activity across Brittany and to support the small and medium enterprises, typically representative of Brittany as a whole. In Brittany, as in other regions, early economic-development policies focused on awarding grants to set up small businesses (PRCE) or to promote employment (PRE). While such grants still exist, they have been surpassed in importance by low-interest loans which recipients have to reimburse. The key activities undertaken by the Economic Development directorate are those of awarding loans and grants; quality control, in respect of such loans or grants; organisation of the marketing of the region and research into the nature of the economic and physical environment. The award of interest-free loans is conditioned by commitments on investment and employment.

With the victory of the Left in 2004, there was a change of emphasis, with less focus on grant distribution and technical conformity and more on the defence of threatened economic interests in traditional (fishing, farming) and new economy (telecommunications, defence) activities. The new regional executive elected in March 2004 made clear its intention to take a much closer control over the economic-development activities financed by the regional council. President Le Drian announced an overhaul of the capital-risk regime; the creation of a Regional Economic Development Agency and the establishment of a Regional Land Authority. Finally, with the experimental transfer of the management of EU structural funds to the regions under the 2004 decentralisation law, the Brittany region made clear its intention to weigh much more heavily in relation to European issues.

In the early years of its existence, much of the economic-development activity of the Brittany regional council was carried out on its behalf by a range of partnership organisations. The Region is the dominant partner in *Bretagne*

International (previously MIRCEB), an agency prospecting for inward investment and promoting Breton products abroad. The Brittany regional council is also an important partner in the Breton SDR and the SEMAEB. The SDR is a regional development bank that specialises in providing risk-capital for Breton firms. The Region's involvement in SEMAEB goes back even further. The SEMAEB is a 'mixed-economy society', a public-private partnership majority-owned by Breton local and regional authorities. Its core business is to buy up land, develop buildings and sell them on to companies. The SEMAEB is original in that it was set up as a regional mixed-economy society as early as 1955. The SEMAEB was closely linked with the CELIB, but survived the latter. For half a century, the SEMAEB has been the lead contractor for many infrastructure developments in Brittany, such as the Rennes TGV station.

As economic development is a cross-cutting area, it impinges upon related policy fields such as spatial planning, transport and the environment. The latter issue is of especial importance in Brittany, where surveys (including that treated in this book) repeatedly demonstrate that environmental pollution is the number-one preoccupation of Bretons. The Brittany regional council has attempted to respond to these concerns by using the State-Region plan to set up an Agency for the Environment or to adopt a Water Plan. It has also been in the forefront of regions exercising the experimental transfer of powers in relation to regional railways (from 2002) and calling for the transfer of the management of ports and airports.

The French State remains genuinely fearful of *Länder*-style regions emerging as powerful policy-makers. Though they have been active players, the regions have not been able to control or federate the economic development activities of the other layers of local government. The 2003 White Paper on decentralisation initially proposed to give the regions control of all economic-development policy, a provision struck down by the French Senate (the second chamber, heavily over-representative of local and departmental authorities) and removed from the text of the Decentralisation Act of July 2004. Regional Economic Development plans (*Schémas régionaux de développement économique*), which were to have given substance to this, would now be experimental.

Human capital: education and training

The governance of education in France has been influenced in various manners by political decentralisation. Education is a major service-delivery function for French local and regional authorities. It is the largest item of budgetary expenditure for the twenty-two regional councils, and generally the second item (after social welfare) in the ninety-six departmental councils' budgets. By 2003, there had been a 250 per cent increase in expenditure by local and regional authorities on education since 1985 (*Monde*, 5 June 2003). Underpinning the (partial) decentralisation of secondary education in 1983 and 1985 lay the belief that the quality of educational services could be improved through increased school autonomy, and the involvement of the meso-level local authorities (the ninety-six departmental and twenty-two regional councils) in educational planning. The involvement of the regional councils in planning infrastructure (buildings and equipment) and making educational forecasts would alleviate the burden on an overloaded central state. Local and regional authorities would contribute to financing the efforts of national education policies. The state retained control over the core policy choices: course curriculum, overall pedagogical content, and the recruitment and management of teachers. Within these narrow limits, the regions have responsibility for the *lycées* (upper secondary schools) and the departmental councils for the *collèges* (lower secondary schools). Decentralisation 'has gone much further than anyone expected' (Van Zanten, 2004), however, as local and regional authorities have intervened at all levels of education, from maternity schools to University.

Beyond secondary education, the French Regions are involved at various levels of the education and training supply chain. During the 1980s and 1990s, the Brittany regional council developed a reputation for innovation and expertise in the policy field of apprenticeships, youth training and lifelong learning. The operation of the policy community in these areas will be considered in rather more detail in Chapter 7. Following from Pasquier's policy register, in the case of Brittany is observed an overarching consensus in favour of promoting education and raising educational standards. Traditions of scholarity have a long pedigree in the Academy of Rennes. In the predominantly rural Brittany of the nineteenth and early twentieth centuries, educational achievement was the only means of social and geographical mobility. This consensus looks to the promotion of education not only as a means of social mobility but also as a tool of regional economic development. There is broad acceptance of the specific role performed by the Catholic education sector in Brittany, with all main local and regional authorities providing the maximum assistance to contracted-in Catholic schools permissible under the law. This consensus encompasses the state field agencies. Insofar as it accepted the policy of 'equal treatment for public and private', the regional field service of the Education ministry in Brittany aligned itself with the prevailing local political culture more openly than in most French regions.

Brittany's regional council has steadily increased its institutional capacity in matters of education and training, with its various education and training plans becoming more and more ambitious. This development repeated the familiar pattern whereby increased expertise, experience and resources led the regional councils to adopt an expansive vision of their educational role. Unlike in some French regions, in Brittany there was no open test of force between the regional council and the field service of the Education ministry (the rectorate). The two partners came to appreciate each other's efforts (Mény, 1990; Fontaine 1992). Sources within the rectorate acknowledged that the Brittany regional council had acquired substantial technical competence in the education sector. Competition sparked emulation and eventually produced co-operation. In the late 1990s, the Brittany regional council took the lead in signing contractual agreements with the heads of the region's secondary schools, a move that initially raised eyebrows within the rectorate. In turn, consistent with the co-operative mode of Breton governance, the field service of the Education ministry also signed contracts with secondary-school heads and consulted with the regional council about avoiding duplication. Though the regional council used the training-plan procedure to define its own regional educational priorities, it never questioned the primacy of the state in pedagogical affairs, nor did it call for regional diplomas.

This belief in the merits of learning spreads to higher education, with the Brittany region an important participant in the University 2000 programme. The key official in the Education ministry acknowledged the role of the Brittany regional council (as well as that of local mayors) in influencing University expansion in the late 1980s and early 1990s: 'We were in permanent discussion with the regional council in 1988/89 over the university 2000 plan, which has massively increased higher education capacity in Brittany'. This appreciation was shared in the Regional council and the prefecture. These beliefs and priorities are widely shared irrespective of political cleavages and institutional rivalries. By 2000, the Brittany region regularly featured in the top two or three French regions as measured by Education ministry league tables and had one of the highest proportions of pupils obtaining the *baccalauréat* outside of Ile-de-France.

Language and culture

Issues of language and culture go to the heart of identity-based versions of regional governance. The 1982 law explicitly allowed regions to make policy to support local and regional identities. In the area of cultural policy, the regions have a distinctive role to play. The influence of regional actors in the cultural domain precedes decentralisation. In the case of Brittany, the French

State, the main local authorities and the regional cultural associations signed the Brittany Cultural Charter in 1977. The Charter, an initiative of President Giscard d'Estaing, recognised the cultural specificity of Brittany and provided for the establishment of new institutions to promote Breton culture and history. The 1977 charter incorporated the five regions of historic Brittany, including the Loire-Atlantique (in the Pays de la Loire Region). This episode demonstrated that the French State would, in certain circumstances, recognise the validity of Breton cultural claims and the artificial character of the Brittany administrative region. By including Loire-Atlantique, the State accorded some legitimacy to the idea of historic Brittany. The 1977 Cultural Charter was followed (eventually, in 1982) by the creation of the Brittany Cultural Institute (ICB) as an executive agency of the regional council. Though financed by the regional council, the ICB conducted much of the Brittany region's cultural policy in an autonomous and controversial manner. The ICB became a focus of Breton nationalist sentiment, provoking President de Rohan into reducing its powers in 2000.

If Breton culture has been promoted by institutions, it has drawn its vitality from the imposing and important cultural movement mapped out in Chapter 3. Breton cultural activities are actively promoted by local and regional authorities. With the laws on decentralisation, the regional councils have become important co-financers of cultural policy. Regions have invested heavily in co-financing contemporary art collections, museums, orchestras and operas. In regions such as Brittany, there has been some conflict between those advocating a priority attention to Breton culture and those resisting such demands in the name of cultural universalism. For the former, the regional authority can make a real difference in supporting region-specific cultural activities. The support of the regional council is a lifeline. The Brittany region is the financial mainstay behind the Brittany Cultural Institute and the Brittany Cultural Council (both of which cater for the five 'Breton' departments). Breton activists are highly critical of the pressures placed by central government on regional councils, such as that of Brittany, to support generic cultural activities (museums, opera) which they believe ought not to compete with limited regional funds. Interviewees from across the board criticised the expansion of the DRAC in Brittany – the regional field service of the Culture Ministry – at the same time as the State was making new demands on regional funds. Even prominent centre-Right politicians called for an expansion in regional influence in the cultural sphere, the suppression of the DRAC, the transfers of their responsibilities and finance to the regions and a re-think of cultural priorities (70 per cent of the French cultural budget being spent in Paris and the Ile-de-France region).

If issues of culture raised the temperature, those of language produced powerful social movements. There is a favourable environment for affirmative public-policy action at the regional level. Public and informed opinion in Brittany strongly believes that the regional authorities *ought* to make the main decisions in the field of regional languages. In Brittany, the region came out way ahead of other levels – national, local or European. In the case of the Breton language, the regional council is identified as the appropriate level by a majority of public-opinion-poll respondents (53 per cent) and in this book's elite survey (57 per cent). The importance of this finding in favour of the region should be emphasised. The French government is seen not only as too distant, but also too ambivalent towards the Breton language which, the findings indicate, is viewed with a capital of cultural sympathy, even though its use is marginal.

The case of regional languages provides a good example of the voluntary basis of much local and regional activity in France. French local and regional authorities have a general administrative competency, allowing them to develop policies in all areas except those specifically forbidden by the law. The law thus opens a policy space within which local and regional authorities can develop more or less proactive policies. In the case of Brittany, most of the drive towards institutionalization has come from the Brittany regional council, a theme developed in more detail in Chapter 7. Its critics amongst the language-advocacy coalition are deeply ambivalent about the regional council. On the one hand, the main cultural and language associations depend upon the region for most of their financial support. On the other, these associations, by their very nature, want the region to go further than it is prepared to. The regional council is, to a large extent, obliged to operate within its regulatory environment. Unlike in Wales, for example, there has been no effort, even symbolic, to use Breton in regional council proceedings. As it stands, such an act would be illegal. The region provides grants to the Breton-medium DIWAN schools and to a host of Breton cultural movements. The region has been active in the pursuit of the interests of the Breton language in other ways. The 1994–99 State-Region plan created a publishing company – TES – whose responsibility is to disseminate teaching and learning materials in Breton (books, but also CD Roms). The creation of the Breton Language office (*Ofis ar Brezhonneg*) in 1999 was a milestone in terms of institutional development. *Ofis ar Brezhonneg* is not, strictly speaking, a language board with statutory powers. Its tools are those of persuasion rather than constraint. But it has been very active in promoting the cause of the Breton language, notably through its commercial technical translation service, its bilingual sign-posting activities (for local government, hospitals, schools) and the advice it provides to firms, agencies and individuals on all Breton-language issues.

The support of the Region has for long sustained the DIWAN Breton-medium schools movement. The agreement between DIWAN and the Education ministry in 2001 was followed by the signing of an additional convention to the 2000–6 State-Region plan, which provided various new sources of finance for promoting the Breton language, including for teacher training. In November 2004, the Socialist-led majority issued the first ever Breton language-development plan, containing an ambitious range of targets for linguistic development. In spite of the best efforts of the region, however, the future of the process of institutionalisation is uncertain. The budgetary line specifically allocated to the Breton language represents around 10 per cent of the Region's cultural budget – or 0.5 per cent of the entire Regional budget.

Environmental constraints and opportunities

The specific constraints identified in Wales are characteristic of the British unwritten constitution. The Brittany regional council functions within a very different state tradition. In the Breton case, the regional council operates alongside (and generally co-operates with) the French state, which deeply penetrates civil society in a manner having no British equivalent. Some of the constraints and opportunities shaping regional political capacity building in Brittany will be considered next. Of specific mention will be four key areas exemplifying the form of interdependent regional governance which can exist in France: first, the Brittany region's experience of the State-Region plans; second, the process of elaborating the regional budget; third, relations between the Brittany regional council and other levels of local government and, fourth, the management of European Union issues.

State-region plans

Traditions of decentralised planning have a long pedigree in Brittany, the legacy of the CELIB being one of co-operation between state modernisers and regionalist-minded Breton politicians. There is a natural sympathy to ideas of decentralised planning in Brittany, 'where we have been talking about decentralisation for a very long time and where we developed an original form of regional governance well before the 1982 law'. The various plans negotiated between the CELIB and the French State in the 1950s and 1960s were precursors to the State-Region plans considered next.

The State-Region plans were introduced in the 1982 decentralisation law, which presented the process of 'democratic planning' as an interaction between regional and national priorities. The sums of money involved in the State-Region plans are considerable. The first round of State-Regions plans (1984–88) cost £6.5 billion, with resources divided between the State (£3.9 billion) and the Regions (£2.6 billion). This figure rose to £10.8 billion in the 1989–93 round (£5.8 billion for the State, £5 billion for the Regions). In 1994–99, the *départements* and communes were invited to co-finance projects, producing an increase of the financial mass to £17.1 billion (£7.1 billion each for the state and the region, £2.6 billion for the other local authorities). In 2000–6, this figure increased yet again, to £20 billion (£10.5 billion for the state, £9.5 billion for the regions and other local authorities). Henceforth, a proportion of the regional budget ranging from 15 to 25 per cent is devoted to ongoing items, co-financed by the regions, the state and the EU. No region can ignore the planning process.

French Regions have adopted very different stances to the process of drawing up the State-Region plans. Under the terms of the 1982 law, the Region first draws up a regional plan. The invitation to negotiate a regional plan was ignored before 1994 by most regions (though not in Brittany), but the incentive of obtaining EU structural funds has changed perspectives. In Auvergne, the first Regional plan was reportedly drawn up jointly by the Regional Prefect and the Region's Head of Operations (*Directeur Général des Services*). Brittany was at the opposing end of the spectrum. The Brittany Region has undertaken vast consultation exercises in the run-up to each of the plans. In 1992–93, for example, it consulted widely with other local authorities, took written representations and held public meetings in the each of the eighteen employment zones (*bassins d'emploi*) within the region. Interest in the regional dimension has been strong. It has been sustained by a strong regional media presence (Ouest-France, the broad-circulation French daily, being based in Rennes), by the pan-Breton organisation of the principal economic interests, as well as by the pressure of regionalist movements and the activism of think-tanks such as the Locarn Institute. Regional cultural associations are much more important in Brittany than elsewhere. In terms of sectoral organisation, the farm sector is also very powerful, with an important lobby group (*Breizh Europe*) defending Breton products in Brussels (Pasquier, 2004).

Unlike in most French regions, in Brittany a tradition of negotiated planning *preceded* decentralisation. One interlocutor declared planning processes to be 'naturally at home here'. Co-financing was experienced as a genuine partnership in Brittany, whereas it was felt to be 'a post-decentralisation form of interference' in others. Brittany was the first region to sign the third State-Region plan in February 1994. In interviews, views from within the regional council and the regional prefecture converged, by and large, on the negotiation of the first four State-Region plans in Brittany. Early on in the process, the Regions were timid (including in Brittany). As the regional councils had few financial and bureaucratic resources, they limited themselves to dealing with specifically regional functions. By the time of the negotiation of the third State-Region plan (1994–98), the Brittany region had become more ambitious. In each of the four State-Region plans negotiated since 1984, there have been a number of clear priorities, such as transport infrastructure, the environment, inter-communal co-operation, cultural identity, the development of technology and internationalisation. Consistent with the tradition of CELIB, Breton policy-makers have argued especially strongly in favour of committing state and regional resources to road construction and improvements in transport infrastructure. Opening up Brittany to the French and European market is more important than anything else.

Even within Brittany discordant voices arose, regretting that 'the state-region plans are giving the state a means of supervising policies it has supposedly decentralised'. Some interviewees regretted the fact that the plans allowed the state to put pressure on the regions to allocate a proportion of regional finances to joint projects in areas such as building universities not falling within their official responsibilities. This motivation was recognised explicitly by one interlocutor in the regional prefecture, for whom 'the State has found an extraordinary means of putting pressure on the regions to co-finance state programmes'. The regional ownership of the plans was limited by the fact that all plans had to be agreed by the Inter-ministerial Territorial Planning Committee (*Comité interministeriel de l'amenagement et du développement du territoire* – CIADT), a structure attached to the Prime Minister's office from which the regional Presidents were excluded.

One overlooked dimension of territorial planning is how the State-Region plans have strengthened the organisational capacity of the regional state. The chief negotiator of the first three plans in the regional prefecture expressed it thus: 'The first two plans (1984–88, 1989–93) were exploratory, and we depended upon Paris for most things. The third plan (1994–98) was entirely different. The regional prefect was now the representative of the State in Region. The prefect had considerable autonomy in defining the State's orientations'. The strengthening of the state field services must be incorporated in any analysis of regional political capacity building. Administrative decentralisation has created more powerful state actors at the departmental and regional levels; this has, in turn, created a more interdependent form of policy-making. Stronger state partners have vested the new regional authorities with credibility in areas such as transport, education, training and economic development. The State-Region plans are a means of implementing the state's priorities in a region, but they also involve negotiation. Regions can refuse to agree to the State's demands. The Regions can pressurise the State to contractualise in areas it had not envisaged. In the case of Brittany, the Environmental Agency and the Water Plan are cases in point. The Brittany region demonstrated its ability to stand up to the state. In the 1994–99 round, the regional council refused to agree to the State's demand that it co-finance old-age people's homes, for example, which did not fall within its competencies. On the other hand, it was able to insist that the road-building programme should be the main priority of the plan, though roads did not form part of the regional council's obligatory responsibilities either. All actors involved are under pressure to agree to the State-Region plans because agreement opens up the prospect of match funding from EU structural funds, mainly Objective Two in the case of Brittany. Perhaps for this reason, a number of interlocutors in Wales looked with admiration at the coherence of the State-Region planning process in France.

Finance

Regional government finances in France are derived, in approximately equal measure, from central government transfers and regional sources of income (from direct taxation, charges for services, borrowing, EU grants and miscellaneous sources). State financial transfers form an important part of regional budgets. In addition to a general central-government block grant (*dotation globale de fonctionnement*), regional councils receive financial support from the decentralisation grant (*dotation générale de la décentralisation* – DGD), a fund specifically designed to compensate for new policy responsibilities under decentralisation. The regions (and the *départements*) also benefit from specific grants-in-aid in order to fulfil their responsibilities in areas such as education, training and apprenticeships, as well as to cover investment items. This hybrid method does not favour transparency. In 2004, for example, there were eight separate central-government transfers to the regions concerning apprenticeships alone. Insiders complain, moreover, that state transfers do not come close to covering the real cost of service delivery.

In France as a whole, the proportion of state transfers as a proportion of local government revenues has diminished progressively since 1982, with around 50 per cent of income derived from local sources of revenue in 2002 (INSEE, 2003). In the case of Brittany in 2004, the figure for regionally derived income was rather less than 50 per cent, the centre-Right majority anxious to keep down direct taxes. The main items of regional expenditure were, in order of importance: spatial planning and transport, secondary and higher education, lifelong learning and apprenticeships, economic development and research, quality of life, culture and sport and interregional co-operation. While the regions used to invest most in the area of economic development, they now spend heavily in the areas of secondary and higher education, training and apprenticeships and transport infrastructure. As new areas of responsibility are transferred to the regions, such as regional rail services in the case of Brittany, the balance between budgetary chapters can shift. In 2004, the regional transport chapter (€162 million) surpassed in importance that of secondary and higher education (€161 million) (Conseil Régional de Bretagne, 2004). With the implementation of the new decentralisation laws from 1 January 2005, the regions are likely to increase their expenditure on education (through their responsibility for ancillary staff), on health, on economic development and on transport infrastructure.

As the regional councils have accumulated new responsibilities, their budgets have increased markedly. In 1995, the total budget of the Brittany region was about the same as that of the *département* of Finistère. By 2002, it was 50 per cent more important. In terms of revenue, the total budget of the Brittany regional council in 2004 was €695.7 million (*c.*£500 million). Of this total, 50 per cent came from central state transfers, 28.4 per cent from regional taxes, 15.6 per cent from borrowing and 6 per cent from other sources (mainly charges and EU funds). The Brittany regional council budget is about one-twentieth that of the Welsh Assembly Government. Such comparisons can be misleading, however. The Welsh Assembly Government receives monies for services it does not deliver – in education, health and social services notably – and which it passes on to local government and the NHS. The Brittany regional council only receives money for the services it delivers itself, or which it directly funds. To compare like with like in budgetary terms would call for adding the budget of the communes, the EPCI and the four *départements*, as well as part of the healthcare regime. The Brittany regional council has tools at its disposal to vary rates of local taxation not available to the Welsh Assembly Government. The total regional budget is likely to grow substantially in future years, as more services are transferred to the regions (together with the promised financial compensation). In March 2003, Premier Raffarin announced that the receipts of fuel duty (TIPP) would be entirely transferred to sub-national authorities, which would also have the right to raise taxes on insurance. Interior Minister Sarkozy announced in October 2003 that €30 billion would thus be transferred to local and regional authorities to allow them to exercise their new duties. Local and regional authorities were still not satisfied, fearing that local taxpayers would have to bear the cost of the transferred responsibilities. The confused situation was made somewhat clearer after a ruling of the Constitutional Council, which determined that the central state would have to make up any financial shortfall occasioned by the new responsibilities.

Interlocutors within the Brittany region (Gaullists as well as Socialists) feared that a satisfactory transfer of funds would not accompany the transfer of functions. Former President de Rohan, in an interview in 2002, expressed some dissatisfaction with the decentralisation of regional rail services to the region. The case of the education ancillary workers (TOS) caused even more bitter disputes: regional politicians simply did not believe central-government guarantees that the newly transferred functions would be adequately covered by financial transfers. Past central-government initiatives led local and regional politicians to fear a lack of joined-up thinking. In 2000, the Socialist government had unilaterally suppressed vehicle levy duty, which had provided an important source of finance for the departments and regions. The Jospin government also reduced the rate of the business tax which the regions could claim. In January 2004, President Chirac announced that the government was looking into ways of abolishing the business tax altogether.

Local government

In Brittany, as elsewhere in France, sub-national governance is characterised by resource-based competition between overlapping layers of sub-national administration: the communes, inter-communal bodies, *départements* and regions. The Brittany region stands out, however, for its high level of cross-communal co-operation, not only in urban centres such as Rennes, but in the rural hinterland as well. In the mid-1990s, long before the Chevènement and Voynet laws of 1999 limited local tax competition, Brittany had the highest level of local tax harmonisation in France. Not only was the Rennes urban district the first city authority in France to introduce a city-wide business tax in France (in 1992), but the four *départements* also targeted resources to encourage inter-communal collaboration. In Ille-et-Vilaine, for example, the departmental council used its influence to secure harmonised local taxation agreements between individual communes in rural areas. The regional council in Brittany has continued this tradition. Under President de Rohan, the Brittany regional council was the first in France to agree contracts with the twenty-one *pays*, voluntary associations of mainly rural communes. This decision was confirmed and strengthened by President Le Drian, who directly associated the *pays* with distributing EU structural funds. Le Drian also announced, in 2004, the new majority's intention to extend contractual agreements to the main cities.

The Breton policy register involves recognising a regional interest over and above that of locality. The best evidence of institutional interconnectivity lies in the close collaboration between the local, departmental and regional authorities in negotiating the state-region plans and in preparing bids for structural funds. The regional council has been anxious to secure the agreement of all major interests before defining its bargaining position in negotiations with the State. Interviewees across the main organisations all stressed the importance of the Breton dimension in securing agreement. The main Breton cities and *départements* have accepted the leadership of the regional council in negotiating contracts with central government, at least when they have an obvious regional dimension (the State-Region plans, the University 2000 programme, EU programmes). If there was support (in the 1994–1999 and 2000–6 exercises) for the regional council as co-ordinator of local and departmental authorities, the counterpart was that the region must not attempt to develop its expertise in areas already occupied by other local authorities. Social policy and housing – both areas where the regional council could legitimately declare an interest – were two cases in point where the region refrained from developing sophisticated policies that might impinge upon those carried out by the *départements* or communes. From this brief presentation it can be concluded that Brittany scores highly in terms of institutional inter-connectivity.

Building European political capacity?

The fundamentally pro-European engagement of Bretons and Brittany was a recurrent theme in interviews. There were different versions of this narrative. For Breton regionalists, Europe would eventually shatter the centralism of the French State and impose a polycentric development. More technocratic sources within the regional prefecture were more inclined to emphasise the good collaboration on European dossiers in the Brittany region. These contrasting narratives converged to identify a harmony between the underlying Breton political culture and prevailing European norms, in terms of social cohesion notably. Brittany, along with Alsace, had voted massively in favour of the Maastricht Treaty in the 1992 referendum, the two most 'peripheral' French regions demonstrating the strongest pro-European engagement. From the period of the CELIB, Breton politicians had adopted an active engagement with Europe. One of the key founding-fathers of European integration was René Pleven, the French premier (1950–51) who launched the abortive European Defence Community. He was also the first President and leading personality of the CELIB. Breton elites 'got into the habit of playing the European card' from an early stage.

If individual Bretons have had important contacts, Brittany as a region has had to contend with the France State tradition. France has traditionally had one of the tightest, most state-centric forms of interaction with Brussels (Wright, 1996; Eymeri, 2003). At an official intergovernmental level, all interactions are supposed to be cleared by the SGCI, a bureaucratic unit attached to the Prime Minister's office. Another central state agency dependent upon the Prime Minister, the DATAR, co-ordinates local and regional bids for funding, in close liaison with the regional prefectures, the SGAR. In practice, French regions are not absent from this process. EU rules for the attribution of regional development and structural funds insist upon the involvement of local and regional authorities and voluntary associations. The Commission has clashed with the French government over the interpretation of these rules. The regional prefectures have associated the regions with the definition and the implementation of structural funds. Since the passage of the 2004 decentralisation law, French regions have been allowed to bid to exercise complete control over the management of structural funds on an experimental basis (the first contender being Alsace). The direction of change is clear, even though French administrative and political elites continue to resist as in many other areas of decentralisation.

On the ground, there was dissatisfaction with the attitude of the French government to EU programmes within both of the policy communities under discussion. In the training-policy area, for example, EU programmes such as Leonardo were managed by the regional field service of the Labour and Training Ministry (DRTEFP), rather than by the regional council itself. Officials within the region complained of not being associated with negotiating EU programmes such as TRACE directly relevant to them. Members of the language-policy community were even firmer. One interlocutor regretted that in France, as minorities did not officially exist, it was difficult for Bretons to lobby on issues such as minority languages, a stance which weakened the French (and Breton) position in institutions such as the European Bureau for Lesser Used Languages.

The influence exercised by the Brittany regional council on European Union issues is relatively minor. The overarching French State context has limited direct interactions between Brittany and the EU institutions. There has certainly been some development of regional capacity in the European sphere. The 1982 Decentralisation Act allowed French local and regional authorities to set up offices in Brussels. The Brittany/Pays de la Loire office, set up in 1991, is one of the older, more-established structures. In comparative terms, however, it is a light structure, with a much more modest policy remit than its Welsh counterpart. In 2004, the office had two full time staff and a number of *stagiaires*. One regional politician in charge of liaison with Brussels offices regretted that the joint Brittany/Pays de la Loire office had only '4–5 people maximum, when we have relations with regional offices with over 40 staff'. The Brittany/Pays de la Loire office performs a similar role to those of other local and regional authorities: information gathering, anticipation of future developments, organising meetings for local and regional politicians with the relevant officials from the Commission. The office performs a limited role. It has no official access to diplomatic papers of officials in the *Représentation Permanente*. Regional politicians are not present in the Council working groups, nor do they represent France in intergovernmental committee structures (as they can do in Wales). The representation of France in Brussels remains, in comparative terms, a state-centric affair.

If the institutional avenues for formal expression are modest, interviews uncovered a rich stream of more covert forms of influence. One interlocutor referred at length to the informal linkages between Breton local authorities and well-placed Bretons within the Commission, praising the helpful role of Commission officials in the preparing of urban dossiers. This type of contact, transparent in many countries and encouraged by the Commission, remains semi-covert and strongly discouraged in France. Other sources referred to the existence of a dense Breton network within the relevant Paris ministries and agencies, most especially the DATAR (the French agency charged with monitoring and selecting projects to be forwarded for European funds). Bretons (rather than Brittany per se) exercise a well-developed informal influence, a model consistent with a strong region operating within a restrictive state context. Rather as in Wales, however, the most effective pressures are those exercised at the level of the French State.

Conclusion

With the victory of the Socialists in twenty out of twenty-two metropolitan regions in March 2004, the latent conflict between State and the Regions threatened to expand into a full-blown controversy. Though Premier Raffarin finally deigned to meet the Presidents of the regional councils in July 2004, the meeting was cut short after less than an hour. The Senate's amendment removing clear unambiguous control of economic development from the regions insulted the spirit of the early texts and was met with fury from the regional Presidents. These complications notwithstanding, the 2002–4 reforms offered the prospect of a renewed phase of political decentralisation and the strengthening of regional political capacity. Whether under Gaullist or Socialist control, the Brittany region has been in the forefront of demands for enhanced decentralisation. The Gaullist-led council of President de Rohan published on 20 September 2002 an ambitious 'Manifesto for Decentralisation' which demanded a *pouvoir normatif régional* and asked that all regional councillors be consulted by the National Assembly before any laws concerning them be passed. As the Socialists in opposition had been even more attuned to regionalist demands, the capture by the Socialists of the Brittany regional council in March 2004 ensured that interesting times would lie ahead. Brittany would continue to be seen as a litmus test for regional advocacy.

6
Political institutions, public and elite opinions in Wales and Brittany

The choice of Wales and Brittany as objects of analysis provided two historic regions with complex but strong identities, functioning regional political institutions and past traditions of demanding more regional autonomy. These regions are exceptional within France and the UK. Chapters 2, 3, 4 and 5 introduced the reader to Wales and Brittany, their respective state contexts, party systems and experience of devolved political institutions. Thus far, a mostly inductive, qualitative approach has been adopted, emphasising diversity and complexity, an approach well adapted to a broader interest in regional governance (Kooiman, 2003). Chapter 6 undertakes a rather different intellectual exercise, presenting findings from opinion surveys commissioned in Wales and Brittany in June 2001 in order to engage in deductive quantitative analysis. Defining support for regional political institutions as the dependent variable, the surveys set out to elucidate general comparative political-science questions about institutional traditions, identity foci, instrumental incentives and political opportunity structures. These surveys were also, more specifically, designed to discover what people living in Wales and Brittany think of their regions, how they envisage their future institutional development, how they conceive of their regional and national identities or how they frame issues of public policy.

Public opinion and regional political institutions in Wales and Brittany

A detailed opinion survey was conducted in the two regions in order to ascertain similarities and differences across a range of variables (political institutions and identities, policy preferences, attitudes to language, training and education) (Cole, 2004). Market Research Wales and *Efficience 3* simultaneously carried out the surveys in Wales and Brittany in June and July 2001. A representative sample of 1008 in Wales (1007 in Brittany), selected by quotas of age, gender, socio-economic group and locality, was interviewed in each region. The polity-building dimension was central to the comparative investigation. Taking support for regional political institutions as the dependent variable, the research started with two basic hypotheses, both of which were drawn from the survey of the governance and new regionalist literature and both of which were applied comparatively. These were labelled as identity focus and instrumental incentive.

The first hypothesis is that of identity focus. Identity is a nebulous concept. As McKenzie (1973) affirms ' the phrase identity does not refer to an "objective phenomenon", and there is no agreed meaning attached to the word'. Identity has a compound sense; identity can be personal, social or collective. Though it can be taken logically to imply either similarity or difference (Le Coadic, 1998), identity has been understood here as common purpose, something that persists through time. It consists of a combination of myths, symbols, rituals and ideology. The opinion survey measured identity by adapting the 'Moreno scale', an innovative comparative method for capturing dual identities, and applying it to Wales and Brittany. The Moreno scale asks respondents to situate themselves along a five-point continuum ('Welsh, not British', 'more Welsh than British', 'As Welsh as British', 'More British than Welsh', 'British, not Welsh'), providing insights into their preferential mix of regional and national identities. It does not capture many of the complexities of multiple and overlapping identities, but it does provide a parsimonious and effective comparative tool. The survey also collected data on a range of independent variables such as gender, age, level of education, level of linguistic aptitude and locality, as well as attitudinal variables in relation to political institutions and public policy preferences.

The initial hypothesis, based upon a reading of the existing literature, was that regional identity would be strong in Wales and Brittany, but that the distinctive historical trajectories of the two regions would produce rather different forms of regional governance. In the case of Wales, it was believed that the divisive history of (pre-) devolution and the demonstration of linguistic, territorial and political cleavages in the 1997 referendum would undermine regional political institutions and prevent the development of regional capacity. In the case of Brittany, on the other hand, the hypothesis was that a regional policy register (*répertoire d'action collective*) based on consensus and a political opportunity structure which remains largely state-centric would combine to promote a limited form of regional advocacy. Identity would either destroy the nascent political institutions in Wales or mould them into a coherent project. In the case of Brittany, the research was expected to discover a form of bounded regionality, a combination of powerful dual identities which underpinned the legitimacy of regional political institutions, yet placed boundaries on the development of autonomous political capacity.

First, a brief further development of the idea of multiple identities. McEwen and Moreno (2005) suggest that, while the classic nation-state was based on the idea of an all-embracing state national identity (rooted in cultural and civic axes), globalisation and internal changes have corroded such a neat fit between state and nation. The concept of dual or multiple identity is a useful tool for interpretation. Individuals share identities in varying degrees. They are tied to competing cultural reference groups, those of locality, region, gender, religion, language or political preference. Compound national identities are arguably becoming the norm in most EU states. In some European states, such as Spain or Belgium, individuals have been pulled between their ethno-territorial and their civic identities, to the extent that the cohesion of the state is openly challenged. In others (France notably), the state project explicitly sets out to limit the expression of intermediary corps in the name of the universal values of equality, reason and progress. There has been a spill-over into intellectual traditions. While Spanish and Belgian scholars are in the forefront of theorising about the nature of new imagined communities, in France there has been an unwillingness to confront the issues of cultural and political relativism (Wieviorka, 1997). In the France case, the social-scientific community itself has been deeply hostile to using tools such as the 'Moreno' identity question that potentially sets regional and national identities in opposition. Underpinning these methodological differences lay broader political concerns. From the traditional republican perspective in France, the rise of regional identities can be read as a challenge to the authoritative allocation of values by the central state and the respect for the neutrality of the public sphere (Schnapper, 1994). From the constructivist perspective gaining currency elsewhere (including in the UK), multiple identities can be viewed as a means of adapting the nation-state to post-modern realities.

The second hypothesis was labelled as *instrumental incentive*. The instrumental incentive hypothesis views the meso-level in instrumental terms, as the most appropriate one for the strategic co-ordination of lower-level authorities and the provision of middle-range services (in economic development, transport infrastructure, training, sometimes education), rather than as an institutional focus for identity-based loyalties. A regional political authority does not necessarily represent the meso-level. Even where – as in Wales and Brittany – such authorities do exist, they will have to contend with other players. The reality of regional capacity building depends to some extent upon whether political, administrative and associative players focus upon meso-level interactions as opposed to state-centric ones. The political opportunity structure is an important component of the instrumental incentive. As political parties aggregate interests, party politicians themselves play a crucial role in shaping regional political demands. The presence or not of a powerful regionalist

Table 6.1 Institutional preferences in Wales and Brittany

Q. There is a debate today in France/Wales on the future of decentralisation/Devolution. Which one of the following options do you prefer?

	Brittany (n.1007) %	Wales (n.1008) %
'Abolish the Regional Council/National Assembly for Wales'	2	24
'Retain a Regional Council/National Assembly with limited powers'	44	24
'Create an elected parliament with tax-raising and legislative powers'	34	38
An independent Brittany/Wales	12	11
Don't know	8	3

Note: Figures rounded up or down to the nearest percentage point for ease of comprehension.

party, the attitudes adopted by national parties to issues of territorial identity, the rewards to be gained by emphasising one or another level of governance: all of these are in part shaped by the party linkage function.

The questions asked in the comparative opinion polls were general ones attempting to capture the rather different situations in Wales and Brittany. The polling evidence revealed a strong demand in both regions for effective regional political institutions (Table 6.1). In Brittany, as in Wales, was observed overwhelming support for consolidating or strengthening existing regional institutions.

The research findings confirmed the existence of a regional political consciousness in both cases. If anything, regional political institutions appeared more embedded in Brittany, where only 2 per cent of the population wanted to abolish the regional council, with the largest single group – 44 per cent – in favour of retaining the current situation ('a regional council with limited powers'). A sizeable minority of 34 per cent was regionalist in the sense of seeking greater powers for the regional council similar to those possessed by the Scottish Parliament ('an elected parliament with tax-raising and legislative powers') and a further 12 per cent wished to see an 'independent' Brittany.[1] A firm foundation of support exists in both countries for more enhanced forms of regional governance. The results of the institutional-preference question for Wales are instructive on two counts. Around 24 per cent opposed devolution and a similar number (24 per cent) supported retaining the Assembly with its existing powers. Around one half of respondents advocated the strengthening of the National Assembly: to give it powers at least equivalent to those of the Scottish Parliament (38 per cent) or advocating independence (11 per cent). Though the trend toward embedding devolution was clear, in 2001 the jury was still out and the Assembly needed to convince a large section of the Welsh public that devolution was producing benefits for the Welsh people.

The survey not only indicated strong support for regional political institutions in Wales and Brittany, but also a desire to strengthen the regional over the local, national and European levels in specific areas (notably in training and language, two fields of policy investigation). According to the surveys, public opinion in Wales and Brittany strongly believes that the regional authorities *ought* to make the main decisions in the two fields of training and regional languages, as well as in other areas of regional ownership. In Wales (50 per cent) and in Brittany (53 per cent) a majority of respondents identified the National Assembly for Wales or the Brittany regional council as the appropriate level for decision-making on language-related issues. The findings for training policy provided further support for the regional level in both countries. Welsh and Breton public opinion was remarkably similar in preferring the regional institution as the 'primary political institution making decisions in the area of training policy' (42 per cent of the Welsh and 43 per cent of the Breton survey), rather than the EU, national government or local government. There are many similarities between these findings and those of other surveys. In the 2003 Assembly election survey undertaken by the Institute of Welsh Politics, for example, a majority of people surveyed (57.6 per cent) believed that the UK government exercised the most influence over policy, but a majority (56 per cent) also believed that the National Assembly ought to (Scully, 2003).

There are other ways of capturing the degree of regionality. Since 1992, the Paris- based Interregional Political Observatory (*Observatoire Interrégional du Politique* – OIP) has asked respondents a rather different question: 'do you feel most attached to your locality, your region or your nation?' In the largest survey of its kind ever carried out in France, the 2003 OIP survey discovered that Brittany was the only region in mainland France where 'attachment to the region' came ahead of 'attachment to the nation' (OIP, 2003; Nicolas, 2004). This finding confirms the view that Breton identities are complex and multiple, a provocation to traditional French Republicans for whom regional identities are the legacy of pre-modern obscurantism and should be eradicated. The findings from the survey for the present study also suggest that Bretons demonstrate a willingness to envisage more advanced forms of political decentralisation than elsewhere in France (Pillet, 2001). On the other hand, twenty years of institutional existence of regional councils has created a measure of institutional loyalty even in areas – such as the Centre – where the regions are completely artificial creations (Dargent, 2001).

If public opinion in Wales has become more favourable to devolution, this is not because the Assembly is perceived to have delivered on policy. The surveys carried out by the Institute of Welsh Politics team in 1997, 1999 and 2003 also noted the paradox of an Assembly growing in legitimacy while not delivering in terms of policy (Scully, 2003). When asked specific questions about the effectiveness of the National Assembly, the Welsh people appeared to be underwhelmed. The majority (60 per cent) of those asked disagreed with the statement that 'the quality of public services has improved under the Assembly', indicating that the Welsh public was still waiting for the Assembly to deliver. Other findings from the survey confirmed the Welsh public's more positive attitude to the devolution process in Wales. When asked the question 'What are your personal views on devolution for Wales?', a majority (51 per cent) were in favour or strongly in favour of devolution, with only 32 per cent against. On the issue of whether the existence of the Assembly had democratised political processes in Wales, respondents were split almost evenly, with a small majority against the proposition that 'the say of people in decision-making has improved under the Assembly'. This posed an immediate problem for the Assembly which appeared to reflect the general disillusionment with politics in the UK, indicated by the low general-election turnout of 2001 and the poor Assembly turnout in 2003. But the future existence of the Assembly was no longer really contested. These findings from the survey in 2001 are backed up, indeed strengthened by more recent surveys – notably those carried out by the Institute for Welsh Politics team. In their overview of the three surveys they conducted in 1997, 1999 and 2003, Scully and Wyn Jones (2003); and Wyn Jones and Scully (2004) conclude that there has been a steady shift towards favouring a Scottish-style parliament and a draining away of support for the pre-devolution arrangements. The institutions of Welsh devolution are now more trusted to act in the Welsh people's best interests than are those of London.

Institutions, identities and partisan preferences

How best can differential attitudes towards regional political institutions in Wales and Brittany be comprehended? From the outset, the argument of non-comparability was rejected because of fundamental differences in identity and institutional preferences. In both regions public opinion was divided, but there was simultaneously a strong sense of regional identity and a widespread demand for powerful regional institutions. The research was initially limited to analysis focusing on two criteria – dual identities, and intended voting behaviour in an Assembly or regional election – which allow for meaningful comparisons to be drawn between Welsh and Breton public opinion.

Table 6.2 The Moreno identity scale for Brittany and Wales

Brittany (n.1007)	%	*Wales (n.1008)*	%
Breton, not French	2	Welsh, not British	20
More Breton than French	15	More Welsh than British	17
Equally Breton and French	57	Equally Welsh and British	35
More French than Breton	17	More British than Welsh	22
French, not Breton	7	British, not Welsh	6
Don't know	2		

Note: Figures rounded up or down to the nearest percentage point for ease of comprehension.

Does identity matter? Table 6.2 presents the results of the Moreno identity question applied to Wales and Brittany. The table is highly revealing. A far higher proportion of the Welsh survey – over one-third – considered itself to be exclusively or primarily Welsh than was the case in Brittany. A sense of Welshness as being essentially opposed to Britishness is firmly rooted in a sizeable minority of Welsh people. In Brittany, by contrast, the sense of regional identity is strong, but this is not considered as being in opposition to an overarching French nationhood (Cole and Loughlin, 2003). There is much less of a conflict between Breton and French identities than is the case for Wales and the UK. The greatest difference between Wales and Brittany therefore lies not so much in institutional preferences for the future as in the linkage between national and regional identities. Dual identities are more easily assumed in Brittany than in Wales.

Cross-tabulations suggest that, in the two cases, there is some sort of relationship between identity and institutional preferences. Tables 6.3 and 6.4 cross-tabulate dual identities (the horizontal rows) with views on the desirable future evolution of Wales and Brittany (the vertical columns). Clear relationships were established between identity and institutional preferences at the two extremes. Those considering themselves to be uniquely or predominantly Welsh or Breton were more likely to advocate either a Scottish-style parliament or independence than were those considering themselves to be primarily or entirely British or French. The median position varied between the two regions, however. In the French region, Breton and French identities were mainly complementary. Not so in the case of Wales, where opinion was far more polarised, a polarity manifested by starkly opposed positions in relation to identity and institutional preferences. These cross-tabulations also threw up some surprising findings, such as the higher than average support for Breton independence from those considering themselves as only French. The most credible explanations would point to the exasperation with Breton

Table 6.3 Identity and institutional preferences in Wales (%)

	Independent Wales (n.112)	Elected parliament (n.380)	Elected assembly (n.238)	No elected assembly (n.238)	Don't know (n.41)	Total
Welsh not British (n.202)	26	41	16	13	4	100
More Welsh than British (n.173)	18	44	24	12	2	100
Equally Welsh and British (n.343)	4	39	26	27	4	100
More British than Welsh (n.224)	4	30.5	25.5	36	4	100
British, not Welsh (n.60)	12	25	27	27	9	100

Note: Table 6.3 excludes the small number (n.6) who refused to answer the Moreno Identity question. The table is read as follows. Of those declaring they were More British than Welsh, a small fraction (4 per cent) wanted to see an independent Wales; a much larger number (30.5 per cent) would be happy with an elected Parliament. Of the remainder only a minority (25.5 per cent) were happy with the Assembly as it currently existed and a plurality (36 per cent) wanted to abolish the Assembly. A small number (4 per cent) did not know. Figures rounded up or down to the nearest percentage point for ease of comprehension.

regionalists on behalf of those who the most firmly reject forms of regional expression. Similar sentiments have been observed by French-nationality hardliners in relation to Corsica.

Do partisan preferences matter? Both populations were asked how they intended to vote if a general or a regional election were to be held tomorrow. Regional voting intention was then cross-tabulated with institutional preferences (Tables 6.5 and 6.6).

In Brittany, we observed surprisingly few differences according to voting intention. PS voters were scarcely more favourable than RPR voters to enhanced regional autonomy. These figures bear out the belief expressed in many interviews that institutional preferences cut across existing parties. Institutional choices cannot be reduced to a simple left–right cleavage. These findings are consistent with existing representations of Breton political cleavages, whereby national political parties within Brittany are infused with Breton cultural values. There is an underlying consensus to defend Breton interests to the outside world and limit political conflict. Brittany's political elite has adapted to the French logic of territorial decentralisation, having itself had a

Table 6.4 Identity and institutional preferences in Brittany (%)

	Independent Brittany (n.120)	*Region with law-making and taxation powers (n.343)*	*Regional Council with limited powers (n.442)*	*Abolish the Regional Council (n.19)*	*Don't Know (n.84)*	*Total*
Breton, not French (n.21)	33	19	29	–	19	100
More Breton than French (n.146)	25	35	32	1	7	100
Equally Breton and French (n.574)	10	36	42	2	10	100
More French than Breton (n.174)	3	33	57	2	5	100
French, not Breton (n.75)	15	20	56	1	8	100

Note: Table 6.4 excludes the small number (n.8) who refused to answer the Moreno Identity question. The table is read as follows. Of those declaring they were More French than Breton, a tiny fraction (3 per cent) wanted to see an independent Brittany; a much larger number (33 per cent) would be happy with an elected Parliament; most (57 per cent) wanted to retain the current arrangement of an elected Regional Council with limited powers, and hardly any wanted to abolish the Regional Council (2 per cent). A small number, 5 per cent, did not know. Figures rounded up or down to the nearest percentage point for ease of comprehension.

major influence in forcing decentralisation onto the political agenda, and in obtaining disproportionate resources through playing up, within limits, its territorial distinctiveness. The model of influence is a traditional one of bringing pressure to bear in Paris (raising the spectre of a powerful regionalist movement), in order to promote the material well-being of the region. Instrumental incentives (the Paris-centric distribution of resources) and the political opportunity structure (the departmental basis of regional elections, the weakness of the Breton regionalist party [UDB] and the strategies of existing parties) combine to promote Brittany's interests primarily through lobbying central government (Cole and Loughlin, 2003; Le Coadic, 1998).

In the 2001 survey, there was much less cross-partisan consensus in the Welsh electorate than in Brittany. Within the Welsh electorate were identified three distinct positions, ranging from a residual Conservative hostility to the

Table 6.5 Voting intentions and institutional preferences in Wales (%)*

	Total	*Con n.111*	*Lab n.329*	*Lib Dem n.74*	*Plaid Cymru n.172*
Wales should become independent	11	4	7	1	28
Remain part of the UK, with elected parliament	38	24	44	43	51
Remain part of the UK, with elected assembly	24	17	30	27	12
Remain part of the UK without an elected assembly	24	54	15	27	6
Don't know	3	1	4	2	3

Note: *Intended vote in an Assembly election. Figures rounded up or down to the nearest percentage point for ease of comprehension.

Table 6.6 Voting intentions and institutional preferences in Brittany*

	Total	*PS (n.184)*	*Greens (n.77)*	*UDF (n.27)*	*RPR (n.49)*
Abolish regional council	2	2	0	4	2
Regional council with limited powers	44	49	46	42	54
Elected parliament with tax-raising and legislative powers	33	36	39	46	32
Independent Brittany	12	8	14	4	6
Don't know	9	5	1	4	6

Note: * Intended vote in a regional election. Figures rounded up or down for ease of comprehension. Figures to be treated with caution on account of the large number of undecided voters, refusals to answer the question or votes for minor parties. But the contrast with figures for Wales is very interesting.

principle of devolution, to overwhelming support from intending Plaid Cymru voters for at least a Scottish-style parliament, with Labour and Liberal democrats occupying a median position favourable to going beyond executive devolution (Table 6.5). Rather like the Assembly members interviewed, few supported the existing settlement, with the status quo option arriving in third position in each electorate ('retain an elected Assembly with limited powers'). The principle of an elected Assembly was accepted overwhelmingly in each electorate, except that of the Conservatives. While divisions remained in each party, the centre of gravity among intending Labour and Liberal Democrats voters (the governing coalition at the time of the survey) had shifted beyond accepting devolution towards advocating a Scottish-style parliament. The Plaid Cymru electorate was the most cohesive, in its large majority dissatisfied with the limited devolution introduced by the Government of Wales Act.

The party system is an important explanatory variable differentiating between Wales and Brittany. There are some similarities between the Welsh and Breton situations. Welsh politicians also reached the heights of political power by operating through the national parties, first the Liberals, latterly Labour. A sense of Britishness was inculcated into Welsh consciousness by the actions of politicians such as Aneurin Bevan, who stressed British public services and uniform national standards, and who sought to defend British sovereignty. While no particular family has claimed a dominant role over time in Brittany, however, Wales remains favourable political terrain for the Labour Party. Labour's traditional hegemony was based on its domination of the North-East, South Wales and the Valleys. It excluded the political representation of important sections of Welsh society, however, notably the Welsh-speaking heartlands in North-West and Mid-Wales. The existence of a powerful Nationalist Party (mobilising support in part on the language issue) reinforced Welsh territorial distinctiveness within the Union State. Plaid Cymru represented, above all, the Welsh-speaking heartlands of North-West and Mid-Wales. The penetration of Plaid Cymru into the non-Welsh-speaking Valleys in the 1999 elections was a major breakthrough, though the 2003 elections mostly reverted to type (Scully, 2003b). The role performed by the nationalist movement is a critical distinguishing feature between Wales and Brittany, involving the politicisation of language issues and heightening territorially based divisions within Wales itself.

The respective party systems reinforce substantive differences between Wales and Brittany. While Brittany is a region with a strong identity, the French political opportunity structure has encouraged party elites to plead common cause in the broader French State (and European Union) context. In the case of Wales, territorial divisions, identity, partisan affiliation and, to a lesser extent, language have prevented Welsh political elite from acting in such a unified manner. As the focus of the political opportunity structure has shifted from London to Cardiff, however, devolution in Wales has encouraged all parties to undertake a territorial adjustment of their core political message. Regional political institutions shape party strategies more obviously in Wales than in Brittany.

What priorities for regional action? Public opinion and public policy in Wales and Brittany

Regional public-spending priorities are indicative not only of actual policy choices but also of the appropriateness of public intervention of different levels in specific policy fields. Even in the most federally inclined system, it would be difficult to imagine defence expenditure being a major priority for a sub-central authority. The survey proceeded to ask an open-ended question ('If your region had more money to spend, where should its first two priorities lie?') seeking to elicit the Welsh and Breton public's preferences for regional public expenditure. Table 6.7 presents a hierarchy of the first preferences. The implications of these figures for Wales and Brittany are considered next.

Public opinion in Wales has fully integrated the significance of devolution into its thinking. Its priorities for future regional expenditure involve generic spending areas such as health and education rather than more narrowly defined Welsh interests such as culture or language. The priorities for Assembly expenditure are broadly in line with those of the UK as a whole. Health and education – two areas where the Assembly has been devolved powers to define and apply Welsh solutions – are the overwhelming concerns. The lessons for the Assembly are mixed. On the one hand, the saliency of these issue areas justifies the search for Welsh solutions to intractable policy problems (of educational

Table 6.7 First priority for regional expenditure in Wales and Brittany

Breton first priority	*%*	*Welsh first priority*	*%*
Environmental issues	20	NHS/hospitals	43
Economic development	9	Schools/education	21
Improving the roads	9	Public transport	6
Tourism	8	Getting people into jobs	4
Training	6	Urban development	3
Culture	5	Improving the roads	3
Education	5	Support for small business	2
Urban development	4	Environmental Issues	2
Rural affairs	3	Children's facilities	2
Public transport	3	Other	5
Sport	2	Don't know/nothing	9
Other	15		
Don't know/nothing	11		

Note: Figures rounded up or down to the nearest percentage point for ease of comprehension.

underachievement or of health standards below the UK average). Not only do health and education present seemingly irresolvable policy dilemmas, both fields also contain their own complex pre-existing actor systems and their own path dependencies. Health and education symbolise the semi-sovereign nature of Assembly policy-making. There is a gulf between the expectations placed on the Assembly and the constraints of devolution (Cole and Storer, 2002). The Assembly can decide to shift resources to health or education, but it has a limited budget and some other policy field will lose out. The counterpart to the Welsh electorate's concern with health and education is that other Assembly priorities – such as the environment, social inclusion, transport, urban development and rural assistance – did not figure particularly highly in the public's perceptions of important spending priorities.

In Brittany, the findings differed in important respects from those observed in Wales, where health and education dominated popular preferences. These results do not imply that the Breton public cares less than the public in Wales about health and education. In the Breton case, expenditure priorities demonstrated a realistic appraisal of the limited powers of the French regions much more than a disinterest in the areas of health and education. Breton public opinion has fully integrated the constraints of decentralisation into its preferences. It is because health and education are not identified as areas of regional policy intervention that they do not appear as high priorities for regional expenditure. We would certainly not expect health to top the list of spending priorities for a French regional Assembly. The French system of healthcare is elaborately – and expensively – managed by a social partnership of employers and trade unions, increasingly closely monitored by the central state. The regions have some responsibilities in healthcare, but these are not well perceived by public opinion. Having said this, the temporal dimension is undoubtedly important. Had the survey been carried out one year later, in 2002, there might have been more open support for regional spending on health, given that several regions had by then made public their desire to exercise greater responsibilities in healthcare under the Raffarin government's 'experimental transfer of functions' initiative.

The low ranking of education is rather more intriguing. Though France prides itself on its national education system, implying uniform standards and practices throughout the country, French regions also have important responsibilities in secondary and higher education. The regions build and maintain upper secondary schools (*lycées*) and some universities, provide equipment, participate in educational planning and – of great importance in Brittany – can make grants to private schools. Though there is intense interest in Brittany in education, this issue area is perceived primarily as either a national or a more localised policy responsibility. The Regional councils have not yet drawn much political capital from their major budgetary investment in education over the past fifteen years. Education is one area where the central state has succeeded in shedding responsibilities to the periphery (regional councils and state field services) while retaining strategic control.

Unlike in Wales, in the case of Brittany the public's expenditure preferences pinpoint issues of specific regional importance, rather than generic spending areas. They suggest a strong 'regional effect'. The first priority was the environment. Environmental issues are high on the political agenda in Brittany, which has to face specific challenges unknown to most other French regions. The second priority for regional expenditure identified in the survey is economic development. There is an established post-war tradition of public intervention in supporting the Breton economy, whether through direct investment or through providing transport infrastructure. By distinguishing economic development as the second priority for regional expenditure, the Breton public again identified an area where regional action could (or should) make a difference. Amongst the other priorities for regional expenditure we can identify two further areas closely linked to the specific attributes of Brittany: tourism and culture. Brittany is one of France's major tourist regions. That Bretons look to the regional authority to promote tourism supports the proximity argument; regional investment is appropriate because the Region has detailed knowledge of local conditions. A similar observation might be made with respect to culture. It is entirely appropriate for the regional authority to promote culture, not only because culture is worth promoting but also because it has a strong regional dimension.

The survey's second series of questions lead to refining the argument somewhat. A logic of appropriateness appears to be at work. Whether consciously or not, the Welsh public appeared to have integrated the evolutionary character of devolution into its calculations. It looked to the Assembly (in an exaggerated manner) to concentrate its resources on remedying deep-rooted problems in health and education. To all extents and purposes, the Welsh public implored its Assembly to act as a government, divided opinions over devolution notwithstanding. The Breton public wanted regional public expenditure to be concentrated in areas where regional institutions might make a difference, or where the image of Brittany itself was involved. This might be conceived of as a form of bounded regionality. There is no equivalent process of state building to that which might be inferred from the findings in Wales. Health and education provide a useful contrast to training and regional languages. In the core areas of health and education, even in regionally minded Brittany, there is a preference for a system of national regulation, consistent with French public-service doctrine, equality of standards and the legacy of 150 years of 'republican' ideology.

Determining attitudes to regional political institutions in Wales and Brittany

The above section dealt in a preliminary way with two important variables influencing attitudes to regional political institutions: dual identities and voting behaviour. The survey contained many other possible predictors. The next step was to undertake logistic regression to distinguish further between devolution and decentralisation in Wales and Brittany.[2] Why was this approach decided upon? Logistic regression is the best tool for indicating the probability of something happening, as opposed to it not happening (Field, 2000). Special interest was laid on trying to discover the range of variables which would help differentiate between the Welsh and the Breton cases and elucidate differing attitudes to the hypothetical situations of independence, full legislative devolution, limited devolution and opposition to any form of regional political institution. What variables come into play when supporting hypothetical independence or devolution? How do these vary between Wales and Brittany? What does this tell about the relationship between public opinion and regional political institutions in the two regions?

In the logistic regression analysis, support for regional political institutions was treated as the principal dependent variable, the heart of the comparative institutional study. A series of independent variables was identified, selected on the basis of the existing literature and in accordance with the theoretical framework. These included classic independent variables such as age, gender, education and place of birth. Also integrated were the attitudinal and opinion variables of identity, language aptitude, preferred level of decision for policies and voting behaviour. There are strong theoretical reasons for considering each of these attitudes as independent variables. The new regionalist literature predicts a strong relationship between identity and institutional preference (Keating, 1998; Keating, Loughlin and Deschouwer, 2003). It is also to be expected that those who speak or understand Welsh well/fluently would be more in favour of independence or of an Assembly with extended powers (Cole and Williams, 2004). As observed above, the regional level is the one preferred for the management of language and training policies. Cross-tabulations also convincingly demonstrated a linkage between voting behaviour and institutional preference, as displayed in Tables 6.8 and 6.9.

In the case of Wales (Table 6.8), the fundamental dynamics are those relating to identity. There is a clear link between identity and views on devolution or independence. Those with the strongest sense of exclusive Welsh identity are also those likely to be the most favourable to independence. The variable contributes negatively, on the other hand, in the case of an elected assembly with limited powers or no devolution at all. Identity is by the far the

Table 6.8 Logistic regression estimates for Wales

Variables	Independence	Assembly with extended competences	Assembly with limited competences	No elected assembly
Age	−0.019 (0.206)	0.169 (0.125)	−0.037 (0.140)	* −0.338 (0.201)
Gender	−0.046 (0.295)	0.069 (0.182)	0.264 (0.203)	** −0.594 (0.281)
Education	−0.099 (0.101)	0.096 (0.062)	−0.089 (0.070)	−0.011 (0.099)
Place of birth	0.225 (0.467)	0.086 (0.236)	0.229 (0.256)	−0.340 (0.346)
National identity	*** 0.685 (0.170)	0.135 (0.102)	** −0.325 (0.119)	** −0.406 (0.174)
Language	0.067 (0.328)	* 0.448 (0.230)	** −0.663 (0.294)	−0.502 (0.424)
Attitude to devolution process	0.588 (0.412)	*** 1.159 (0.220)	*** 0.933 (0.255)	*** −2.912 (0.320)
Level of decision (language)	0.317 (0.358)	0.169 (0.211)	* 0.438 (0.243)	*** −1.127 (0.313)
Level of decision (training)	−0.164 (0.333)	** 0.479 (0.207)	0.061 (0.235)	** −1.051 (0.340)
Voting	** 0.344 (0.137)	0.034 (0.082)	−0.153 (0.094)	*** −0.138 (0.129)
Constant	* −6.057 (0.822)	*** −2.753 (0.635)	−0.557 (0.459)	3.711 (0.673)
Log-likelihood	325.166	709.057	597.431	343.365
Predicted (%)	90.00	66.00	76.40	87.10
R2 Cox & Snell	0.094	0.149	0.068	0.404

* p < 0.10, ** p < 0.05, *** p < 0.001

Table 6.9 Logistic regression estimates for Brittany

Variables	Independence	Regional Council with extended competences	Regional Council with limited competences	No Regional Council
Age	*** 0.668 (0.182)	** −0.421 (0.124)	0.168 (0.115)	−0.138 (0.391)
Gender	0.375 (0.264)	** −0.368 (0.169)	* 0.329 (0.163)	* −1.095 (0.605)
Education	*** 0.712 (0.130)	*** −0.247 (0.057)	0.025 (0.056)	0.128 (0.207)
Place of birth	* 0.511 (0.310)	−0.016 (0.200)	−0.267 (0.194)	0.353 (0.622)
National identity	*** 0.863 (0.179)	** 0.255 (0.113)	*** −0.587 (0.113)	0.107 (0.321)
Language	−0.135 (0.447)	0.434 (0.267)	−0.314 (0.272)	−0.689 (0.990)
Attitude to devolution process	−0.481 (0.350)	0.391 (0.278)	0.243 (0.263)	** −1.700 (0.566)
Level of decision (language)	-0.293 (0.266)	0.141 (0.174)	0.040 (0.168)	−0.507 (0.595)
Level of decision (training)	−0.186 (0.278)	−0.018 (0.175)	0.151 (0.169)	* −1.282 (0.715)
Voting	−0.200 (0.165)	0.015 (0.094)	0.049 (0.091)	0.135 (0.294)
Constant	*** −9.225 (1.301)	** 0.227 (0.703)	1.084 (0.677)	−2.592 (2.090)
Log-likelihood	409.327	841.489	886.650	121.605
Predicted (%)	88.20	65.00	61.10	97.80
R2 Cox & Snell	0.118	0.072	0.063	0.030

*p < 0.10, ** p < 0.05, *** p < 0.001

most significant of the 'independent variables' for determining attitudes to independence, followed by voting behaviour. There is a clear relationship between strong attitudes, such as feeling primarily or exclusively Welsh, and voting for parties supporting enhanced devolution or independence. Focusing on language, the initial hypothesis was that Welsh and Breton speakers were likely to be more in favour of enhanced devolution or independence than others. This finding is backed up in the case of Wales (but not Brittany). The model demonstrates a clear linkage in Wales between language competency and institutional choices. Those who speak or understand Welsh well or fairly well are more inclined to support enhanced devolution (legislative and tax-raising powers) than they are to favour the status quo (an Assembly with limited powers). Other variables were less conclusive. Levels of decisions concerning public policies in the areas of language and training are not fully correlated with support for devolution. Unsurprisingly, there is a strongly negative correlation between those favouring the Assembly as the level of decision for language and training and those opposed to the Assembly. In other respects, the 'levels of decision' variable is not a particularly good predictor. There were no clear patterns for most of the socio-demographic variables (age, education, gender or place of birth).

In the case of Brittany, Table 6.9 shows a number of similarities with Wales, the most significant relationship in both cases being that between the intensity of feelings of identity and support for independence. The contrasts between Wales and Brittany are more striking than the similarities. While a strong relationship between intended vote in a regional election and institutional preference in Wales is noted, there was no significant relationship in Brittany. There are some very interesting contrasts between Wales and Brittany. In Brittany, there is a slight negative relationship between language competency and support for independence or for enhanced forms of devolution. This finding backs up the traditional literature in the field, emphasising a lingering sense of shame and inferiority amongst native Breton speakers (almost by definition in the oldest age categories) and an over-compensation of loyalty to France and the French state (Hoare, 2000). On the other hand, there were significant contrasts according to the socio-demographic criteria. In the case of Brittany, support for independence was strongly correlated with age, gender, education and, to a lesser extent, place of birth. The youngest Bretons, especially those born in Brittany, the most educated people and women were the most inclined to support independence. It can be observed that the revival in Breton culture has mobilised the youngest and most educated age cohorts and deduce that there has been some spillover from culture into broader support for independence.

These findings confirm the differentiation of processes of regional governance in Wales and Brittany. In the Welsh case, cleavages are deeply embedded and there is a real debate between independentists, devolutionists and unionists. Support for enhanced devolution (and even more so independence) is party political, with a powerful regionalist party mobilising support for more enhanced devolutionary solutions and maintaining pressure on the other parties. Voting choice clearly influences attitudes towards independence. A strong relationship is also noted between attitudes to the level of decision concerning language and the strength of the attitude against devolution. From this it is deduced that the Welsh language reinforces polar attitudes towards independence. In the case of Brittany, there is a latent Breton consciousness, but this is not a political resource which can be mobilised by regionalist political parties and no significant relationships are noted between regional voting choice and attitude to independence. Unlike in Wales, moreover, in Brittany there has never been a strong Breton autonomist movement using language as a tool of regional identity. While the Breton cultural movement has been very powerful, it has built its regional advocacy on cross-partisan support and has avoided politicising language issues.

Political institutions and informed opinions in Wales and Brittany

To what extent are the opinions of informed groups faithfully reflected in that of public opinion? How, if at all, does this vary according to the region concerned? In the ensuing section, mass and informed opinions about political institutions in Wales and Brittany are compared. The information presented below is obtained from two sources. Around 200 semi-structured interviews were carried out, using the snowball sampling technique to gather data. At the end of each interview, an 'elite' questionnaire was also left which proved to be a source of valuable additional information.[3] Many of the same questions asked in the mass survey were repeated in the questionnaire. It should be emphasised, however, that no *statistical* associations can be drawn from the interview sample; the figures presented below are for illustrative purposes only. But the evidence collated from the questionnaire returns in particular is especially relevant for identifying lessons, specifying contacts, indicating the saliency of particular types of policy concern and testing the cohesion between attitudes within the policy-making community and public-opinion polls.

A broad consistency of viewpoints was discovered between informed and popular opinion samples in Brittany, and to a lesser extent Wales. It was possible to measure this consistency in two distinct ways. First, responses to the public-opinion question on regional expenditure priorities were compared with those to the same question asked in the elite surveys. In Wales, the elite sample identified health and education as the principal priorities for regional expenditure. In Brittany, the environment and economic development were favoured as objects for any increased available spending. In a separate question, the interview samples were asked in an open-ended question to identify the three principal problems which their regions would face in the next five years. In Wales, the order of priorities was education, healthcare and devolution. The Breton sample identified the main challenges as the environment, followed closely by economic development and the future of regionalism. There exists a broad consensus in both regions about the nature of the salient policy problems. According to this most basic of yardsticks, elite and public opinion in both countries is broadly convergent.

Consider further the case of Brittany. The high response rate to the elite survey in Brittany allows drawing firmer conclusions than in Wales and provides a wealth of information. There was almost a 70 per cent response rate in the Brittany survey. In Table 6.10 can be seen a high degree of cohesion between mass and informed opinion in relation to the future of regionalisation, expenditure priorities for the Brittany region, and the future of the Loire-Atlantique department. There is a broad agreement over the importance of decentralisation, favouring expenditure on environmental issues and economic development, and bringing the Loire-Atlantique back into Brittany.

In relation to the Moreno identity question, the similarities between the interview samples and mass opinions are more striking than the – predictable – differences. Though the interview sample was more likely than the mass survey to adopt a Breton identity, the median position – 'as Breton as French'– prevailed comfortably. This finding is interesting. Even many of those working for greater Breton autonomy (the case for many in the sample) felt a deep sense of their French identity and declared themselves proud to be French. This finding highlights the paradoxes and limitations of the Breton autonomist cause. Those with the strongest Breton identity were also deeply influenced by their Frenchness. This duality came out clearly in interviews, when Breton autonomists expressed their support for France taking a stance against the linguistic domination of Anglo-American and the political domination of the United States. There was also much cohesion between the interview sample and mass opinion in Brittany in relation to the questions on the appropriate level for the governance of language and training issues. A reasonable conclusion is that Breton decision-makers can feel confident that their activity rests upon a solid core of shared beliefs.

Great care must be taken over the interpretation of the Wales findings. Table 6.11 reveals that the response rate to the questionnaire was lower in Wales, though still respectable (60 per cent). Other researchers have noted a certain interview fatigue, though actors were very generous with their time in

Table 6.10 Interview and mass opinions in Brittany compared

Proposition	Public Opinion (n.1007)	Interview sample (n.68)
Elected parliament with tax-raising and legislative powers	34	54
Regional council with limited powers	44	25
An independent Brittany	12	21
Abolish the regional council	2	–
First priority for more public expenditure (open-ended)	Environment	Environment
Second priority for more public expenditure (open-ended)	Economic Development	Economic Development
Identity: Breton, not French	2	18
Identity: More Breton than French	15	17
Identity: As Breton as French	57	41
Identity: More French than Breton	17	18
Identity: French not Breton	7	4
Reunify Brittany and the Loire-Atlantique (agree and strongly agree)	61	81
'Regional council should determine policy over the Breton language'	53	57
'Regional council should determine training policy in Brittany'	43	65

the present case. In some cases questionnaires were returned unanswered with an apologetic note explaining that the individuals concerned had been advised not to respond to any questionnaires. In terms of institutional futures and identities, the informed sample appeared somewhat less representative of public opinion in Wales than in Brittany. There was a greater propensity to entertain ideas of independence from the UK than amongst the population

Table 6.11 Interview and mass opinions in Wales compared

Proposition	Public Opinion (n.1008)	Interview sample (n.59)
Abolish the National Assembly	24	8
Keep an Assembly with limited powers	24	36
An elected parliament with tax-raising and legislative powers	38	39
An independent Wales	11	17
First priority for more public expenditure	Health	Health
Second priority for more public expenditure	Education	Education
Welsh, not British	20	37
More Welsh than British	17	16
Identity: equally Welsh and British	35	27
More British than Welsh	22	11
British, not Welsh	6	9
'National Assembly should determine policy over the Welsh language'	50	83
'National Assembly should determine training policy in Wales'	41	90

as a whole. There was also a more marked tendency for respondents to perceive of themselves as being wholly or primarily Welsh, a trait particularly marked amongst those intending to vote for Plaid Cymru at the next Assembly election. There was overwhelming support for language and training issues to fall within the sphere of authority of the National Assembly for Wales, even more so than within public opinion as a whole. These findings lend weight to the idea that devolution is an elite-driven project.

Conclusion

Identity foci, institutional demands, instrumental incentives and political opportunity structures all produce substantive differences between Wales and

Brittany. Regional governance in Wales is driven more by the force of identity politics and the dynamic of polity building (hypothesis one), whereas in Brittany regionalism has been limited because the prevalent mode of regional advocacy has proved to be very effective and because the political opportunity structure has pre-empted the development of a regionalist party (hypothesis two). Though identity and instrumentalism are presented here as two distinctive hypotheses, the researchers are aware that identity-based and instrumental concerns can be mutually self-reinforcing. There is a strong institutional dimension to this linkage. Citizens identify with effective and/or proximate institutions. Welsh citizens are unconvinced by the policy performance of the Assembly, but they identify with the institutions of devolution as a sign of Welshness. Bretons are, by and large, trusting of their regional institutions and want to see them perform a more important role in the future. But support for regionalisation in Brittany is rather more instrumental (the region as the appropriate level for good services) rather than identity-based (the region at the service of a distinct identity, separate/adversarial from that of the rest of France). In Wales can be read no such straightforward instrumentalist intent from the figures. Cleavages are much more deeply embedded within Welsh society, and there is a more complex relationship between identity, institutions and partisan preferences than in Brittany.

Notes

1 In the case of Brittany, the expression 'independence' is used with some caution. The precise wording of the Breton question was that of 'autonomy', not 'independence'. This wording was used upon the strong insistence of the Breton advisory group, for whom autonomy portrayed an advanced state of political self-government. Independence, they argued, made little or no sense in the French context.

2 The data are based on 1,008 individuals surveyed across Wales (and 1,007 in Brittany) aged 16 and above. Interviews were carried out in June 2001 in both regions. Most questions in the two surveys were identical; some were functionally equivalent and some specific to the region concerned. The survey was divided roughly into four parts, corresponding to specific research questions – namely, attitudes to political institutions; to language; to education and training issues; and socio-demographic characteristics. The four-point scale used for the question on regional political institutions is consistent with similar exercises carried out in Wales. (As far as can be ascertained, an equivalent survey has never been carried out in Brittany.) For the purposes of establishing comparative relationships, data were recoded to develop multivariate models of institutional preference, and logistic regression was run to explain individual support for each of the possible institutional situations.

For the Welsh case, four different dependent variables were extrapolated from the institutional scale, and coded as follows: 1 'independent Wales', 0 'others' ("independence" column in table); 1 'elected assembly with law-making and taxation powers', 0 'others ("Assembly with extended competences" column); 1 'elected assembly with limited law making and taxation powers', 0 'others' ("Assembly with limited competences" column); 1 'no elected assembly', 0 'others' ("No elected Assembly" column). Independent variables used included the classic ones such as: age (3 '16–24 years', 2 '25–44 years', 1 '45 years and more'); gender (0 'male', 1 'female'); education (1 'lowest or no degree' to 6 'upper degree'); place of birth (0 'other', 1 'Wales'). In addition, the following attitudinal and opinion variables were integrated: identity (1 'Welsh not British', 2 'More Welsh than British', 3 'equally Welsh and British', 4 'More British than Welsh', 5 'British not Welsh'); language (0 'not Welsh speaker', 1 'Welsh speaker'); level of decision for policies (0 'other', 1 'Wales') voting behaviour (1 'Conservative', 2 'Labour', 3 'Liberal Democrat', 4 'Plaid Cymru').

In the case of Brittany, the dependent variable was reversed in the questionnaire. For facilitating comparisons, the scale in the four dependent variables was reversed: 1. ' independent Brittany', 0 'others' ("independence" column in table); 1 'regional council with law-making and taxation powers', 0 'others' ("regional council with extended competencies" column); 1 'regional council with limited law-making and taxation powers', 0 'others' ("regional council with limited competencies" column); 'no regional Council', 0 'others' ("No regional council" column). The same independent variables were selected in Brittany as in Wales. These were age (3 '16–24 years', 2 '25–44 years', 1 '45 years and more'), gender (0 'male', 1 'female'), education (1 'lowest or no degree' to 6 'upper degree'), place of birth (0 'other', 1 'Brittany'), identity (1 'Breton not French', 2 'More Breton than French', 3 'equally Breton and French', 4 'More French than Breton', 5 'French not Breton'), language (0 'not Breton speaker', 1 'Breton speaker'), level of decision for language and training (0 'other', 1 'Brittany') voting behaviour (1 'UDF', 2 'Socialist party', 3 'RPR', 4 'Regionalist party').

3 The Wales elite survey recorded the views of members of the Welsh policy community, as determined on the basis of snowball sampling and the advice of the advisory group. The dataset derived from the questionnaire consists of 59 cases and 93 variables, a 60 per cent response rate. The dataset is divided into socio-demographic and attitudinal variables. The socio-demographic variables are those of region, locality, gender, occupation of the chief income earner, level of education, country of birth, intended vote in a general election, intended vote in an Assembly election; working status; time spent in Wales; age; marital status; children in full-time education and level of interest in politics. Most of the survey material is in the form of detailed analysis of attitudinal and opinion variables on matters relating to devolution, Welsh identity and attitudes (preferences) toward issues of the Welsh language, education and training. The principal attitudinal questions investigate views on devolution for Wales; the 'Moreno' identity scale; opinions on the performance of the National Assembly for Wales; beliefs about the main challenges facing Wales; future expenditure priorities; preferences for regional political institutions; relations between the Assembly and similar bodies elsewhere in Europe; the importance of organisations and levels of government for the governance of Wales; understanding of the Welsh language; views on the

Welsh language; public policy and the Welsh language; decision-making arenas and the Welsh language; lessons from linguistic experiences elsewhere; attendance at a training course in the past 24 months; priorities for spending money on training in Wales; decision-making arenas and training in Wales; priorities for improving the training of young people and attitudes toward adopting more interventionist policies (the importance of qualifications against employment, the desirability of training levies and whether there should be a legal requirement to undertake training) and lessons from experiences elsewhere.

The Brittany elite survey dataset consists of 68 cases and 92 variables, a 70 per cent response rate. The dataset is divided into socio-demographic and attitudinal variables. The socio-demographic variables are those of region, locality, gender, occupation of the chief income earner, level of education, country of birth, intended vote in a general (parliamentary) election, intended vote in a regional council election; working status; time spent in Brittany; age; marital status; children in full-time education and level of interest in politics. Most of the survey material is in the form of detailed analysis of attitudinal and opinion variables on matters relating to decentralisation, Breton identity and attitudes (preferences) toward issues of the Breton language, education and training. The principal attitudinal questions investigate views on decentralisation in Brittany; the 'Moreno' identity scale; the Loire-Atlantique and the administrative region of Brittany; views on the performance of the Brittany regional council; future expenditure priorities; preferences for regional political institutions; relations between the Brittany regional council and similar bodies elsewhere in Europe; the importance of organisations and levels of government for the governance of Brittany; understanding of the Breton language; views on the Breton language; public policy and the Breton language; decision-making arenas and the Breton language; Breton language in schools; lessons from linguistic experiences elsewhere; attendance at a training course in the past 24 months; priorities for spending money on training in Brittany; decision-making arenas and training in Brittany; priorities for improving the training of young people and attitudes toward the importance of qualifications against employment and lessons from experiences elsewhere.

Both surveys are deposited with the ESRC Data archive at Essex University

7
Policy communities, public policy and policy learning in Wales and Brittany

In Chapter 1 it was argued that relationships and coalitions are vital in understanding sub-national politics and administration. A direct linkage between modes of regional governance and the internal quality of regional relationships was posited. While good horizontal (and vertical) relationships can increase governing capacity, negative-sum inter-organisational rivalries can have a detrimental effect on the quality of policy outputs. The use of community implies regular personal relationships and shared values. If policy networks represent new forms of policy-making to deal with the complexity of modern governance, it was argued, the metaphor of community best captures the close personal linkages between actors involved in relationships in specific policy sectors and/or territories. The classic policy-community literature was focused upon vertical policy sectors, rather than horizontal territorial communities. Keating and Loughlin (2004) argue that 'a territorial policy community is one where the territorial framework is of primary importance in the construction and frames of reference of that community'. Engagement with this assumption was sought in selecting two distinctive policy communities, one with an obvious territorial base, which was expected to be rooted in identity politics (regional languages), another with a strong sectoral logic (training and lifelong learning). For each of the cases, answers were sought for the following research questions. Can a territorial policy community be recognised? What is the relationship between territorial and sectoral policy communities? Have the institutions of devolution and decentralisation made a difference?

In this chapter, an attempt is made to reconstruct the beliefs of the chosen policy communities, based on responses to a detailed questionnaire and upon data from the interviews themselves. The method of snowball sampling was used as a useful aggregate indicator of the policy communities in the regions and issue areas involved (see Devine, 1995). The mass surveys analysed in Chapter 6 have the advantage of being compiled on a representative basis of the entire population. An elite sample requires a much greater use of interpretative skills. In an attempt to ensure that comparable actors were being investigated in the two regions, three conceptual sub-groups were developed within the elite samples, labelled as the generic group, the training and education group and the Breton/Welsh language-advocacy groups. The generic group consisted of regional politicians, officials and those with an overarching Breton or Welsh view. The training and education group, as its name suggests, was composed of individuals representing organisations involved in policy formulation or the supply chain in education and training. The Welsh and Breton language groups brought together organisations and individuals involved, at various levels, with language policy or advocacy. These actors occupied distinctive worlds in both cases, and entertained quite antagonistic relationships.

Around 200 face-to-face interviews lay at the heart of the empirical research. The primary function of these interviews was to acquire detailed information about political and policy dynamics in the two regions. The basic interview schedule allowed for free-flowing discussion in interviews. However, a number of common questions were asked in both countries. The common core of questions concerned the role of regional authorities; the main achievements and political/policy challenges for the five years ahead; the operation of policy communities; the role of 'national regions' in a broader perspective, attitudes to institutional reform and lessons from experiences elsewhere. As well, certain more specific questions were tailored to each of the interlocutors. Following below, each of the six groups identified above is considered in turn: the Wales and Brittany generic groups, then the language-advocacy and training and education groups in Wales and Brittany. The discussion concludes in considering whether there are any lessons to be drawn from comparative experience.

Wales: the unfinished business of devolution

Interviews were carried out across Wales from 2001 to 2004. The answers from free-flowing interviews can be regrouped under five broad themes: the operation of devolution; the future of the devolved institutions; the main challenges facing Wales; the operation of the Welsh policy community and the role of Wales as a national-region within the United Kingdom and the European Union.

Devolution and policy difference

Does devolution make a difference? There was a measure of consensus that devolution has many achievements to its credit. First and foremost was the promoting of a Team Wales approach, signifying closer patterns of co-operation between 'post-devolution' institutions and centred on the National Assembly. Observed as well was a measure of residual distrust between the devolved and non-devolved agencies, especially in the area of employment policy. There was a belief, in the early stages at least, that the Assembly as a corporate body had been closely involved in policy development within the National Assembly, but that this influence had diminished under the partnership agreement and even more during the second term. There was a degree of pride that the Assembly had been able to differentiate itself from England (and Scotland), even within the confines of the existing devolution settlement. This belief was coupled with a conviction that devolution had created a new policy style, one based on social inclusion (in health and education notably). There was also a strong feeling, expressed across many interviews, that the new institutions (however flawed) were becoming the focus of identity. This was summarised in several interviews in terms of the emergence of a new devolutionary political family and a belief that the small size of Wales facilitated closer contacts.

This understandable pro-Assembly sentiment was not always echoed outside of the Assembly government or the National Assembly. Local government and the business communities in particular were critical of many of the decisions taken by the Assembly. All agreed, however, that the devolved institutions had made a conscious effort to develop policy formulation and implementation in close collaboration with civil society. The Assembly's lack of institutional capacity was counterbalanced by the active involvement of social partners. For their part, representatives of local government, of the voluntary sector or of the business or labour communities knew that ignoring the Assembly was no longer an option. Whether through idealism or pragmatism, the mainstream view in interviews across Wales was that there was a need to make the devolved institutions work. There was a gradual acceptance of the devolved institutions as *our* institutions, across the political spectrum and across the range of policy actors. This refocusing of attention upon a contested institution augurs well for its future survival.

The future of the devolved institutions

In Chapter 6, it was concluded that, though still divided, public opinion in Wales was beginning to warm to the Assembly as an institutional expression of Welsh identity. Within and around the National Assembly, there was a sense of pessimism that the existing devolution settlement would be able to work in the longer term, coupled with certainty (amongst political actors especially) that there would eventually be a move to a full parliament. The backbench Assembly members interviewed in 2001 and 2002 were clearly politically inexperienced and bewildered by the complexity of the governing arrangements. In most interviews with Assembly members from all parties, strong demands were formulated for new powers. A majority of members interviewed favoured moving to a more transparent system based on full legislative and tax-varying powers. The consensus view was that, deprived of full legislative powers in the transferred domains, the National Assembly lacked the legal and political means for its policy ambitions. Even the Conservative group accepted that a clarification of the Assembly's powers was essential. Interviews in 2001 and 2002 thus largely anticipated the findings of the Richards Commission reporting in March 2004, which advocated a gradual move to primary legislative (though not tax-varying) powers by 2011.

The challenges facing Wales

When the interviews moved to challenges, two themes prevailed above all others, the first institutional, the second relating to the perceived weakness of Wales in terms of economic development and basic skills. The need to complete the settlement was the first and foremost challenge that Wales faced. Following this institutional demand, there was virtual unanimity that everything had to be done to raise the Welsh GDP level, and that promoting general skills and up-skilling the workforce was the best means to achieve this. More focused interviews amongst members of the Welsh advocacy group and the training and education group revealed more specific concerns. Language activists maintained very firm positions, which went well beyond those supported by public opinion. There was overwhelming support for the Assembly as the only legitimate site for managing Welsh language-related issues. There is much more language mainstreaming in the case of Wales than in Brittany. Unlike in the French region, in Wales interviewees from across the board were willing to answer questions on language. The main concerns of those identified as forming part of the training and education group were rather different, far more focused on issues of economic development and training, rather than on linguistic planning. These themes explored are explored in more detail on pages 150–156.

The operation of the Welsh policy community

The operation of the emerging policy community in and around the National Assembly gave rise to a mixture of traditional and more innovative themes. Predictably, there was a good deal of resentment against the role of Cardiff in the new devolved Wales which transcended party affiliation. There were strong partisan rivalries – between Labour and Plaid Cymru in particular –

which cut across the cross-cutting themes of social inclusion, environmental sustainability and gender equality. During the first round of interviews (2001–2) many interlocutors emphasised the innovative methods of working within the Assembly, especially the role of the subject committees. Follow-up interviews in 2004 pointed to a degradation of relationships since May 2003, a feeling amongst opposition members that the single-party government created by Rhodri Morgan went against the spirit of the all-inclusive Assembly set up by devolution. Paradoxically, as party politics came more to the fore, the joint commitment to making the devolved institutions work strengthened. The Assembly has acted as the focus of institutional and 'national-regional' loyalties, however critical Assembly members have been of its operation. The Assembly method of partnership working has also gradually imposed itself upon (if not endeared itself to) the varied groups affected by devolution, though certain interests (the voluntary sector) were more supportive than others (business community, local government).

Wales within the UK and the European Union

The vast majority of those interviewed considered Wales as a nation/country, rather than a region. The Welsh Assembly Government itself has played up the role of Wales as a small nation within the United Kingdom as a Union-State. Hence the usefulness of Rawling's (2003) characterisation of Wales as a national region. In pursuing the aims of Wales as a national region, however, even those politicians most favourable to autonomy accepted that future institutional developments would only occur in a broader UK and European context. The UK context has been dealt with elsewhere. The interdependency between Cardiff and London is most obvious in the field of European policy. In the words of one well-placed source, 'UK Policy towards Europe is made in London. It is not made in Brussels' (interview, March 2004). Hence the emphasis placed on developing informal relationships and operating within the UK policy family. As a counterpart to the development of its European paradiplomacy, the Assembly Government has worked closely with UKRep, the permanent representation of the United Kingdom government in Brussels.

Outside of the narrow European Union community, interviewees evoked European issues overwhelmingly in distributional terms. There was no rhetorical appeal to Wales in Europe comparable to that associated with the SNP in Scotland (Elias, 2004). European issues were domesticated: the role of Objective One funding as an issue of domestic competition for resources and rivalry between areas was uppermost in interviews. Objective One funding also pitted the business community against the Assembly and the voluntary sector. Members of the well-organised Business Forum were highly critical of the criteria perceived to determine the distribution of Objective One funds. There was no real debate in Wales on Europe, apart from specialised concerns (from the WDA) about the impact of the Euro delay on Welsh manufacturing and the opportunities (and threats) for Wales of enlargement.

In sum, the Welsh policy community was convinced that devolution has made a difference, but wanted a strengthening of the devolved institutions and a clearer statement of their competencies. There was a broad measure of consensus that human capital needed to be strengthened if Wales was to overcome its chronic skills and education deficits. There was a gradual convergence around the devolved institutions as comprising the heart of the policy community. There was a reluctance to challenge the pre-eminent role of the UK government in relation to the management of EU issues, however, coupled with a belief that strong Welsh institutions would eventually make an impact on the role Wales could play in Europe.

Brittany: cultural identity and political ambiguity

Intensive interviews in Brittany were undertaken in two distinct stages of the research. Most interviews were conducted from April to September 2001, when the Socialist government led by Jospin promised to lead France down the path of asymmetrical devolution. Follow-up interviews occurred in July–September 2002, with the Raffarin government preparing to introduce a major new reform recognising French regions in the constitution. As with Wales, the answers from free-flowing interviews can be regrouped under a number of broad themes: the future of decentralisation and the regional institution; the policy challenges facing Brittany; the operation of the Breton policy community and Brittany, France and Europe.

The future of decentralisation and the regional institution

There was very strong support in the interviews for strengthening the regional political institution and for vesting the Brittany regional council with a leadership role in relation to other sub-national authorities. These findings must be interpreted with some caution. Interviews took place principally with members of the regional political and policy communities, rather than with local or departmental politicians. Having said this, most of the politicians interviewed combined a regional with a local, departmental or national mandate. There was no blanket support for the regional level. Even the leader of the Breton Democratic Union (UDB), for example, refuted the suggestion that there could be a regional police force, or that the social-security system should be regionalised. But there was widespread support for enhanced regional powers in the spheres of education, culture, historic monuments, transport, training, regional languages and, to a lesser degree, health. Almost everybody interviewed in the Summer of 2002, irrespective of party, was favourable to the extension of the policy responsibilities of the regional councils then proposed by the Raffarin government. The structured elite questionnaire backed up the findings of the interviews. When asked to indicate which level of governance was the most appropriate for matters of training and language policies, the region emerged as the clear favourite amongst all types of interviewees, way ahead of the central state, the regional state or other levels of sub-national authority.

The policy challenges facing Brittany

There was a remarkable cohesion between the attitudes expressed rather informally in interviews, the findings from the elite questionnaire and evidence from the public-opinion poll survey about the nature of the policy problems facing Brittany. All interviewees were asked what they considered to be the main policy problems facing Brittany in the years ahead, an option repeated in the elite questionnaire.

This was an open-ended question, with responses coded into fourteen separate responses. Three types of response came way ahead of all others: first, problems related to the environment and, specifically, to water provision and pollution of water supplies; second, the need for more regional economic development and, third, the need for a strengthening of the powers for the regional council. How should these findings be interpreted? To take the last one first, informed opinion in Brittany supports more regional responsibility to tackle deeply rooted problems which in face-to-face interviews were often attributed to distant decisions taken by technocratic Parisian elites. A certain amount of blame avoidance in the facility with which Breton decision-makers attributed Brittany's malaise to outside forces was identified, a phenomenon typical of a region with a consciousness of being on the periphery. Upon further prompting, several interviewees acknowledged that environmental pollution was made worse by the intensive-farming model and practices associated with Breton farmers during the post-war economic miracle. Alongside deep environmental concern, there was also strong support for regional economic development and for help for the agricultural sector. The paradox was not lost on decision-makers themselves. Awareness of the environmental damage caused by intensive farming (pollution, water contamination, soil erosion) has been a painful discovery for one of France's main agricultural regions. The policy priorities of environmental policy and economic development illustrate a certain dilemma and uncertainty faced by Bretons. On the one hand, they wish to continue their story of the Breton 'economic miracle'. On the other hand, this very success, based as it was on intensive agricultural methods, has endangered one of Brittany's greatest assets, its reputation for unspoiled natural products.

If there was much support for enhanced regional governance, little direct linkage was made between the objectives of political governance and the symbols of Breton identity such as language or culture. Support for regionalisation was rather more instrumental (the region as the appropriate level for good services) rather than identity-based (the region at the service of a distinct identity, separate/adversarial from that of the rest of France). This conclusion should be qualified. There *was* general support in the interviews, the questionnaire and the opinion poll for allowing more regional influence over the definition of language policy and for more public support for Breton-language education. But the salient issues of concern were those of economic development, agriculture, the environment and education, rather than these rooted in the politics of identity. It was observed with interest that in Brittany, unlike in Wales, very little mention was made of education or training as a policy problem. This should not be surprising: Brittany has an excellent education system with standards amongst the highest in France, and education is perceived as a success story, not a problem. Many interviewees were worried about the inability of Brittany to retain their highly trained young people, who continued to export their skills to Paris or abroad.

The operation of the Breton policy community

Many interviewees spontaneously volunteered the information that, in the words of one, 'in Brittany we do things differently'. A number of interviewees referred to a Brittany effect, particularly in relation to the outside world. Though conflicts within Brittany could be fierce, there was a common front presented to the outside, whether the French state, the European Union or other regions and countries. A number of interviewees referred to Brittany's past as an independent Duchy, a degree of autonomy which they equated with pre-unification Scotland rather than Wales. There was some nostalgia about pre-1532 Brittany, a 'prosperous maritime trading state larger than Belgium or the Netherlands'. Unlike Scotland, however, Brittany had had to face a formidable centralising machine in the form of the post-Revolutionary French State. In order to defend Breton interests in a hostile environment, Bretons of all persuasions had developed powerful codes to recognise each other across formal divides. More than one interviewee spoke of a Breton 'network' in Paris, linking key positions in the ministries with the defence of Breton interests. Whatever the nostalgia for the past, there was a general feeling that the existing pattern of representing Breton interests had served Brittany fairly well, though this coexisted with a demand for more regional autonomy.

Brittany, France and Europe

Bretons are distinctive not only because of the strength of their regional sense of belonging but also by their European attachment. Pro-European sentiment is stronger in Brittany than in most French regions. This European identity has been identified in numerous monographs and was graphically illustrated by the results of the 1992 referendum on the Maastricht treaty. Along with Alsace and Lorraine, Brittany was the strongest pro-Maastricht region in France, with the three peripheral regions securing the victory of the Yes vote. This public opinion evidence is supported by elite-level surveys in which the peripheral status of Brittany is identified as a major obstacle for future prosperity and closer European integration as a major opportunity (Cole and John, 2001). Brittany was for long the main French beneficiary of European structural fund grants (in the 1960s and 1970s) and has always benefited from the Common Agricultural Policy (Phlipponneau, 1993). On the other hand, the reform of the CAP in the 1990s and the introduction of milk quotas and set-aside in particular have hardened the opinion of some Breton farming organisations against 'Brussels'.

Many interviewees stressed the fundamentally pro-European sentiment existing within Brittany. Europe is part of the 'Christian-democratic' stock in trade, which remains alive in Brittany, in spite of the creation of a unified conservative party in November 2002 (the UMP). Several interviewees also linked the pro-European sentiment in Brittany with the peripheral location of Brittany at one of the westernmost points of continental Europe. Bretons looked to the European Union, as much in faith as in expectation, as the best guarantor of their future prosperity. On the other hand, a number of interviewees expressed frustration at the tight control over European issues exercised by the French government, while secretly congratulating Bretons for maintaining networks in Brussels allowing local and regional politicians to side-step the French state.

In sum, there was very strong support in the interviews for strengthening the regional political institution. There was an emphasis on the environment and economic development as principal policy challenges in the years that lie ahead. Support for regionalisation was framed in terms of policy challenges, rather than for the region being at the service of a distinct identity separate from that of the rest of France. There was widespread belief in the existence of a Brittany effect, however, a legacy of past forms of collective action which sets Brittany apart from other regions. There was a sense of satisfaction that Brittany had come a long way, combined with apprehension about the future.

Language policy communities in Wales and Brittany

Almost by definition, regional languages have a strong link to territory. It is argued here that the influence of language policy communities depends on the extent to which they are cross-sectoral (that is, they attempt to influence all policy fields), which is, in turn, highly dependent on the legitimacy they are accorded within their respective state-nations. While language policy has established itself as a cross-cutting (if contested) agenda in Wales, formidable obstacles have been dressed against it in Brittany.

As regions with closely related minority Celtic languages, Wales and Brittany face comparable problems of regional language preservation. Both languages face similar challenges due to their spatial concentration, their differential comprehension by generations and (in the case of Wales at least) the partisan affiliations of the language. While a language-policy community can be referred to in Wales, however, such a label is less appropriate in the case of Brittany. The overarching characteristic of the Welsh language-policy community has been its ability to mainstream and institutionalise its concerns and to spearhead demands for enhanced regional autonomy. In Brittany, on the other hand, the language-advocacy group has faced enormous regulatory and constitutional obstacles to enacting lesser-used language policies in France and has adopted a defensive posture. Before the operation of the language-policy communities in Wales and Brittany is considered, there now follow some preliminary data on the state of the languages and the regulatory environment within which language policies are formulated and implemented.

The twentieth century witnessed the collapse of Welsh as a dominant medium of communication in most parts of Wales. From 1901 to 1991, the proportion of the population speaking Welsh declined from 43.5 per cent to 18.7 per cent, before rising to just over 21 per cent in 2001. In the 2001 census, there were 576,000 Welsh speakers aged three and over. In broad socio-economic terms, Welsh has expanded its usage considerably since the late 1980s and the language is now used widely in education, the media, leisure and selected public services (Williams, 2003). Language-survey data suggest that social context, family, language transmission and exposure to formal bilingual education are the key factors in language reproduction. In the case of Wales, community and family are less powerful agents of language reproduction than they were previously, but formal bilingual education and language planning has slowed the rate of absolute decline.

The situation for Welsh is much more optimistic than for Breton. At the turn of the twentieth century there were around 1,500,000 Breton speakers according to Gourvil (1952). A later estimate was that by 1962 this figure had dropped to 686,000 speakers. In the survey for the present study, conducted in 2001, around 200,000 people claimed to speak Breton fluently, to which can be added 100,000 who are able to speak and understand quite well. This represents 10 per cent, at most, with any sort of Breton-language competency. These figures would appear to be broadly consistent with other recent surveys (Gemie, 2002; *Télégramme de Brest*, 2001). Apart from the total number of speakers, the demographic and age structure together with the geographical profile is deeply pessimistic for the future of the language. Almost no one under 40 today was born and brought up in a Breton-speaking household. Unlike in Wales, there has been no formal language planning, though bilingual education and community activism have slowed the rate of decline. When the language interviewees were asked whether they were optimistic or pessimistic for the future of the language, a standard response was one of 'pessimistic activism'. Members of the language-advocacy group are not optimistic, but they remain very active.

The regulatory framework of language governance in France is hardly propitious to the diffusion of regional languages (Poignant, 1998; Denez, 1998). As France has become ever more deeply embedded in multilateral and international structures, the French State has sought to defend what it deems to be the core of French sovereignty: namely the French language. One example above all others illustrates this. There was an explicit linkage between identity and language in the Maastricht referendum of 1992, when France committed itself simultaneously to an enhanced degree of European integration and to the codification of French as the official language of the Republic. The reformed Article 2 of the French Constitution declares that French is the official language of the Republic. In 1997, France signed the European Charter of Regional Languages. In 1999, however, the Constitutional Council declared the Charter to be contrary to the French Constitution, the Council arguing that Article 2 of the French Constitution prevented French ratification. There are, in short, formidable structural obstacles to the development of regional languages, whether relating their usage in the public sphere, or regarding public support for forms of language-medium education.

The British 'Union State' was never quite as hostile to forms of regional distinctiveness as the French unitary and indivisible Republic. The Welsh language has performed an important role in the process of institution building in Wales. The passing of the Welsh Courts Act of 1942 rescinded the provisions prohibiting the use of Welsh by the Acts of Union 1536–43. Further legal recognition was given in the Welsh Language Act of 1967, which offered an initial definition of equal validity of English and Welsh in Wales. During the 1960s and 1970s a number of statutory and non-statutory bodies called for greater state support for the language. The Education Reform Act of 1988 set up a National Curriculum for Wales, with Welsh becoming a core subject. The Welsh Language Act of 1993, the major piece of language-related legislation in the twentieth century, went even further. The 1993 Act provided a statutory framework for the treatment of English and Welsh on the basis of equality and inaugurated a new era in language planning. Its chief policy instrument is the Welsh Language Board, established by the Act as a non-departmental statutory organisation. The Act detailed key steps to be taken by the Welsh Language Board and by public-sector bodies in the preparation of Welsh language schemes, designed to treat Welsh and English on the basis of equality. Since 1995 more than 200 language schemes have been approved, covering all twenty-two local authorities.

Policy community and advocacy group

The Welsh language has performed an important, if not primordial, role in this process of institution building. The language-policy community in Wales forms a constellation of actors and interests revolving above all around two key institutions: the National Assembly for Wales and the Welsh Language Board. The National Assembly for Wales has been active in its pursuit of a bilingual policy. In the most comprehensive elaboration of its language policy, made public in 2002, the Assembly advocated, *inter alia,* the further development of bilingual education and the normalisation of bilingual service provision in local government, health and social services. Neither language planning, nor Welsh-medium education had to await devolution, but both have been given a boost by the National Assembly. The National Assembly has had a major role in disseminating Welsh, as well as providing employment for Welsh speakers. The Assembly has used the Welsh Language Board (WLB) as its policy instrument to implement the bilingual policy. In over ten years of existence, the Welsh Language Board has fulfilled five core functions (Cole and Williams, 2004). It has promoted and facilitated the use of the Welsh language. It has advised UK central government, the National Assembly and other public-sector bodies on issues relating to the Welsh language. It has initiated and overseen the process of preparing and operating language schemes.

It has distributed grants for promoting and facilitating the use of the language. It has maintained a strategic overview of Welsh-language education.

The regulatory frameworks for language management differ in almost all respects between Wales and Brittany. A formal bilingual policy in Wales contrasts with a constitutionally entrenched unilingual policy in the case of Brittany. Despite such structural dissimilarity, the beginnings of an institutional strategy for rescuing Breton can be discerned. Most of the drive towards institutionalization has come from the Brittany regional council, in ways described in Chapter 5 (support for DIWAN schools, for teacher training, for Breton-language teaching, for the Breton Language Office). The Breton Language Office (*Ofis ar Brezhonneg*) is the most important institutional innovation. The Office sees its work as mainly technical, a tool at the service of public and private users. It looks to the Welsh Language Board and other language agencies for inspiration. The Office seeks to divorce the language debate from issues of identity or culture. Ideally, as in Wales, language planning should concern issues of planning permission, building regulations or obligatory education. Here are met concerns which, although mainstreamed in Wales, are of much more limited relevance in Brittany.

If Breton is beginning to make headway in public administration, this is also a result of local-government initiatives. While there are no comparable planning dilemmas for Breton officials as for their Welsh counterparts (Breton having no statutory existence), sympathetic councils have adopted a range of measures to promote the language. These range from the symbolic (signposting) to the eminently practical, such as providing buildings for DIWAN schools or, in two precise cases, providing land for a Breton enterprise zone (Carhaix) or a Breton cultural district (Quimper). Local councils sometimes provide buildings for adult-training courses in Breton, which have traditionally been provided on a voluntary basis by organisations such as STUMDI and ROUDOUR. This support for Breton has been pushed furthest in Carhaix, a commune in central Brittany, which elected an 'autonomist' mayor in 2001. Though business stands apart from this advocacy group, Breton firms are rarely hostile to the language, which forms an important part of the overall Breton identity that firms seek to utilize.

There is no mainstreaming of the Breton language within Brittany comparable to that witnessed in Wales. This being said, the embattled status of the Breton language gave this group an extraordinary cohesion in adversity. If it is impossible to detect any single actor, a constellation of individuals, semi-official agencies and voluntary associations can be identified, gravitating for the most part around the regional council. These actors form part of a language-advocacy group drawing its strength not from institutionalisation but from shared beliefs and from the capacity to mobilise the powerful Breton cultural movement. This advocacy group includes actors within local and regional authorities, semi-autonomous agencies such as the Breton Language Office and the cultural federations regrouped in the Brittany Cultural Institute and the Brittany Cultural Council.

In the case of Wales, language and institutions matter. Centred around the National Assembly and the Welsh Language Board has been identified a cohesive territorial policy community which has succeeded in diffusing a cross-sectoral message and in defining the core issue of language in terms of public policy and regulation, rather than in terms of identity. The territorial policy community preceded the creation of devolution, but received a major boost from the setting up of the Assembly. In the case of Brittany, it is more difficult to identify a territorial policy community. The Breton language-advocacy group adopted a defensive posture, on account of the difficult regulatory environment within which it functioned. Defining language issues in terms of regulatory conformity was not an option in the Breton case. Though the concerns that dominated the agenda in Wales were highly unlikely to become rooted in Brittany, the Brittany regional council has made some difference in restoring the fortunes of the language.

Human capital and the emergence of territorial policy communities in Wales and Brittany

In their relationship to territory, the closely linked areas of higher education, training and lifelong learning are subject to countervailing pressures. On the one hand, the development of knowledge-driven economies has arguably enhanced the importance of local and regional innovation, especially in terms of niche markets. As Lash and Urry write, 'The specificity of place, of its workforce, the character of its entrepreneurialism, its administration, its buildings, its history and especially its physical environment, become more important as temporal and spatial barriers collapse' (1994, 303). Comparative studies indicate, moreover, that the regional space is an appropriate one for developing learning policies addressing specific demands of the local and regional economy (Brown *et al.*, 2001). On the other hand, higher-education policy dynamics in particular are rooted in challenges which can rarely be reduced to specific places. Diplomas ensuring national or European mobility are more highly valued by high achievers than narrow vocational qualifications seeking to match local employment and training possibilities. In their attention to issues of youth and adult training and lifelong learning policies, regional policy-makers occupy a policy space that lies somewhere between classic education, the economy and social inclusion. The presence of competing interests makes it extremely difficult for regional authorities to define authoritative frames of reference.

The issue area of training and lifelong learning has similarities with, but is distinct from that of education. The well-documented policy field of education mobilises strong professional interests (teachers, educational administrators) in both countries, to the extent that it has sometimes been considered a closed, impenetrable policy community (Duclaud-Williams, 1993). Moving from the easily identifiable field of education to that of training and lifelong learning, it becomes much more difficult to define precise contours. As Shackleton (1995) argues, there is no common definition of training and some lack of clarity about its purpose. There are recognisable market segments, which mobilise different sets of actors and resource dependencies. Training is understood as a generic definition to cover various related (but distinctive) processes, namely: school-based forms of professional education and work placement; work-based youth training; work-based adult training (or lifelong learning) and individual learning. The terminology used to describe these human capital processes varies: education, training, learning, skills. The first step to understanding the dynamics of training lies in comprehending how the issue is defined in a particular context. In both Wales and Brittany, regional politicians and officials have justified the considerable effort spent on developing regional training programmes in terms of matching employment supply and training needs. Interestingly, however, though the meso-level authorities have varying degrees of competency over training and skills policies in both countries, neither has a statutory competence for employment policy, reserved for the central state in France and a UK-wide agency (Jobcentre plus) in the UK.

It is essential to comprehend both institutional legacies and relationships in order to understand the dynamics underpinning policy formation in post-devolution Wales and in Brittany. Next, each case in turn is briefly considered.

Brittany: the strength of weak ties

In the case of France and Brittany, the institutional legacy is best described as an interaction between state-centrism, social partnership and new forms of territorial governance. Social partnership forms the cornerstone of public discourse about training and employment, the belief being that social partners (employers and trade unions) are the key stakeholders in determining priorities for increasing skills in the workforce. The social partnership approach was most clearly articulated in the 1971 Training Act. The 1971 law introduced a legal requirement for firms to spend a proportion of their wage costs on training (the 'levy') and to develop a training plan. The 1971 law strengthened social partnership, insofar as it involved the trade unions and employers in negotiating plant-level training plans. The logic of the social partnership is usually top-down. In most economic branches, national agreements are negotiated between trade unions' and employers' peak organisations, and applied more or less uniformly irrespective of local conditions.

The regional-capacity approach, on the contrary, is underpinned by a horizontal logic, one based on inter-organisational co-operation and the adaptation of local training supply to local labour-market conditions. Faced with the resistance of pre-existing networks of solidly implanted institutions, the ability of the regions to make a difference depends upon the quality of the relationships they maintain. French regions have adopted a variety of responses (OIP, 1997). In Brittany, good relationships have provided a bridge across competing organisational interests. This can be illustrated briefly with two examples: the ARGOS programme and the 'Contracts of Objectives' procedure.

The ARGOS programme was first experimented in the Brittany region in the 1980s. ARGOS is a methodological approach, rather than a fully fledged policy. ARGOS, put simply, provides a single set of statistics allowing the region concerned to match the training courses offered with predicted future employment needs at a sub-regional level. In Brittany, all the main players agreed from the start to accept ARGOS as a common set of statistics upon which to base future policy. ARGOS provides an overview of training supply and demand in relation to a territory – the region – rather than dealing with one particular industrial sector. The first ARGOS programme in Brittany defined 455 distinct types of employment, regrouped into professional families. ARGOS estimates how many jobs there are in each professional family and which training courses are needed to place people in these jobs. Training courses are funded on the basis that they respond to the needs of one or more professional family. Understanding the regional labour market is, therefore, of critical importance in order to facilitate the formulation of regional training policies. Insofar as the Brittany region defined its policy objectives in terms of training for employment, it situated itself as part of a diffuse employment advocacy coalition.

The Contract of Objectives procedure provided another indicator of good relationships underpinning inter-organisational co-operation. The tension between the elected regions and the social partners was a recurrent theme in interviews. These tensions were less acute in Brittany than in most other regions, however. There were more sector-specific contractual agreements between the Brittany region, the French State and the social partners than in any other French region. The procedure known as the Contract of Objectives is an attempt to involve business more closely in the definition of its training objectives. Contracts are signed between the state, the region and a particular profession; each party agrees specific commitments, financial or otherwise. The regions and economic branches define together their training needs for the duration of a five-year planning contract. By 2001, twenty-one agreements known as 'Contracts of Objectives' had been signed in Brittany, more than in any other French region.

In the area of training *stricto sensu* we should speak of a realm of interdependent decision-making, since the French State retains important powers and the domain regulated by the social partners escapes in most respects from regional oversight. The challenge for the Regions has always been to substitute a territorial for a functional logic. In theory, only the regions can pull together all the various strands on their territory, but their record is a mixed one. French regions are secondary stakeholders in each of the interlocking policy fields that together comprise 'training'. Though they have precise legal responsibilities, they do not control alone any of the essential policy instruments. The social partners (employers and the trade unions) and the State decide the number of youth-training contracts to be financed in any given year, and these are mainly paid for by a training levy on firms. The professional branches work out the details of on-the-job training and the content of professional training courses. The central state has kept control of most social-inclusion activities or job-promotion schemes with a training dimension (the *emplois-jeunes* under Jospin, the *contrats-jeunes* under Raffarin). The natural market niche of the regions is neither the army of employed (social partners) nor the unemployed (the ministry or its agencies). Its policies touch both constituencies, but, arguably, on the margins. The approach adopted by the Brittany region was one of horizontal co-ordination and inter-organisational dialogue, which, in the circumstances, was the most rational strategy available.

Wales: the top-down temptation

There are some similarities and many differences with the case of Wales. While it is possible to observe a strong territorial dimension to training policy under devolution, for most of British post-war history training policy was not a devolved area. Wales had to accept a similar range of institutions to those operating in England and Scotland. In Wales, as in Brittany, the emphasis on 'training' policy oscillated from social partnership to state interventionism to encouraging local and regional influences and to emphasising individual choice. The one ingredient present in Wales but missing in Brittany was that of a distinctly neo-liberal version of individual choice during the Conservative period in office. Next, revisiting briefly this institutional heritage will allow a better appreciation of the distinctiveness of devolution.

Ideas of social partnership were at their strongest during the period of social-democratic consensus that held sway from 1945 to 1974. The Industrial Training Act of 1964 introduced a Central Training Council, run on the basis of tripartite management, including government, unions and employers. It also introduced the Industrial Training Boards to administer a system of compulsory levies and grants. This gave way in 1973 to the Manpower Services Commission (MSC), another tripartite body which was centrally organised and funded. The MSC survived until the 1988 Employment Act, enacted under the Conservatives, which replaced ideas of social partnership with those of consumer choice. The creation of the Training and Enterprise Councils (TECs) represented a shift from government provision to employer responsibility for training. For the Conservative government, business involvement would attract more private investment to training and allow for better types of training, more adapted to the needs of business. Opponents, of which there were many within Wales, complained that there were no real means of controlling the TECs, private firms entrusted with very large amounts of public expenditure. The political and policy environment changed with the arrival of New Labour in power at the UK level and the advent of devolution shortly afterwards. From the devolutionary perspective, the TECS were not adapted to considerations of territory, certainly not to building Wales as a distinctive political community. In place of the TECs, the Assembly introduced the National Council for Education and Learning Wales (ELWa). The research reported in this book accompanied the evolution of ELWa throughout its course, as a series of interviews was undertaken across Wales in 2001–4 with actors from all parts of the policy community.

ELWa began life on 1 April 2001. Described by one interviewee as 'a single giant quango', ELWa was born out of the fusion of the four Welsh Training and Enterprise Councils and the further and higher education funding councils (FEFCW, HEFCW). In March 2003 the decision was taken to de-merge these two organisations, with the ELWa label reserved for the former. From the start, the new organisation had a steep learning curve. Morale was lowered by large-scale redundancies in 2002 and 2003 from amongst the former staff of the TECs. The public image of the organisation was seriously damaged by a number of the early funding decisions it made and by acrimonious changes of leadership at the top. By 2004, the National Council had strategic responsibility for all post-16 education, training and lifelong learning in Wales (except for higher education), including school sixth forms, further education colleges, the training programmes previously funded by the TECs and local-authority adult education. The story of ELWa has been expertly narrated elsewhere, but the focus here is upon the policy-community interactions around ELWa and the institution-building dimensions of the devolution project in the domain of education and training.

Interviews from 2001 to 2003 revealed a rather fragmented policy community. Three types of policy actor were identified: those working for the National Assembly, the business community and educational providers. There was, in equal measure, broad agreement amongst politicians and officials of the devolved Assembly that ELWa was essential for the devolutionary project, and broad dismay at the logistical and financial difficulties faced by the organisation during its first three years of existence. Other stakeholders were divided. The main business organisations were suspicious of ELWa, criticising the organisation for not focusing on work-based training and for laying too much emphasis on education and generic skills. For the CBI, ELWa was a massive quango with a public-sector ethos. The CBI lamented the lack of direct business representation on ELWa, in contrast to the Learning and Skills Councils in England. The CBI, FSB and IoD all agreed, however, that ELWa had made a determined effort to seek out business advice and to work closely with employers. Interviewees in the secondary and further-education sector expressed the most doubt and anxiety about ELWa. Heads of schools with sixth forms were worried about the creation of ELWa, fearing the organisation would be biased against them in favour of the further-education colleges. Such preoccupations were also expressed in interviews with local authorities across Wales, which would lose all control over school sixth forms. Representatives of the further-education sector were initially confident they would prosper under the new regime, but relations soured as cuts across the FE sector were announced in 2003 and 2004.

Across all groups of interviewees, there was a belief that ELWa was too broad and top-down an organisation to achieve the aims ascribed to it. The challenge for ELWa was to be able to identify the solutions to deep-seated policy problems in institutional terms. The result was one of organisational overload. Institutional ambition produced short-termism, a response to the pressures for rapid, quantifiable results from the Assembly Government. In the case of post-devolution Wales, there has been a strong emphasis on institutions and their capacity to drive change. When institutions fail (or are perceived to fail), policy-makers have searched for new institutional solutions. In 2001, the Assembly looked to ELWa to provide a long-term strategic approach; by 2004, the Assembly Government had decided to exercise direct control over post-16 education and learning. In June 2004, First Minister Morgan announced that ELWa, along with the WDA and WTB, would be wound up and its duties administered directly by the Assembly Government. In one sense, this move was a recognition of failure, as it damaged the myth of Team Wales which the Assembly had tried so hard to foster.

In the area of training and lifelong learning, comparison illustrates similarity, as well as difference. In both policy communities, tensions were observed between regionally focused political actors and economic actors whose perspectives remained national. These tensions were especially important in Brittany, where the regional council had great difficulty imposing its views on business organisations, trade unions and individual firms. In the case of Wales, tensions were also observed between regional players and nationally focused social partners (unions, business), played out in the tender relations between ELWa and the UK-wide Sector Skills Councils. From this brief overview it can be concluded that Wales has suffered poor outcomes on account of its difficult management of interorganisational relationships and an overly directive, strategic approach. Whether or not to the taste of ELWa or the Assembly, interdependent relations were crucial. Devolution in Wales has placed excessive confidence in institutional solutions, at the expense of managing delicate relationships. In Brittany, there was a weaker strategic oversight for the region, but the disadvantages of strategic command and control were offset by a more harmonious set of inter-organisational relations.

Lessons from comparative experience

Are there any relevant political and policy lessons to be drawn from cross-national comparison? Insofar as the research interested itself as much in the similarities between Wales and Brittany as in the contrasts between them, this question was central to the investigations. From the outset, the thirst of the National Assembly for Wales for information relating to experiences in other EU countries was striking, as was the fascination displayed by regionalists everywhere with the experiences of devolution in Wales and Scotland. In this final section, the voyage within the Welsh and Breton policy communities continues with a view to elucidating the political models and policy lessons which decision-makers draw from observing what goes on elsewhere.

Comparative public-policy analysis is increasingly focused upon how public policies can be improved by observing practice elsewhere (Rose, 1993; Evans and Davies, 1999; Dolowitz and Marsh, 2000; James and Lodge, 2003). Best-practice, benchmarking and policy evaluation are all predicated upon the belief that narrow institutional knowledge is inadequate for resolving complex policy dilemmas. These various approaches can be subsumed under the general heading of policy transfer.

There are two distinctive approaches to policy transfer. The first can be labelled as hard policy transfer. It is based on understanding how and when policies initiated in one place and time can be transplanted to another. There requires a strong political will and an *a priori* belief that solutions appropriate for one context can be equally important in other contexts. In practice, there is daily evidence of policy transfer. The European Union operates not only as a melting pot of ideas coming from different national traditions but also, on occasion, as an authoritative institution constraining member-states to adopt policy instruments designed elsewhere and viewed with suspicion. EU competition policy, for instance, has often gone against the grain of policy-making in France, Germany and a number of other states. This type of policy transfer usually relies upon a strong normative belief about the best types of policy instruments and their appropriateness irrespective of context. A second approach can best be described as one of reflexive learning. Policy actors reflect upon their own practices as they accumulate experience, learn how to identify weaknesses and interact with others. Reflexivity can induce a form of soft policy transfer, or lesson-drawing.

If Rose (1991) is accurate in saying that lesson-drawing requires the thirst for inquiry, information, comparability and the exchange of knowledge, then it ought to be deduced that the existence of contacts between decision-makers and/or awareness of policy programmes elsewhere are a precondition for drawing lessons The theme of lesson-drawing was pursued both in face-to-face interviews and in an elite questionnaire. Respondents were asked in an open-ended question in both elite surveys to identify lessons from practice elsewhere. The main conclusion drawn for Wales and Brittany is that the policy communities are not epistemic communities and that reference frames are primarily regional or national.

Where direct comparisons were drawn in interviews with experiences elsewhere, they were idealised comparisons, rather than being rooted in policy-relevant knowledge of 'what happens elsewhere' (as opposed to general perceptions of the state of political institutions). In both Wales and Brittany, there was a measure of confusion between lessons and models. In both regions, when respondents evoked 'lessons' from abroad, they tended to respond in terms of particular regions rather than specific policies or programmes. When the 'lessons' related to training policy, responses in both regions were given in terms of models, the most popular model being that of the German Dual system. In the case of training and lifelong learning especially, there was a lack of knowledge or a misrepresentation of the practice in other countries and regions. In both regions also, when the 'lessons' related to language policy, the Spanish region of Catalonia was the most cited, rather than any specific policy programme. A number of Breton respondents held the Welsh model of interventionist language policy in great esteem. Interestingly, however, even fervent supporters of bilingualism in Wales or

Catalonia were much more reserved when it came to France itself. A bilingual policy was not generally considered to be an option in the French context, emphasising the importance of national paths in shaping perceptions of policy norms.

Interestingly, when the research moved to the more general question of models, there was a measure of convergence between the Welsh and Breton samples. The interviews and questionnaire uncovered a small number of strong models in 'third party' countries. When asked which models they looked to abroad, Catalonia (and Spain more generally), the Basque Country, Ireland and Wales emerged as the principal regions to which Bretons (all categories included) would look for inspiration. In Wales, the foreign models were Ireland, Canada, Catalonia (and Spain more generally), the German *Länder* and the Scandinavian democracies. On the specifics of the Wales-Brittany comparison was observed a certain asymmetry, following logically from the more enhanced form of regional governance in Wales. Regional actors in Brittany were more likely to refer to Wales as a model of devolution than were those in Wales to advocate adopting lessons from Brittany. Speaking in Cardiff in March 2003, First Minister Morgan evoked a continuum of experiences of regional autonomy, placing Wales in the same camp as Catalonia, the German *Länder* and other legislative regions, eventually setting Wales as a model for Brittany to follow. At the level of political institutions, the Welsh policy community considered that it enjoyed a more advanced form of devolution than in Brittany, a belief shared by many (but not all) regional policy actors in Brittany. In response to Morgan's claims, the then President of the Brittany Region, Josselin de Rohan, pointed out that French regions had much greater leeway in raising revenue than the devolved Assemblies in the UK.

With whom were members of the policy communities in contact? In Brittany, a majority of respondents indicated that they had no foreign contacts. Upon further investigation, those members of the elite sample with pro-regionalist tendencies were seen as much more likely than the others to be engaged in international networks, a finding which suggests a powerful pan-European network of regionalist activists. On the contrary, those intending to support the mainstream parties – PS or UMP – were less likely to be involved in international networks. An uncharitable observer might draw the conclusion that international contact was a surrogate activity for the exercise of real political influence. When foreign contacts were specifically mentioned, the most important (in order) were with Catalonia, the European Bureau of Lesser Used Languages and Wales. In the Welsh case, a majority of the sample claimed to be in contact with decision-makers in other countries, but few could specify who these were. In Wales in particular was observed a basic incongruity between idealised visions of where Wales ought to be (the aspirational comparisons with, in order of frequency, Ireland, Catalonia or the Scandinavian democracies) and a lack of precise policy knowledge about experiences elsewhere.

In both cases – Wales and Brittany – the knowledge of experiences elsewhere should not be overestimated. Contacts between policy stakeholders in Wales and Brittany were few, limited mainly to the cultural domain. In both countries, the training-policy community was more insular than its language counterpart. There were very few contacts with foreign countries, much fewer than in the area of regional languages. Only EU programmes such as Leonardo brought training-policy actors together with counterparts from other countries, an experience most interviewees found useful but peripheral to their main concerns. In both regions, the language-policy communities were rather less inward-looking than the training-policy communities. The pre-eminence of parochial concerns is a rational response to operating within precise regional and national contexts, which shape the forms assumed by regional political institutions and policy communities. This is not to imply staticity; rather, that exogenous challenges are filtered in accordance with precise ideas, interests and institutions which make sense first and foremost in a regional or national context. The comparative survey and elite interviews thus revealed the limitations of the policy-learning approach amongst meso-level policy communities.

Conclusion

The evidence presented in this chapter allows the drawing of some firm conclusions about Wales, Brittany and the interaction of territorial and sectoral policy communities. Territorial policy communities are more easily identifiable in the field of regional languages than in that of training and lifelong learning. Regional languages are owned by meso-level political authorities in a much more explicit way than training or lifelong-learning policies. Obviously the case for Wales, this conclusion is also valid in Brittany. From the above evidence it can be deduced that sectoral policy communities, such as those described by Marsh and Rhodes (1992) or Marsh and Smith (2000), do not naturally have a territorial dimension. To be successful, territorial policy communities need to span distinctive policy sectors and invest them with a sense of territoriality. In the case of Wales, the devolved political institutions acted as a focus for the interaction of the territorial policy community in both areas surveyed. Regional language policy was an important symbol of Welsh distinctiveness and fully embraced by the main actors of devolution. The case of training and lifelong learning was rather different. Not only was the policy field marked by an embarrassing case of institutional failure (ELWa), the present investigation demonstrated the persistence of powerful intervening variables, especially in the form of pre-existing actor systems and the limited legal competencies of the Assembly.

The case of regional languages revealed distinctive forms of territorial policy community in both Wales and Brittany. In Wales the language-policy community was effective because it is cross-cutting, rather than linked to a single recognisable policy sector. In Brittany, a strong Breton language-advocacy group was identified, one which is possibly in the process of transforming itself into a recognisable policy community. In terms of political capacity, however, this group was much weaker than its Welsh counterpart. In contrast to regional languages, in both Wales and Brittany there were many obstacles to building unified policy communities in the area of training and lifelong learning. In both regions, there was competition from sector-specific forces (the professions or industrial branches) and professional associations looking to a larger regulatory framework. In neither region did the decentralised political authorities exercise convincing control over economic policy. In spite of differences of national context, there were thus many similarities between the policy communities in training and lifelong learning. Multi-layered policy sectors such as education and training are not easily shaped in line with the wishes of devolved or decentralised political authorities.

In both areas surveyed, as well as in others such as economic development and agriculture, the institutions of Welsh devolution matter rather more than those of Breton decentralisation. Devolution in Wales is having an effect on territorial policy communities. It is making them more territorially focused. New sets of relationships have emerged and existing patterns have been disrupted. This process of institutionalising and regulating relationships works better in areas of obvious regional ownership, such as language, than in multi-actor areas, such as training or even economic development. In the case of Brittany, it is less easy to diagnose an institutional effect. In both areas surveyed, however, the regional council managed to place itself at the centre of territorialised networks.

Where does this leave the argument in terms of regional political capacity? Overarching national contexts matter. Territorial policy communities focus their attentions more explicitly upon the National Assembly in Wales than they do upon the Brittany regional council, testament to the more advanced form of political devolution in Wales. In Brittany, there is a more explicit process of bargaining between organisations, rather than the top-down command-and-control approach experimented on with mixed success in Wales. If in Wales the institutions are too directive, in Brittany the institutions are too weak to provide uncontested leadership.

8
Regional political capacity in Wales and Brittany

This book set out to deepen the understanding of processes of comparative regional governance by investigating two historic regions (Wales and Brittany) in two neighbouring European Union states. Chapter 1 presented a theoretical framework based on regional political capacity, defined as an inter-active process encompassing institutions and institutional processes, actors and their relationships, socially constructed identities and forms of overarching regulation (Kooiman, 2003; Le Galès, 2002; Loughlin, 2001; Keating, 1998). The framework for analysis combines criteria drawn from institutions (and political opportunity structures), relationships, identities and regulation (Cole, 2004). Next, a set of concluding evaluative judgements about regional governance in Wales and Brittany is presented, in an attempt to draw out some more general conclusions about regional political capacity.

Institutions and institutional capacity

Institutions are of primary importance for understanding regional political capacity. In the comparison between Wales and Brittany, old and new institutional variables assume great importance. From the insights of new institutionalist theory, regional political institutions can be understood as players in the broader development of regional public spheres, especially through their role in embodying collective beliefs and their linkage with popular identities (François and Neveu, 1999; Gaudin, 2002). But, consistent with older institutional traditions, the rule-making potential of regional political institutions and their ability to define norms were also scrutinised. The ability to shape public policies is a fundamental feature of regional political capacity building. It draws upon both formal rules and informal understandings about the role of regional players. Regional institutions, predicated upon precise legal rules and the ability to define norms, can provide avenues through which to develop more autonomous regional capacity. At the purely regional level, it can be concluded that in most respects the regional institutions provide more opportunities for the pursuit of territorially specific policies in Wales than in Brittany. The institutions of devolution are weightier than those of decentralisation, whether measured in terms of budgets, personnel or legal powers. In some respects, the Brittany regional council is able to adopt territorially specific public policies in a less problematical way than in Wales. Elected French Regions have limited tax-varying powers not available to the National Assembly for Wales. In the French case, all sub-national authorities, including the regions, are recognised with a general administrative responsibility in law: they can do what they want, unless explicitly forbidden by the law. In Wales, not only the National Assembly but also local government can only act where precise statutory competence exists.

Though the institutions of devolution in Wales are more consequential than those of decentralisation in Brittany, the future development of Welsh devolution is more uncertain. A lack of constitutional embeddedness for the devolution project has acted as a source of constant political tension. London can change the rules of engagement, either through its control of detail (its ability to define what is primary and what is secondary legislation) or through act of parliament. The lack of defined generic competencies for the National Assembly acts as the main countervailing force to the polity-building tendency observed at various stages of the book. In Brittany, though the institutions are in most respects weaker, at least their existence is constitutionally ensured.

New institutionalist frames place importance upon the ability to construct identities and adapt discourses. Within the contrasting national administrative frameworks represented by the British and French states, there are varying opportunities and incentives for the construction of autonomous 'national-regional' futures. The theme of polity building has been pushed further in the Welsh case than in the Breton one, though it is also highly contested in Wales. Though the formal powers of the National Assembly for Wales are limited, the historical evolution of the UK, a curious mix of unitary and union-state, has been much more accommodating for the construction of competing visions, at least in its Celtic regions. In France, the reality is somewhat different. The institutional and political structures of opportunities have emphasised the conquest of national (French) power, and this has only partially been called into question with decentralisation. In Wales, the future of devolution is at least as dependent on evolutions at the UK as at the Welsh level, and the UK context provides the primary focus for the (all-UK) political parties. But devolution has also been accompanied by the development of a Welsh party system focused upon the conquest of political power in the National Assembly for Wales.

On balance, the scorecard is favourable to Welsh devolution. In spite of its lack of tax-varying or primary legislative powers, the Welsh Assembly Government can make a difference. The Assembly can make primary legislation within secondary legislation (through statutory instruments and circulars), conferring upon it a distinctive policy-formulation role. There have been a number of independent policy initiatives in Wales since devolution. These are conceptualised in Chapter 4 in terms of incremental changes, institutional capacity building, identity markers, interdependency and policy inflation. The Assembly has made many incremental changes designed to bolster the image of Wales as a small country committed to social justice and equality. It has also engaged in far-reaching structural reforms in health and education, testament to its belief in the efficacy of institutional solutions to resolve policy dilemmas. Politicians in Wales have used the devolved institutions to embed policies designed to strengthen the sense of Welsh national identity, especially in language policy. The Assembly has attempted, moreover, to go beyond the strict parameters of the 1998 Act and spillover into non-devolved areas. Such initiatives have complicated inter-organisational relations, as other players resent the Assembly's interference. Its ambition notwithstanding, the Assembly has had to manage a set of interdependent relations that restrict the possibilities for autonomous action, especially in the non-devolved areas (such as employment policy) and in the field of European Union policy. Party political ties have limited policy divergence over policies and institutional futures, though they create the prospect of future instability.

In the case of Brittany, the ability of the regional political institution to make a difference is less easy to appreciate. The Brittany regional council has a weaker capacity to impose norms than the National Assembly for Wales, though this is to some degree variable on policy issue area. The regions in France have had to make their mark in a dense institutional setting. Regions were superimposed upon pre-existing departmental councils, while large cities and towns have also become powerful levels of sub-national government. The type of authority exercised by French regions is much more one of networked governance than of strategic command and control. The elected regions are, in theory, the lead authorities in matters deemed to be strategic, such as economic development, vocational training, infrastructure, some secondary education, some transport (and regional rail services since 2002). Formal legal competencies are virtually never exercised alone. Building political capacity in the case of a French region involves developing trusting relationships and engaging with other major players to ensure positive-sum outcomes. Chapter 5 uncovered the existence of a Breton framework of policy, which emphasises the importance of the regional space, the desire to build regional consensus over and above departmental and local rivalries and a belief in the need to negotiate with the state in an equal-to-equal negotiation. The Breton mode of operation builds upon regional capacity, but is focused upon lobbying the central state. The regional policy community seeks a collaborative mode of governance and believes in building a measure of trust in relations with central government. Chapters 5 and 7 observed the very different way in which the Brittany Regional council made a difference in the areas of economic development, training and lifelong learning, education and regional languages.

Regional political capacity in Brittany is of the soft variety. There is no real equivalent in Brittany of the National Assembly for Wales's capacity to adapt primary Westminster legislation. There are some examples in the overseas French territories, in New Caledonia and French Polynesia especially, but not yet in mainland France. The 2002 law gave the Corsican Assembly some powers to make regulations, though the Constitutional Council ruled as unconstitutional Article 1, which would have vested legislative powers in the Corsican Assembly. It is premature to affirm that the direction of change in France is the same as in the UK, but important movement is afoot. The 2003 constitutional amendment granted constitutional recognition to French regions for the first time, alongside that for communes and departments, as well as allowing for the experimental transfer of new powers from central government to sub-national authorities. Whether under Gaullist or Socialist control, Brittany has been in the forefront of French regions in demanding enhanced devolutionary powers. There remain many divergences between the French model and those of France's principal neighbours. There are no provisions to provide legislative powers for regions, unlike in Germany, Spain or Italy. On the other hand French governments are slowing moving towards the obvious truth: that a modern complex democracy can not be administered in exactly the same way across all of its territory.

On the basis of 'old' institutional criteria, however, regional governance is more advanced in Wales than in Brittany, in spite of the newness of regional institutions. The scorecard is less uneven in relation to the softer variables, which are also important for appreciating regional governance, most especially those relating to relationships, socially constructed identities, patterns of partisan behaviour and environmental constraints and opportunities.

Actors and relationships

Institutions can also be understood in a softer sense. Institutional capacity is relational; it depends upon relationships, shared values and the effective interlocking of organisations. Effective regional institutions need to be well interconnected with lower- and higher-level political and administrative echelons, as well as being deeply embedded within civil society. How the development of regional political institutions has acted as a focus for territorial identities is one important measure of institutional capacity. How institutions have become arenas for the mobilisation of social and economic actors is another.

Chapter 1 posited a direct linkage between modes of regional governance and the internal quality of relationships. In normative terms, effective regional governance is predicated upon good relationships and shared values, as well as upon powerful institutions. These various qualities were conceptualised in terms of political capacity. Political scientists understand capacity in a variety of ways (Stone, 1989; John, 2001). Capacity building is used as a generic term to identify a virtuous circle of resource synergy, and most obviously comprises regional political institutions, but also involves developing trusting horizontal and vertical relationships. There is a value-added dimension, insofar as good relationships are required to make institutions function effectively and to maximise policy outputs. Capacity building is also linked with trust and interconnectivity (Brown *et al.*, 2001; Randles, 2001; John, 2001).

What evidence is found of trusting relationships, interconnectivity and shared visions and values amongst political, economic and societal decision-makers in Wales and Brittany? Schematically, Brittany builds upon territorial solidarity and a broad consensus to promote institutional interconnectivity and to enmesh institutions within civil society. In Wales, on the other hand, linkage between civil society and political institutions is still in its infancy. This weakness of 'civic culture' is in part a consequence of the absence of genuine Welsh political institutions until 1999.

The comparison can be developed further by focusing upon the related themes of trust and interconnectivity. Trust evokes sentiments of honesty, a culture of co-operation and a high level of social capital. In the case of Brittany, the opinion survey revealed a high degree of trust in the regional council, a belief that the region defends Brittany's interest well in other arenas and a preference for the region over other levels in many important areas of public policy. An overwhelming majority of the Breton poll – 82.1 per cent – expressed their 'trust' in the Brittany regional council to assure the development of Brittany, while three-quarters of the survey – 74.2 per cent – believed that the existence of the regional council was important for defending Brittany's influence in Paris. These findings are consistent with mainstream representations of Breton political culture, which emphasise political moderation, the cohesive traditions of the co-operative movement in farming and banking, the robust state of participation in voluntary associations, consensual Breton political traditions and a developed sense of regional identity (Le Coadic, 1998; Le Bourdennec, 1996; Favereau, 1993). In Wales, there is less trust in the devolved institutions and a more distinctive set of political cleavages, a theme developed in the next section of this chapter.

Trust has an iterative dimension linked to interconnectivity. In other words, relationships need to be built upon repeated contacts. The small scale of policy-making in both Wales and Brittany facilitates frequent relationships. This proximity is increasingly obvious in the case of post-devolution Wales. All the main players know each other personally and there are close linkages not only between civil servants and ministers but also between politicians, officials and representatives of Welsh civil society. Devolution created several new all-Wales organisations, such as Careers Wales and Education and Learning Wales (ELWa), and reformed old ones such as the Welsh Development Agency (WDA). Metaphors of Team Wales rang hollow after June 2004, however, when First Minister Morgan announced the Assembly Government's intention to take over direct control (in 2006) of the WDA, the Wales Tourist Board (WTB) and ELWa. If the logic of institution building arguably explained this move, this was at the expense of maintaining good territorial relationships – the leaders of the WDA, ELWa and WTB manifestly did not want to be integrated into the civil service.

The jury is out about the future of devolution. There was some evidence that the first term of devolution provided the mobilising project necessary to embed the Welsh polity and to build Welsh civil society, in the long run potentially overcoming an important social capital deficit. On the other hand, a 37 per cent turn-out in the 2003 Assembly election was disappointing, down almost 10 percentage points from that of 1999. Devolution has produced a more cohesive (though still divided) party system, the equilibrium of which is favourable to making the devolved institutions work. There are much closer contacts between Welsh Assembly government officials and Assembly-sponsored public bodies than in the pre-devolution era (Cole, Jones and Storer, 2003). There is the appearance, finally, of all-Wales organisations within civil society and the gradual recognition by professional organisations (the CBI and TUC notably) of the need to take devolution into account in their own organisation.

In Brittany, observers have long noted a deeply rooted territorial solidarity. Though modern Brittany harbours the divisive political memory of wartime 'collaboration', the dominant political culture is one of political accommodation. In a rather paradoxical manner, Breton political capacity is strong because of the weak intensity of domestic cleavages, confirmed in the survey findings. There is an underlying consensus to defend Breton interests to the outside world and limit political conflict. This consensual model is broadly shared within Breton public opinion. In practice, French sub-national governance, in Brittany as elsewhere, is characterised by resource-based competition between overlapping layers of sub-national administration: communes, inter-communal bodies, departments and regions. The Brittany region stands out, however, for its high level of cross-communal co-operation, not only in urban centres such as Rennes, but in the rural hinterland as well. Brittany scores highly in terms of institutional interconnectivity, embodied by traditions of inter-communal co-operation, normally harmonious relationships between regional politicians and representatives of the state field services, and high levels of social capital, measured by an active associative life, high electoral participation and strong social networks acting as a barrier to the extreme right (weaker in Brittany than anywhere else in France).

The linkage between governing capacity, shared values and the quality of inter-organisational and interpersonal relationships is central to the debate over regional capacity. The horizontal enmeshing of regional political institutions with public-, private- and voluntary-sector bodies is one gauge of interconnectivity. If institutions are primordial in the Welsh case, it can be surmised that relationships are more important in the case of Brittany. Relationships based on trust and regional advocacy exist both at the horizontal (within Brittany) and vertical levels. At the horizontal level, interlocutors in Brittany were virtually unanimous in praising the capacity of Breton actors to join forces to promote their common interests and to defend Brittany against attacks from the outside world. There was no such unanimity in Wales, in spite of the Assembly's espousal of all-inclusive politics. These qualities are not necessarily innate to Brittany and absent in Wales. It was noted above that actors believed in the beginnings of a 'Wales effect' and the emergence of a more unified Welsh political culture post-devolution. The temporal dimension is important: devolution in Wales is only seven years old, undoubtedly too short a period of time to allow firm conclusions to be drawn about the capacity for institutional or policy learning.

It can be surmised from the above that effective regional capacity building requires regional political institutions to be interconnected with lower- and higher-level political and administrative echelons, as well as being deeply embedded within civil society. It also appears axiomatic that effective regional governance must rest upon a strong sense of regional awareness and a linkage between identity and institutions, a theme addressed next.

Identities and institutions

The linkage between identity and institutions was a core concern of the survey. In the case of Wales, an initial hypothesis was that the divisive history of (pre-)devolution Wales and the demonstration of linguistic, territorial and political cleavages in the 1997 referendum would undermine regional political institutions and prevent the development of regional capacity. Identity would either destroy the nascent political institutions in Wales, or mould them into a coherent project. In the case of Brittany, on the other hand, it was conjectured that a regional policy register (*répertoire d'action collective*) based on consensus and a political opportunity structure remaining largely state-centric would combine to promote a limited form of regional advocacy.

On the basis of the evidence presented in Chapter 6, it was concluded that multiple identities (regional and national) are more easily assumed in Brittany than in Wales. A sense of Welshness as being essentially opposed to Britishness is firmly rooted in a sizeable minority of Welsh people. In Brittany, in contrast, the sense of regional identity is strong, but this is not considered as being in opposition to an overarching French nationhood (Cole and Loughlin, 2003). In the French region, Breton and French identities are mainly complementary. The greatest difference between Wales and Brittany therefore lies not so much in institutional preferences for the future as in the linkage between national and regional identities and in the party political dynamics.

Most Bretons are conscious of the limits of regional capacity building within the context of French republicanism. The salient issues of concern in Brittany were those concerning public policy rather than the politics of identity. In Wales, no such straightforward instrumentalist intent can be read from the figures. Cleavages are much more deeply embedded within Welsh society and there is a more complex relationship between identity, institutions and partisan preferences than in Brittany. The main achievement of devolution in Wales has been to harness a diffuse sense of Welshness in support of the devolved political institutions. This finding, backed up by the survey evidence, was not a foregone conclusion. In Wales, the institutions of devolution are to some extent supplanting the role of language as the critical marker of identity.

One essential differentiation between devolution in Wales and decentralisation in Brittany is of a (party) political order. As political parties aggregate interests, so party politicians play a crucial role in shaping political demands. It was demonstrated in Chapter 6 that there are no significant relationships between regional voting choice and attitudes to autonomy in Brittany. Why is this the case? Two fundamental reasons were highlighted, concerning first, the legacy of the past and, second, the contemporary political opportunity structure. Breton-style identity politics were discredited by the collaborationist activities of a minority of Breton activists during the war. The prevailing post-war model of political activism has been one of territorial solidarity. There has been a strong political consensus among the regional elites in favour of enhanced regionalisation, but also a recognition of the need to enter into a dialogue with the French state.

The counterpart to the ongoing dialogue with the central state is that national political parties operating within Brittany are infused with Breton cultural values, and local or regional politicians are aware of the need to combine strong regional and national messages. The successful articulation of mixed messages helps explain why the Breton political scene has been dominated by national parties, rather than regionally specific ones. Regionalist parties have been ineffective because they are unable to influence the centres of political and economic power in Paris. Not only have national parties adapted their message while in Brittany, but Bretons have been spectacularly successful in positioning themselves as leaders of national parties. Brittany's political elite has adapted to the French logic of territorial decentralisation.

There are some similarities with the situation in Wales, where Welsh politicians also reached the heights of political power by operating through the national parties, first the Liberals, latterly Labour. The critical distinguishing marker in Wales related to the existence of a powerful Nationalist Party whose core electorate is the Welsh-speaking heartland of north-west and mid-Wales. The influence of Plaid Cymru can be measured by the issues placed upon the political agenda, as well as the pressure placed upon other party players to incorporate explicit territorial demands in their programmes. In the Welsh case, cleavages are deeply embedded and there is a real debate between independentists, devolutionists and unionists. Support for enhanced devolution (and even more so independence) is party political, with a powerful regionalist party mobilising support for more enhanced devolutionary solutions and maintaining pressure on the other parties. Voting choice clearly influences attitudes towards independence, as does competency in the Welsh language. Unlike in Wales, Breton identity is not a diacritical political marker of difference. Bretons can vote for any party (save the FN) while retaining their dual sense of Breton and French identity. There is a latent Breton consciousness, although this is not a political resource that can be mobilised by regionalist political parties. But beyond that, it can be said that regional capacity in Brittany prospers because the prevalent mode of regional advocacy has proved to be very effective and because the political opportunity structure has pre-empted the development of a regionalist party.

Regional governance in Wales, on the other hand, is driven by the dynamic of polity building and the explicit attempt to construct the devolved political institutions as the focus of identities. This enterprise has been only partially successful. All parties now accept that the Assembly is here to stay. The fate of the Richard Commission report demonstrates, however, that the overarching party and national (UK) context remains a powerful countervailing force.

Welsh Labour members of the Westminster parliament were in the forefront of those opposing the Richard report, with the ruling Labour Party itself deeply divided on the issue.

Environmental constraints and opportunities

Understanding regional governance in Wales, Brittany or any other region requires cognisance of the overarching context within which regional institutions operate and the interplay between micro-, meso- and macro-level processes. Next, a brief comparison of the legal-constitutional order, provisions for asymmetry and the mode of intergovernmental relations will be undertaken. Other themes – such as Europeanisation and the influence of subnational players in the European arena – are manifestly important, but they have not formed a central focus of this comparative study. Notwithstanding the rhetoric of a Europe of the Regions, the empirical investigation reported on in this book has demonstrated that the National Assembly for Wales and the Brittany regional council were minor bit players in European Integration. Both France and the UK are the EU member-states, not the devolved or decentralised authorities. If the French State is more centralised than the British in controlling the interactions of its sub-national units with Brussels, the difference is one of degree. In neither case is there a real equivalent of the influence of German *Länder* in shaping national EU policy positions.

The legal/constitutional order

The British and French governments have devolved powers to regional assemblies; they have not transformed themselves into federal states. Though considerable circulation of ideas and policy models has been noted at the level of the two regions, the two overarching states – France and the United Kingdom – were less open to exogenous influences. Neither France nor the United Kingdom has an interest in cultivating a formal, artificial federalism of the German variety, the product of specific historical circumstances. In neither case was the Belgium model of separate community development openly embraced, nor the asymmetrical devolution of Spain, much vaunted by politicians in Wales and Brittany. The British unwritten constitution, by definition, does not embed federalism in a series of constitutionally entrenched rules. The French constitution explicitly rejects federalism in its Article 72, though it refers to subsidiarity. In both instances, legal-constitutional frameworks impose constraints and create opportunities. In the UK, First Minister Morgan has expressed his belief in the advantages for Wales of the British unwritten constitution. Pragmatic, negotiated and flexible responses have underpinned an innovative and dynamic role for Wales, which would have been more difficult in a codified context. On the other hand, the current piecemeal approach is a source of fragility, especially in the event of different political majorities in Cardiff and London. In the case of France, where all twenty-two regions are in theory treated exactly the same, there is a greater appearance of consistency, though this is rather misleading. Constitutional provisions for equality have served as a brake on the development of forms of regional distinctiveness, in a manner that would be unacceptable in the context of the UK as a Union State.

Asymmetry or uniformity?

The UK model of asymmetrical devolution has produced variable outcomes across the Kingdom: full legislative devolution in Scotland, a (suspended) devolutionary process in Northern Ireland, secondary legislative, or 'executive' devolution in Wales and a commitment to regional referendums in England. From the start, there has been an explicit distinction between the four nations forming the United Kingdom. In the French unitary context, such 'imagined communities' are less acceptable.

In France, the dominant referential frames and legal/constitutional rules combine to ensure that there is less disparity in outcomes across the territory. The lack of asymmetry in mainland France has limited the extent to which regions with strong identities can pursue distinctive institutional paths. Is this about to change? The 'special statute' clause of the 2003 constitutional reform provides potentially for a radical break with the past. The constitutional-reform bill enables the creation of authorities with a 'special statute'. There have been calls, from traditional regionalists and others, for the Brittany region to recover the Loire-Atlantique *département* (including Nantes, the historic capital of Brittany) and to restore Brittany in its historic boundaries. With the left now in control of both the Brittany administrative region and the Loire-Atlantique departmental council (for the first time ever), this issue is at the forefront of regional concerns. Alongside support for the unification of historic regions such as Brittany, Normandy and Savoie, there have also been arguments, notably by former President Giscard d'Estaing as former President of the European Convention, for the creation of a few large regions to be comparable with German *Länder*.

Modes of intergovernmentalism

Evaluating regional capacity must also refer to the overarching national administrative contexts within which meso-level authorities function, for example the style of intergovernmental relationships. The mode of inter-governmental relations in post-devolution Britain is one of informality, secrecy and incremental adjustments. Concordats, departmental guidance notes, party meetings and unwritten understandings form the core of post-devolution intergovernmental relations, along with the Joint Ministerial Committee. Whether this empiricist approach will be able to survive a change in political majority in London is a moot point.

In the case of France, intergovernmental relations are more formalised and codified. In the Breton case, the regional council operates alongside (and generally co-operates with) the French state, which deeply penetrates civil society in a manner that has no British equivalent. Decentralisation in France can in some respects be interpreted as a central response to governing complexity through 'steering at a distance'. The State-Region plans provide powerful evidence for this. The elected regions are tied into five-year contracts negotiated with the regional prefectures. Typically, the state puts pressure on the regions to allocate a proportion of regional finances to joint projects in areas such as road building or university construction, which do not fall within their official responsibilities. On the other hand, stronger state partners have vested the new regional authorities with credibility in areas such as transport, education, training and economic development. In the French context, a strong, decentred state might even be a pre-condition for the emergence of strategic regional authorities capable of assuming their responsibilities.

The development of enhanced regional capacity has had an impact upon intergovernmental relations in both countries. The responses adopted to deal with increased complexity – codified and formal, in the one case, informal and irregular in the other – represent distinctive modes of intergovernmentalism embedded in specific politico-administrative traditions, but modes which pose challenges to and are gradually reshaping these traditions.

National context and regional capacity in Wales and Brittany

Chapter 1 set out to establish comparative dynamics in Wales and Brittany. What weight should be given to national institutional and administrative traditions in both countries? How important are regionally specific explanations and how can these be conceptualised? Can distinctions be drawn between the policy issue areas and, if so, what does this tell about the operation of regional institutions in the two countries?

National institutional effects are more important than territorial effects in the case of France and Brittany, though the relationship is a two-way one.

In the case of France, the institutional balance and structure of incentives is state-centric. As a region, Brittany is replete with curious paradoxes. There is a widespread demand for more powerful regional political institutions within public opinion, and an even stronger demand amongst regional politicians. But Breton regional politicians also occupy important positions within all the leading French parties. In an ideal situation, attention would be focused upon the regional level, but in the real world, where powerful vestiges remain of the centralised model of territorial administration, Breton politicians concentrate their primary efforts on Paris. An element of ambiguity is calculated to serve Brittany's interests. Playing up Breton identity performs a useful function, insofar as it encourages the central state to channel scarce resources to its peripheral and potentially rebellious region. However deeply felt the attachment to Brittany, the motivations are primarily instrumental.

The Bretons play the Paris card well, undoubtedly, but this is a limited form of self-governance. The interpenetration of political personnel at local, regional and national levels comforts the traditional French model of exercising influence at the centre. That leading Breton politicians are also national players (the ex-President of the regional council, for example, is head of President Chirac's supporters [UMP] in the French Second Chamber) makes eminent sense in the French context, but confirms the Paris-centric distribution of resources. The absence of a specifically Breton political class is a logical consequence of the weaker form of decentralisation in France and the persistence of the tradition of multiple-office holding. Evidence has been presented from the public-opinion survey that Bretons would be willing to accept a more thoroughgoing regionalisation, which would in no sense limit their attachment to the broader French nation. As there is little or no conflict between French and Breton identities, the French government ought to be able to reform with a clear conscience.

Regional political capacity has been defined in institutional terms in Wales, more so than in Brittany

The overarching-state context also matters in the Welsh case. The 1998 'settlement' clearly establishes the Assembly as a subordinate institution. On the other hand, the Assembly has proved its ability to make a difference in policy terms and has laid a powerful claim to institutional relevance. In addition to developing institutional capacity, various other quantifiable regional effects can be denoted, such as the emergence of a specifically Welsh political class, the development of a recognisably Welsh party system and the role performed by the Assembly as a focus for territorial policy communities. In the case of

Wales and the UK, after a difficult period of apprenticeship, there is evidence that the institutions of devolution have captured a measure of popular and partisan support, including general acceptance by the main parties and by public opinion. Not even the Conservatives advocate a return to the pre-devolution arrangements, and, though Plaid Cymru and some within the Liberals and Labour would like to go further, all can operate the institutions as they stand. In the case of Wales, institutions have performed an important role in embedding ideas and creating political capacity. The initial hypothesis – that devolution would be undermined by cross-cutting linguistic, political and territorial cleavages – appears not to have been vindicated.

Though the pattern is different in Brittany, it is no less momentous. According to the 2003 *Observatoire Interrégional du Politique* survey, Bretons feel more attachment to their region than to their nation (France), thus undermining traditional republican hierarchies (Reynié, 2004). There was very strong support in the interviews for strengthening the regional political institution and for vesting the Brittany regional council with a leadership role in relation to other sub-national authorities. There is also a degree of realism about what the French State will and will not accept.

In Wales and Brittany, territorial policy communities are mediated by sectoral and institutional effects

The sectoral policy communities described by Marsh and Rhodes (1992) or Marsh and Smith (2000) do not naturally have a territorial dimension. Of the issue areas surveyed in this study, territorial policy communities are more easily identifiable in the field of regional languages than in that of training and life-long learning. Regional languages are owned by meso-level political authorities in a much more explicit way than training or lifelong learning policies. Obviously the case for Wales, this conclusion is also valid in Brittany. On the other hand, in neither region did the decentralised political authorities exercise convincing control over training and lifelong learning. In spite of differences of national context, there were many similarities between the policy communities in this area. Multi-layered policy sectors such as education and training are not easily shaped in line with the wishes of devolved or decentralised political authorities. In Wales and Brittany, territorialised policy communities are also influenced by the nature of regional political institutions. They focus their attentions more explicitly upon the National Assembly in Wales than they do upon the Brittany regional council, testament to the more advanced form of political devolution in Wales. In Brittany, there is a more explicit process of bargaining between organisations, rather than the top-down command-and-control approach experimented with, but with mixed success, in Wales.

Thus, country, sector and place all matter. In the case of the French region of Brittany, the overarching national context strongly influences the interactions of policy sector and place and distorts regional political capacity by introducing powerful state-centric incentives. In the case of Wales, the UK context is less pervasive, though its importance, if and when tested, might eventually be as great. In both Wales and Brittany, certain types of issue area are more amenable to control by regional political institutions or networks than others.

Beyond Wales and Brittany

What general lessons might be inferred from the Wales–Brittany comparison? In terms of institutions, it is possible to reason *up to a point* in terms of a spectrum. Strong regions require directly elected regional institutions with specific fields of policy responsibility, as well as a general right of policy initiative. Strong regions need to possess tax-varying powers, or else to be able to manage global budgets of the type provided by the Barnett formula for Wales and Scotland. In some respects, German *Länder* are very powerful in their areas of responsibility, but they are so deeply embedded into a system of joint decision-making and central financial control that their autonomy is circumscribed. Strong regions also need guaranteed legal or constitutional rights, something notably lacking in the case of the UK. Strong regional institutions need to act as a powerful focus for interest-group activity.

Even with such a basic definition, the spectrum of regional capacity varies, encompassing powerful regional institutions with fiscal and/or legislative powers (Scotland, the Belgian and Italian regions, the Spanish Autonomous Communities, the German *Länder*); rather less powerful bodies with secondary legislative and/or regulatory powers (Wales, Corsica); regional authorities with a shared general competency and some tax-varying powers (Brittany and the mainland French regions) and essentially honorific regions (in Portugal, Greece, the Netherlands or a number of the enlargement countries). The essential point, however, is that classification of regional authorities in terms of their legal functions is of limited value. Legal descriptions of powers are a necessary but by no means sufficient tool for appreciating regional capacity. Tax-varying powers can provide additional resources, for example, but if they are politically inoperable they are worthless. In the case of the French regions, modest tax-varying powers have been used, but they have proven to be a double-edged tool for the regions themselves, as they have encouraged central government to offload functions to local and regional authorities, and have forced the regions to take the blame for unpopular tax rises. In the case of Scotland, the tax-varying powers have not been used and would prove difficult to operationalise. Another example is that of regional legislative powers, which depend for their operation upon the nature of party politics. The most symbolic reforms enacted in Scotland since 1999 – the abolition of university tuition fees for Scottish students, or free residential care for the elderly – have been enacted as a result of Liberal Democrat pressures within the Labour/Liberal Democrat coalition. A dry legal reading tells us little. If powerful and autonomous political institutions are a sine qua non of effective regional capacity, comparative case studies are needed to test their effective functioning on the ground.

The prospects for regional capacity building are conditioned to some degree by overarching patterns of national public administration, which offer variable degrees of freedom. The French unitary and British union states offer contrasting opportunities for the construction of credible autonomous polity-building visions. In this respect, Wales benefits from a far more permissive environment than Brittany. The history of administrative decentralisation in Wales before 1999 encouraged the development of a relatively sophisticated administrative machinery which could later be placed at the service of an autonomous-minded National Assembly with its own directly elected mandate. The decentralised regional institution in Brittany has had to coexist with powerful field services of central state ministries and has had to operate within an over-crowded institutional space where *départements* and large cities vie for influence. The 'Brittany effect' is real, insofar as co-ordination is rather more effective here than in other French regions, but this is a limited form of autonomous regional development.

Ideational frameworks are essential in giving a sense to specific territories as regions or small nations. Throughout the book, the importance of diffuse underlying political and policy beliefs, especially in Brittany, has been emphasised. Herein lies a paradox. In the broadest ideational sense, the history of modernity in France links ideas of progress, social cohesion, justice with the object of a neutral and distant central state. These ideas (especially progress and social cohesion) are also those underpinning the Breton policy register. Though the role of regional actors as courtiers of these ideas is greater in Brittany than in other regions, the overarching political opportunity structure in France is state-centric. A strong sense of *regional* awareness in Brittany thus translates itself into a primary emphasis upon lobbying for the redistribution of resources and interacting with the French State, rather than upon pursuing the theme of self-government (though the latter theme is more developed than in any other mainland French region). In the case of Wales, it was not possible to diagnose an equivalent of the Breton policy register, but the development, under the impetus of devolution itself, of a powerful new narrative of Wales as a *nation* reborn was noted, widely diffused amongst political elites (though less so in public opinion).

From these general themes can be extrapolated the observation that effective *regional* governance relies upon effective and functioning regional institutions whose action is underpinned by a coherent regional narrative. Regions combine these qualities in different proportions. The most effective regional governance is typically based upon a strong sense of regional awareness and an uncomplicated linkage between identity and institutions. A strong measure of 'national-regional' identity can underpin effective regional institutions (as in Scotland), though it can also produce societal divisions which damage consensus (as in the Spanish Basque Country or, to a degree, Wales). At its best, the belief in community gives sense to this level of public administration. Comparing Wales and Brittany has the advantage of focusing upon historic regions with specific territorial identities. In both Wales and Brittany, some aspects of the small-country dynamics were uncovered ('team Wales', 'Brittany effect', 'Breton diaspora'), which the interlocutors themselves identified in small countries such as Ireland or Denmark. In both regions also there was a belief in the pertinence of the All-Wales or All-Brittany levels as appropriate given the sense of community, the size of the region and the modes of political and policy interaction.

It has also been noted that effectively functioning regional political institutions with a link to territory are the exception, rather than the rule, in France, the UK and probably most other countries as well. The examples from Germany considered in Chapter 1 went in the same direction. The *Land* governments are efficient levels of government for the formulation and delivery of services, but they do not capture the public imagination, nor do they correspond to traditional regional boundaries. Even in Spain, a powerful model for decision-makers in Wales (especially) and Brittany, the Autonomous Communities vary considerably in their ability to give a sense of territoriality to their public administrations.

Regions such as Wales and Brittany are exceptional within France and the UK. In the UK, regional institutions are likely to be limited for the foreseeable future to the Celtic nations. In France most regional councils do not correspond to specific historical regions, but were designed to avoid them. In most regions in France and the UK there is no comparable stock of historical myths upon which to found regional institutions to those available in Wales and Brittany. In most areas of France and England, there is little support or demand for regional political institutions. Political loyalties are vested in localities, cities, the nation or Europe, rather than on a regional level which where it exists, can appear as technocratic and remote. The example of the North-east of England referendum in November 2004 demonstrated how, when put to the test, hypothetical regional institutions could be squeezed between local and national loyalties. In England in particular, there would appear to be a lack of interest in regional institutions without a link to territory.

The case in France is rather different because regional councils have now existed for more than twenty years. Some French regions have developed a powerful institutional existence without a pre-existing territorial identity, either as a result of determined political leadership (Nord/Pas-de-Calais) or economic power (Rhône-Alpes, Ile-de-France). These cases are testament to the ability of effective institutions to make a difference. In other areas, regions have been much less effective. Regions are not the only contenders for the sub-central space. In both France and the UK, the city-government route can produce political leaders of international reputations, such as Bernand Delanöe in Paris or Ken Livingstone in London. Direct election of French mayors ensures that the mayoral office, rather than the presidency of a departmental or a regional council, continues to be the most coveted amongst politicians with a base in local government. In larger cities in France and the UK, city-based administrations can emerge as powerful competitors to elected or imaginary regions.

In the light of the referendum result in north-east England, it would be hazardous to accept the description of the UK as a whole as a model of asymmetrical devolution or quasi-federalism. The character of the United Kingdom as a Union State, however, has undoubtedly been strengthened by its experience of devolution and by the redefining of the implicit contractual relationship between its four component nations. Contemporary France, on the other hand, remains wedded to a model of the unitary state that has proved remarkably resilient and which forces regional players to adopt multiple strategies in order to survive.

The intention in this final chapter has been to deepen an understanding of processes of comparative regional governance. A framework for analysis has been offered for combining criteria drawn from institutions, relationships, identities, political opportunity structures and environmental constraints and opportunities. If Welsh devolution is above all shaped by the institutional avenues opened in the Government of Wales Act of 1998, regional capacity in Brittany is built upon a dense network of relationships and tested forms of horizontal and vertical linkage. The linkage between identity, territory and institutions is primordial for comparing regions, the Wales-Brittany comparison suggesting that strong regional identities are important for building institutions, but that divided identities do not necessarily add value to regional political institutions. Political opportunity structures are vital for understanding comparative regional dynamics, notably the political space available for the development of a regionalist party, the interlocking of regional and social movements and the structure of incentives for regional players to engage in local, regional, national or European games. Understanding regional governance, finally, requires cognisance of the overarching environment: the importance of constitutional rules, mechanisms of financial transfer, inter-institutional linkages, the capacity of central government to intervene in devolved areas or the Europeanisation of specific policy sectors. Environmental constraints weigh heavily in both regions, but the model of territorial administration and the political opportunity structure in France is more state-centric than in Wales. As in the case of Wales and Brittany, processes of regional political capacity building in other regions can best be comprehended by combining explanations based on institutions, relationships, identities, political opportunity structures and environmental constraints and opportunities.

Bibliography

Adams, J. and Robinson, P. (2002) (eds) *Devolution in Practice: Public Policy Differences within the UK* London: IPPR/ESRC.

Arthur, P. (2003) *The Government and Politics of Northern Ireland* London: Longman.

Ascher, F. (1998) *La République contre la ville: Essai sur l'avenir de la France urbaine* Paris: Editions de l'Aube.

Ashford, D. (1982) *British Dogmatism and French Pragmatism: Central-local Policymaking in the Welfare State* London: Allen & Unwin.

Balme, R. (1999) *Les Politiques de néo-régionalisme* Paris: Economica.

Balsom, D and Burch, M. (1980) *A Political and Electoral Handbook for Wales* Farnborough: Gower.

Baudewyns, P. and Dandoy, R. (2003) 'Federalism and Social Security in Belgium', *European Consortium for Political Research* (ECPR), Edinburgh University, 28 March–2 April.

Benz, A. (1998) 'German Regions in the European Union: From Joint Policy-making to Multi-level Governance'. In P. Le Galès and C. Lequesne (eds) *Regions in Europe* London: Routledge.

Berthet, T. and Merle, V. (1999) *Les Régions et la formation professionnelle* Paris : LGDJ.

Biarez, S. (1989) *Le Pouvoir local* Paris: Economica.

Boeuf, J.-L. (2004) *Les Collectivités territoriales et la décentralisation* Paris: Documentation française.

Boguenard, J. (2004) *La Décentralisation* Paris: Presses Universitaires de France (PUF).

Breuillard, M. and Cole, A. (2003) *La Gouvernance locale du changement éducatif en Angleterre et en France* Paris: l'Harmattan.

Brown, P., Green A. and Lauder, H. (2001) *High Skills: Globalisation, Competitiveness and Skill Formation* Oxford: Oxford University Press.

Bulpitt, J. (1983) *Territory and Power in the United Kingdom* Manchester: Manchester University Press.

Burch, M. and Gomez, R. (2002) 'The English Regions and the European Union' *Regional Studies* 436:7, 767–778.

Canevet, C. (1992) *Le Modèle agricole breton* Rennes: Presses Universitaires de Rennes.

Caro, P. (1998) 'La Dimension régionale de la relation formation-emploi des jeunes' *L'Information Géographique* 5, 203–215.

Carter, C. and Scott, A. (2003) 'Making Multi-level Governance Work: The View from the Devolved Administrations'. Paper to the Political Studies Association conference 15–17 April, 13 pp.

Chartier, E. and Larvor, R. (2003) *La France éclatée?* Spézet: Coop Breizh.

Chavrier, G. (2004) 'L'expérimentation locale: vers un État subsidiaire?' Paper presented to the GRALE colloquium on *Réforme de la Décentralisation, Réforme de l'État*, National Assembly, Paris, 22–23 January.

Cheney, P., Hall, T. and Pithouse, A. (eds) (2001) *Post-Devolution Wales: New Governance – New Democracy?* Cardiff: University of Wales Press.

Christiansen, T. (1998) 'Plaid Cymru: Dilemmas and Ambiguities of Welsh Regional Nationalism'. In L. de Winter and H. Tursan (eds) *Regionalist Parties in Western Europe* London: Routledge, pp. 125–142.

Clift, B. (2003) *French Socialism in a Global Era* London: Continuum.

Cole, A. (1999) 'Les réseaux et l'espace publique: leçons de France et de Grande-Bretagne'. In B. François and E. Neveu (eds) *Espaces publics mosaïques: Acteurs, arènes et rhétoriques des débats publics contemporains* Rennes: Presses Universitaires de Rennes.

Cole, A. (2001) 'The New Governance of French Education' *Public Administration* 79:3, 707–724.

Cole, A. (2004) 'Devolution and Decentralisation in Wales and Brittany, 2001–2002', UK Data Archive (*www.data-archive.ac.uk*), Study Number 4802.

Cole, A. and John, P. (2001) *Local Governance in England and France* London: Routledge.

Cole, A. and Loughlin, J. (2003) 'Beyond the Unitary State? Political Institutions, Public Policy and Public Opinion in Brittany' *Regional Studies* 37:3, 265–276.

Cole, A. and Storer, A. (2002) 'Political Dynamics in the Assembly: An Emerging Policy Community'. In J. Barry Jones and J. Osmond (eds) *Building a Civic Culture* Cardiff: Institute of Welsh Affairs.

Cole, A. and Williams, C. (2004) 'Identities, Institutions and Lesser Used Languages in Wales and Brittany' *Regional and Federal Studies* 14:4, 1–26.

Cole, A., Jones, J. B., and Storer, A. (2003) 'Inside the National Assembly for Wales' *Political Quarterly* 74:2, 223–232.

Cole, A., Jones, J. B., Loughlin, J., Storer, A. and Williams, C. (2003) 'Political Institutions, Policy Preferences and Public Opinion in Wales and Brittany' *Contemporary Wales* 16, 88–110.

Collier, D. (1991) 'The Comparative Method: Two Decades of Change'. In D. A. Rustow and K. P. Ericson (eds) *Comparative Political Dynamics* New York: HarperCollins.

Comas, J. M. (2003) 'Spain: The 1978 Constitution and Centre–Periphery Relations'. In J. Ruane, J. Todd and A. Mandeville (eds) *Europe's Old States in the New World Order: The Politics of Transition in Britain, France and Spain* Dublin: University of Dublin Press.

Conseil Régional de Bretagne (2000) *Contrat de Plan Etat-Région Bretagne, 2000–2006* Rennes: Conseil Régional de Bretagne.

Conseil Régional de Bretagne (2002) *Plan Régional Ariane 2 en Bretagne* Rennes: Conseil Régional de Bretagne.

Conseil Régional de Bretagne (2004) *Projet de budget primitif 2004* Rennes: Conseil Régional de Bretagne.

Cooke, P. (2003) 'Devolution and Economic Development in Wales'. Paper presented to the Economic and Social Research Council conference on Devolution in Wales, Cardiff University, 18 March 2003.

Cooke, P. and Morgan, K. (1998) *The Associational Economy* Oxford: Oxford University Press.

Cressard, J.-P. (2000) *Quand la Bretagne s'est réveillée* Spézet: Coop Breizh.

Crozier, M. (1992) 'La décentralisation est-elle une réforme de l'Etat?' *Pouvoirs Locaux* 12, 130–134.

Dargent, C. (2001) 'Identités régionales et aspirations politiques: l'exemple de la France aujourd'hui' *Revue Française de Science Politique* 51:5, 787–806.

DATAR (2003) *Une Nouvelle Politique de l'aménagement du territoire et de la décentralisation* Paris: Documentation française.

Denez, P. (1998) 'Brittany: A Language in Search of a Future' European Bureau of Lesser Used Languages: Dublin.

De Rinck, S. (1998) 'Civic Culture and Institutional Performance of the Belgian Regions'. In P. Le Galès and C. Lequesne (eds) *Regions in Europe* London: Routledge, pp. 199–218.

Devine, F. (1995) 'Qualitative Analysis'. In D. Marsh and G. Stoker (eds) *Theory and Methods in Political Science* London Macmillan, pp. 137–153.

Dogan, M. and Kazancigil, A. (eds) (1994) *Strategies in Comparative Research* Oxford: Blackwell.

Dogan, M. and Pelassy, D. (1990) *How to Compare Nations: Strategies in Comparative Politics* New Jersey: Chatham House.

Dolowitz, D. and Marsh, D. (1996) 'Who Learns What from Whom: A Review of the Policy Transfer Literature' *Political Studies* 44:4, 343–357.

Dolowitz, D. and Marsh, D. (2000) 'Learning from Abroad: The Role of Policy Transfer in Contemporary Policy-Making' *Governance* 13:1, 5–24.

Dowding, K. (1995) *The Civil Service* London: Routledge.

Duclaud-Williams, R. (1993) 'The Governance of Education in Britain and France'. In J. Koojman (ed.) *Modern Governance* London: Sage, pp. 235–248.

Dupoirier, E. (1998) *Régions, la croisée des chemins* Paris: Presses de Sciences Po.

Duran, P. and Thoenig, J.-C. (1996) 'L'état et la gestion publique territoriale' *Revue Française de Science Politique* 45:4, 580–622.

Durand-Pringborne, C. (2003) 'A propos de la politique de décentralisation: vers de nouveaux transferts de compétences en éducation et formation?' *Actualité Juridique-Droit Administratif* 2, 65–71.

Dutercq, Y. (2000) *Politiques éducatives et évaluation: querelles de territoires* Paris: PUF.

Dyson, K. (1980) *The State Tradition in Western Europe* Oxford: Martin Robertson.

Elias, A. (2004) 'From Full National Status to Independence in Europe: The Case of Plaid Cymru – the Party of Wales'. Paper presented at the European University Institute conference on Minority Nations and European Integration, Florence, Italy, 7–8 May.

Evans, D. G. (2000) *A History of Wales, 1906–2000* Cardiff: University of Wales Press.

Evans, M. and Davies, J. (1999) 'Understanding Policy Transfer: A Multi-Level, Multi-Disciplinary Perspective' *Public Administration* 77:2, 361–385.

Eymeri, J.-M. (2003) 'Définir la position de la France dans l'Union européenne: La Médiation interministérielle des généralistes du SGCI'. In A. Smith (ed.) *Le*

Gouvernement du compromis: courtiers et généralistes dans l'action politique Paris: Economica, pp. 149–175.

Favereau, F. (1993) *Bretagne contemporaine: Langue, culture, identité* Rennes: Skol Breizh.

Field, A. (2000) *Discovering Statistics Using SPSS for Windows* London: Sage.

Flatres, P. (1986) *La Bretagne* Paris: PUF.

Flora, P., Kuhnle, S. and Urwin, D. (1999) *State Formation, Nation-Building and Mass Politics in Europe* Oxford: Oxford University Press.

Fontaine, J. (1992) 'Une région, des lycées, un rectorat: l'incidence politique de la décentralisation en Bretagne' *Savoir* 4:4, 669–691.

Fontaine, J. and Warin, P. (2000) 'Retour des évaluations: les politiques publiques territorialisées entre affichage et incertitude de leur régionalisation' *Pole-Sud* 12, 1–12.

Ford, C. (1993) *Creating the Nation in Provincial France: Religion and Political Identity in Brittany* Princeton: Princeton University Press.

Foster, J. J. (2001) *Data Analysis: Using SPSS for Windows* London: Sage.

Fourcade, B., Ourliac, G. and Ourtau, M. (1993) 'ARGOS: Une démarche d'aide à la décision en matière de formation professionnelle'. In CEREQ *La Décentralisation de la formation: marché du travail, institutions, acteurs.* Collection des Etudes 64, 141–161.

Fournier, B. (1995) 'La formation professionnelle gérée par les conseils régionaux: d'une décentralisation à l'autre' *Premières Synthèses* 55:100, 1–8.

François, B. and Neveu, E. (eds) (1999) *Espaces publics mosaïques: acteurs, arènes et rhétoriques des débats publics contemporains* Rennes: Presses Universitaires de Rennes.

Fréville, Y. (2004) 'Les transferts de compétences'. Communication presented to the GRALE colloquium on *Réforme de la Décentralisation, Réforme de l'Etat*, National Assembly, Paris, 22–23 January.

Galliou, P. and Jones, M. (1996) *The Bretons* Oxford: Blackwell.

Gaudemet, Y. and Gohin, O. (2004) *La République décentralisée*, Paris: Editions Panthéon-Assas.

Gaudin, J.-P. (1999) *Gouverner par contrat: l'action publique en question* Paris: Presses de Sciences Po.

Gaudin, J.-P. (2002) *Pourquoi la gouvernance?* Paris: Presses de Sciences Po.

Gemie, S. (2001) 'The *Marée noire*, Vintage 1999: Ecology, Regional Identity and Politics in Contemporary France' *Modern and Contemporary France* 9:1, 71–86.

Gemie, S. (2002) 'The Politics of Language: Debates and Identities in Contemporary Brittany' *French Cultural Studies* 13:38, 145–164.

Gourvil, F. (1952) *Langue et littérature bretonnes* Paris: PUF.

Hall, P. (1986) *Governing the Economy: The Politics of State Intervention in Britain and France* Cambridge: Polity.

Hall, P. and Taylor, R. (1996) 'Political Science and the Three New Institutionalisms', *Political Studies* 44:4, 936–957.

Hanley, D. (1984) *Keeping Left: CERES and the French Socialist Party* Manchester: Manchester University Press.

Harding, A. (1998) 'American Urban Political Economy, Urban Theory and UK Research'. Paper presented to the UK Political Studies Association Conference, University of Keele, 11 pp.

Heald, D. and McLeod, A. (2002) 'Beyond Barnett? Financing Devolution'. In J. Adams and P. Robinson (eds) *Devolution in Practice: Public Policy Differences within the UK* London: IPPR/ESRC, pp. 147–175.

Heclo, H. and Wildavsky, A. (1974) *The Private Government of Public Money* London: Macmillan.

Heinz, W. (1994) *Partenariats publics-privés dans l'aménagement urbain* Paris: L'Harmattan.

Hirst, P. and Thomson, G. (1999) *Globalisation in Question* Cambridge: Polity.

Hoare, R. (2000) 'Linguistic Competence and Regional Identity in Brittany: Attitudes and Perceptions of Identity' *Journal of Multilingual and Multicultural Development* 21:4.

Hoffmann-Martinot, V. (1999) 'Les grandes villes françaises: une démocratie en souffrance'. In O. Gabriel and V. Hoffmann-Martinot (eds) *Démocraties urbaines: l'état de la démocratie dans les grandes villes de 12 démocraties urbaines* Paris: L'Harmattan.

Howarth, D. (ed.) (2001) 'Comparing Public Administrative Reform in France and the UK' Special issue of *Public Policy and Administration* 16:4.

Huggins, R., Morgan, K. and Rees, G. (2000) 'Devolution and Development: The Welsh Assembly and the Governance of Regional Economic Policy'. Welsh Governance Centre working paper no. 1, Cardiff University, 2000.

Institut Français d'Opinion Publique (1994) 'Les français et les langues régionales' Paris: IFOP, 5 April, PC/MCD No. 1.365. 27 pp.

INSEE (2003) *Tableaux de l'économie française* Paris: Documentation française.

James, O. and Lodge, M. (2003) 'The Limitations of "Policy Transfer" and "Lesson Drawing" for Public Policy Research' *Political Studies Review* 1, 179–193.

Jeffery, C. (2000) 'Sub-national Mobilisations and European Integration' *Journal of Common Market Studies* 38:1, 1–23.

Jeffery, C. (2004a) 'Devolution: What Difference has it Made?' Economic and Social Research Council (ESRC) Briefing Paper, February.

Jeffery, C. (2004b) 'The Report of the Richard Commission: An Evaluation'. ESRC Briefing Paper no. 12, June 2004, ESRC Devolution and Constitutional Change Programme, 4 pp.

Jobert, B. and Muller, P. (1987) *L'Etat en action: politiques publiques et corporatisme* Paris: PUF.

John, P. (2001) *Local Governance in Western Europe* London: Sage.

John, P. and Cole, A. (2000) 'When do Countries, Sectors and Localities Matter?' *Comparative Political Studies* 33:2, 248–268.

Jones, J. B. (1986) 'Welsh Local Government: A Blueprint for Regionalism?' *Local Government Studies* 12:4, 61–74.

Jones, J. B. (1990) 'The Welsh Office: A Political Expedient or an Administrative Innovation?' *Transactions of the Royal Society of Cymmrodorion* Cardiff.

Jones, J. B. (2000) 'Changes to the Government of Wales, 1979–1997'. In J. B. Jones and D. Balsom (eds) *The Road to the Assembly* Cardiff: University of Wales Press.

Jones, J. B. (2003) 'Wales and the European Union: Refining a Relationship'. In J. Majone (ed.) *Regional Institutions and Governance in the European Union* London and Westport CT: Praeger, pp. 120–133.

Jones, J. B. and Balsom, D. (2000) (eds) *The Road to the Assembly* Cardiff: University of Wales Press.

Jones, J. B. and Osmond, J. (eds) (2000) *Inclusive Government and Party Management* Cardiff: Institute of Welsh Affairs.

Jones, J. B. and Osmond, J. (eds) (2002) *Building a Civic Culture* Cardiff: Institute of Welsh Affairs.

Jouve, B. (1995) 'Réseaux et communautés politiques'. In P. Le Galès and M. Thatcher (eds) *Les Réseaux de politiques publiques* Paris: L'Harmattan, pp. 121–140.

Jouve, B. and Négrier, E. (eds) (1998) *Que gouvernent les régions d'Europe* Paris: l'Harmattan.

Julien, C. (1998) *Les Politiques régionales de formation professionnelle continue* Paris: L'Harmattan.

Kassim, H. (2000) 'The United Kingdom'. In H. Kassim, B. G. Peters and V. Wright (eds) *The National Co-ordination of EU Policy: The Domestic Level* Oxford: Oxford University Press.

Keating, M. (1998) *The New Regionalism in Western Europe: Territorial Restructuring and Political Change* Cheltenham: Edward Elgar.

Keating, M. and Loughlin, J. (2004) 'Territorial Policy Communities in the United Kingdom' EUI (European University Institute) Working Paper, SPS No. 2002/1, European University Institute, Florence, Italy.

Keating, M. and McGarry, J. (eds) (2001) *Minority Nationalism in the Changing State Order* Oxford: Oxford University Press.

Keating, M., Loughlin, J. and Deschouwer, K. (2003) *The New Regionalism in Europe: A Comparative Study of Eight Regions* Cheltenham: Edward Elgar.

Kingdom, J. (1991) *Government and Politics in Britain* Cambridge: Polity.

Kooiman, J. (ed.) (1993) *Modern Governance* London: Sage.

Kooiman, J. (2003) *Governing and Governance* London: Sage.

Laffin, M. (2002) *A New Partnership? The National Assembly for Wales and Local Government* York: Joseph Rowntree Foundation.

Laffin, M. and Thomas, A. (2000) 'Designing the National Assembly for Wales' *Parliamentary Affairs* 53:3, 557–576.

Laffin, M. and Thomas, A. (2001) 'New Ways of Working: Political–Official Relations in the National Assembly for Wales' *Public Money and Management* 21:2, 45–51.

Laffin, M., Shaw, E. and Taylor, G. (forthcoming) 'The Role of the Labour Party in Intergovernmental Relations'. In Alan Trench (ed.) *Devolution and Power in the UK* Manchester: Manchester University Press.

Lagrée, M. (1988) 'Les Bretons, Dieu et la modernité de 1789 à nos jours'. In Institut Culturel de Bretagne, *Bretagne: Clés en mains*. Rennes: Institut Culturel de Bretagne.

Lagroye, J. (1973) *Société et Politique: Jacques Chaban-Delmas à Bordeaux* Paris: Pédone.

Lagroye, J. and Wright, V. (eds) (1979) *Local Government in Britain and France* London: Allen & Unwin.

Lambert, D. and Navarro, M. (2004) 'The Legislative Scope of the Assembly'. Paper presented to the ESRC conference on 'Devolution in Wales: the Scorecard', 24 June 2004.

Lash, S. and Urry, J. (1994) *Economies of Signs and Space* London: Sage.

Lebesque, M. (1970) *Comment peut-on être breton?* Paris: Seuil.

Le Bourdennec, Y. (1996) *Le Miracle breton* Paris: Calmann-Lévy.

Le Coadic, R. (1998) *L'Identité bretonne* Rennes: Presses Universitaires de Rennes.

Le Faou, P. and Latour, J-L. (2000) *La Dynamique culturelle bretonne* Rennes: Conseil Economique et Social de Bretagne.

Le Galès, P. (1993) *Politique urbaine et développement local* Paris, L'Harmattan.

Le Galès, P. (1995) 'Du gouvernement local à la gouvernance urbaine' *Revue Française de Science Politique*, 45:1, 57–95.

Le Galès, P. (1999) 'Crise de gouvernance et globalisation' *Revue Internationale de Politique Comparée* 6:3, 627–652.

Le Galès, P. (2002) *European Cities: Social Conflicts and Governance* Oxford: Oxford University Press.

Le Galès, P. and Lequesne, C. (eds) (1998) *Regions in Europe* London: Routledge.

Le Galès, P. and Thatcher, M. (eds) (1995) *Les Réseaux de politiques publiques* Paris: L'Harmattan.

Le Guirrec, P. (1994) *Le Pouvoir en campagne: formes locales du politique en Bretagne* Rennes: Apogée.

Le Nail, B. (1996) 'L'identité bretonne', *Pouvoirs Locaux*, 31:4, 85–92.

Les Echos (2003) 'La France des Regions'. Special issue, 8 March.

Le Télégramme de Brest (2001) 'Le breton tel qu'on le parle'. Supplement to the *Télégramme de Brest*, 10 April.

Levy, J. (2001) 'Territorial Politics after Decentralization'. In A. Guyomarch, H. Machin, P. Hall and J. Hayward (eds) *Developments in French Politics 2* Basingstoke: Palgrave, pp. 92–115.

Loughlin, J. (2000) 'Regional Autonomy and State Paradigm Shift in Western Europe' *Regional and Federal Studies* 10:2, 10–34.

Loughlin, J. (ed.) (2001) *Subnational Democracy in the European Union: Challenges and Opportunities* Oxford: Oxford University Press.

Loughlin, J. and. Keating, M. (eds) (1997) *The Political Economy of Regionalism.* London: Frank Cass.

Loughlin, J. and Mazey, S. (eds) (1995) *The End of the French Unitary State? Ten Years of Regionalization in France* London: Frank Cass.

Loughlin, J. and Peters, B. G. (1997) 'State Traditions and Regional Reform'. In M. Keating and J. Loughlin (eds) *The Political Economy of Regionalism* London: Frank Cass.

Mabileau, A. (1997) 'Les génies invisibles du local: Faux-semblants et dynamiques de la décentralisation' *Revue Française de Science Politique* 47:3–4, 340–376.

Majone, J. (ed.) (2003) *Regional Institutions and Governance in the European Union* London and Westport CT: Praeger.

March, J. and Olsen, J. (1989) *Rediscovering Institutions* New York: Free Press.

Marcou, G. (1992) 'Les collectivités territoriales et l'éducation nationale' *Savoir* 4:2, 189–215.

Marcou, G. (ed.) (2003) *Les Régions en Europe, entre l'État et les collectivités locales* Paris: Ministry of the Interior.

Marin, B. and Mayntz, R. (eds) (1991) *Policy Networks* Frankfurt: Campus.

Marinetto, M. (2001) 'The New Settlement and the Process of Devolution: Territorial Politics and Governance under the Welsh Assembly' *Political Studies* 49:2, 306–322.

Marsh, D. and Rhodes, R. A. W. (eds) (1992) *Policy Networks in British Government* Oxford: Clarendon.

Marsh, D. and Smith, M. (2000) 'Understanding Policy Networks: Towards a Dialectical Approach' *Political Studies* 48:1, 4–21.

Martray, J. (1983) *Vingt ans qui transformèrent la Bretagne: L'épopée du CELIB* Paris: France Empire.

Mayntz, R. (1993) 'Governing Failures and the Problem of Governability: Some Comments on a Theoretical Paradigm'. In J. Kooiman (ed.) (1993) *Modern Governance* London: Sage.

Mazey, S. (1995) 'French Regions and the European Union'. In J. Loughlin and S. Mazey (eds) *The End of the French Unitary State?* London: Frank Cass.

McAllister, L. (2000) 'The New Politics in Wales: Rhetoric or Reality?' *Parliamentary Affairs* 53:3, 591–604.

McDonald, M. (1989) *We Are Not French* London: Routledge.

McEwen, N. (2003) 'Welfare Solidarity in a Devolved Scotland'. European Consortium for Political Research, University of Edinburgh, 28 March–2 April, 18 pp.

McEwen, N. and Moreno, L. (eds) (2005) *The Territorial Politics of Welfare* London: Routledge.

McKenzie, W. J. M. (1973) *Political Identity* London: Allen & Unwin.

Mény, Y. (ed.) (1990) *Les Politiques décentralisées de l'éducation: analyse de quatre expériences régionales* GRAL-CNRS report for the French Ministry of the Interior.

Michel, H. (1992) *Les Politiques de formation professionnelle continue et d'apprentissage du Conseil régional de Bretagne, 1983–1991.* Rennes: DEA thesis, University of Rennes 1.

Mitchell, J. (2004) 'Core Executive and Devolution', *Conference of Europeanists*, 11–13 March, Palmer House Hilton, Chicago,

Monnier, J.-J. (1994) *Le Comportement politique des Bretons* Rennes: Presses Universitaires de Rennes.

Moreno, L. and McEwen, N. (2003) 'The Welfare State and Territorial Politics: An Under-explored Relationship'. European Consortium for Political Research, University of Edinburgh, 28 March–2 April, 43 pp.

Morgan, K. O. (1982) *A History of Modern Wales* Cardiff: University of Wales Press.

Morgan, K. and Mungham, G. (2000) *Redesigning Democracy: The Making of the National Assembly for Wales* Bridgend: Poetry Wales Press.

Morvan, Y. (1997) *Demain, La Bretagne ou La métamorphose du modèle breton* Rennes: Editions Apogée.

Muret, J.-P. (1994) *Connaître le Conseil Régional* Paris: La Découverte.

National Assembly for Wales (1998) 'Concordat on European Affairs' Cardiff: National Assembly for Wales.

National Assembly for Wales (2001) *BetterWales.com* Cardiff: National Assembly for Wales.

National Assembly for Wales (2001) *The Learning Country: A Comprehensive Education and Lifelong Learning Programme to 2010 in Wales* Cardiff: National Assembly for Wales.

National Assembly for Wales (2002a) *Our Language: Its Future* Culture Committee Report, Cardiff: National Assembly for Wales.

National Assembly for Wales (2002b) *Dyfodol Dwyieithog: Bilingual Future* Cardiff: National Assembly for Wales.

National Assembly for Wales (2004) *Report of the Richard Commission* Cardiff: National Assembly for Wales.

Nay, O. (1997) *La Région, une institution: La représentation, le pouvoir et la règle dans l'espace régional* Paris, l'Harmattan.

Négrier, E. and Jouve, B. (eds) *Que gouvernent les régions d'Europe? Échanges politiques et mobilisations* Paris: L'Harmattan.

Nicolas, M. (1982) *Histoire du mouvement breton (Emsav)* Paris: Syros.

Nicolas, M. (1986) *Le Séparatisme en Bretagne* Brasparts: Editions Beltan.

Nicolas, M. (2004) 'Breton Identity Highlighted by European Integration'. Paper presented to the Conference of 'Nations, Minorities and European Integration', European University Institute, Florence, Italy, 7–8 May 2004, 17 pp.

L'Observatoire Interrégional du Politique (1995, 1996, 1997, 1998, 1999, 2000, 2001, 2002, 2003) *Le Fait régional* Paris: OIP.

Ohnet, J.-M. (1996) *Histoire de la décentralisation française* Paris: Hachette.

Osmond, J. (2001) 'The Engima of the Corporate Body'. In J. B. Jones and J. Osmond (eds) *Inclusive Government and Party Management* Cardiff: Institute of Welsh Affairs.

Page, E. (1991) *Localism and Centralism in Europe* Oxford: Oxford University Press.

Page, E. and Goldsmith, M. (1987) *Central and Local Government Relations* Beverly Hills: Sage.

Parkinson, M., Bianchini, F., Dawson, J., Evans, R. and Harding, A. (1992) *Urban Change and the Function of Cities in Europe: A Report to the European Commission of the European Communities* Liverpool: Liverpool John Moores University.

Parry, R. (2001) 'Devolution, Integration and Modernisation in the United Kingdom Civil Service' *Public Policy and Administration* 16:3, 53–67.

Pasquier, R. (2004) *La Capacité politique des régions: Une comparaison France/ Espagne* Rennes: Presses Universitaires de Rennes.

Patchett, K. (2000) 'The New Welsh Constitution: The Government of Wales Act 1998'. In J. Barry Jones and D. Balsom (eds) *The Road to the National Assembly for Wales* Cardiff: University of Wales Press.

Patton, M. Q. (1990) *Qualitative Evaluation and Research Methods* London: Sage.

Pearce, G. and Martin, S. (2003) 'Building Multilevel Governance in Britain? The Engagement of Subnational Government in EU Programs and Policies'. In J. Majone (ed.) *Regional Institutions and Governance in the European Union* Westport CT and London: Praeger.

Peters, B. G. (1999) *Institutional Theory in Political Science: The 'New Institutionalism'* London: Cassell.

Phlipponneau, M. (1977) *Changer la vie, changer la ville* Rennes: Skol Breiz.

Phlipponneau, M. (1993) *Le Modèle industriel breton 1950–2000* Rennes: Presses Universitaires de Rennes.

Pierre, J. (ed.) (2000) *Debating Governance* Oxford: Oxford University Press.

Pillet, B. (2001) 'La Bretagne: un modèle? Non, un exemple' *Ouest-France*, 23 November.

Poignant, B. (1998) *Langues et cultures régionales: rapport au Premier ministre* Paris: Documentation française.

Pontier, J.-M. (1998) *Les Contrats de plan entre l'État et les régions* Paris: PUF.

Poussier, J-L. (1997) *Bretagne* Paris: LEC Edition.

Powell, W. and DiMaggio, P. (1991) *The New Institutionalism in Organisational Analysis* Chicago: University of Chicago Press.

Przeworski, A. and Teune, H. (1970) *The Logic of Comparative Social Inquiry* New York: Free Press.

Putnam, R. (1993) *Making Democracy Work: Civic Traditions in Modern Italy* Princeton: Princeton University Press.

Ragin, C. (1987) *The Comparative Method: Moving Beyond Quantitative and Qualitative Strategies* Berkeley: University of California Press.

Randles, S. (2001) 'Geographies of Collective Reflexivity? Thinking Futures, Doing Urban Governance and Influencing Economic Development in Manchester and Lyons'. Unpublished paper presented to the First European Conference of the *Observatoire International de Prospective Régionale* Lille, France.

Rapport Mauroy (2000) *Refonder l'action publique locale : rapport au Premier ministre* Paris : La Documentation française.

Rawlings, R. (1998) 'The New Model Wales' *Journal of Law and Society* 25:4, 461–509.

Rawlings, R. (2001) 'Quasi-legislative Devolution: Powers and Principles'. Unpublished paper considered by the *Assembly Review of Procedure* ARP-04-01 (P3), 22 pp.

Rawlings, R. (2003) *Delineating Wales* Cardiff: University of Wales Press.

Rees, G. (2002) 'Devolution and the Restructuring of Post-16 Education and Training in the UK'. In J. Adams and P. Robinson (eds) *Devolution in Practice: Public Policy Differences within the UK* London: IPPR/ESRC, pp. 104–114.

Reynié, D. (2004) 'L'Apport des assises des libertés locales'. Paper presented to the GRALE colloquium on *Réforme de la Décentralisation, Réforme de l'Etat*, National Assembly, Paris, 22–23 January.

Reynolds, D. (2002) 'Developing Differently: Education Policy in England, Wales, Scotland and Nortnern Ireland'. In J. Adams and P. Robinson (eds) *Devolution in Practice: Public Policy Differences within the UK* London: Institute of Public Policy Research, pp. 93–103.

Rhodes, R. A. W. (1997) *Understanding Governance: Policy Networks, Governance, Reflexivity and Accountability* Buckingham: Open University Press.

Richard, B. (2001) 'Oui au Breton s'il n'est pas obligatoire' *Ouest-France*, 23 November, p. 8.

Richardson, J. (1996) 'Actor-based Models of National and EU Policy Making'. In H. Kassim and A. Menon *The European Union and National Industrial Policy* London: Routledge, pp. 27–51.

Richardson, J. J. and Jordan, G. (1979) *Governing under Pressure* London: Martin Robertson.

Rokkan, S. and Urwin, D. (1982) *The Politics of Territorial Identity* London: Sage.

Romani, C., Richard, A. and Méhaut, P. (1997) 'Décentralisation de la Formation professionnelle et coordination de l'action publique' *Travail et Emploi* 73:4, 97–109.

Rose, R. (1993) *Lesson-drawing in Public Policy: a Guide to Learning across Time and Space* New Jersey: Chatham House.

Ruane, J., Todd, J. and Mandeville, A. (eds) (2003) *Europe's Old States in the New World Order: The Politics of Transition in Britain, France and Spain* Dublin: University of Dublin Press.

Sabatier, P. (1999) *Theories of the Policy Process* Boulder CO: Westview.

Sadran, P. (1992) *Le Système administratif français* Paris: Montchrestien.

Sandford, M. and Maer, L. (2003) 'Scrutiny under Devolution: Committees in Scotland, Wales and Northern Ireland' London: The Constitution Unit, University College London, 51 pp.

Sartori, G. (1991) 'Comparing and Miscomparing' *Journal of Theoretical Politics* 3:3, 243–257.

Sawicki, F. (1993) *La Structuration du Parti socialiste: Milieux partisans et production d'identités* Paris: PhD thesis, University of Paris 1.

Scharpf, F. W., Reissert, B. and Schnabel, F. (1976) *Politikverflechtung: Theorie und Empirie des kooperativen Föderalismus in der Bundesrepublik* Kronberg: Scriptor.

Schlesinger, P. (1998) 'L'ecosse fait sa révolution tranquille' *Le Monde Diplomatique*, April.

Schmidt, V. (1990) *Democratizing France: The Political and Administrative History of Decentralization* Cambridge: Cambridge University Press.

Schnapper, D. (1994) *La Communauté des citoyens: sur l'idée moderne des nations* Paris: Gallimard.

Scully, R. (2003) 'Coming Home to Labour? The 2003 Welsh Assembly Election'. Paper presented to the Annual Conference of EPOP, Cardiff, 12–14 September.

Scully, R. and Wyn Jones, R. (2003) 'A Settling Will? Wales and Devolution Five Years On' *British Elections and Parties Review* 13: 86–106.

Shackleton, J. R. (1995) *Training for Employment in Western Europe and the United States* Aldershot: Edward Elgar.

Sharpe, L. J. (ed.) (1993) *The Rise of Meso-government in Europe* London: Sage.

Smith, A. (1996) *L'Europe au miroir du local: Les fonds structurels en France, en Espagne et au Royaume Uni* Paris: l'Harmattan.

Smith, A. (1997) 'Studying Multi-level Governance: Examples from French Translations of the Structural Funds' *Public Administration* 75:4, 711–29.

Stoker, G. (ed.) (2000) *The New Politics of British Local Governance* Basingstoke: Macmillan.

Stone, C. (1989) *Regime Politics: Governing Atlanta, 1946–1988* Lawrence KS: University Press of Kansas.

Storer, A. (2001) 'Confrontation and Consensus: The Economic Development Committee'. In J. B. Jones and J. Osmond (eds) *Inclusive Government and Party Management* Cardiff: Institute of Welsh Affairs, pp. 79–95.

Storer, A. and Parsons, N. (2003) 'Redundancy, Training and Employment in South Wales: The Case of Corus'. Unpublished paper.

Storper, M. (1997) *The Regional World: Territorial Development In A Global Economy* New York: Guildford.

Sullivan, M. (2002) 'Health Policy:Differentiation and Devolution'. In J. Adams and P. Robinson (eds) *Devolution in Practice: Public Policy Differences within the UK* London: Institute of Public Policy Research, pp. 60–68.

Todd, J. (2003) 'The British State since Devolution'. In J. Ruane, J. Todd and A. Mandeville (eds) *Europe's Old States in the New World Order: The Politics of Transition in Britain, France and Spain* Dublin: University of Dublin Press.

Trench, A. (2004) 'The Richard Commission'. Paper presented to the Institute of Welsh Affairs conference on 'Responding to Richard', Cardiff, April 2004.

Uguen, J.-L. and Urvoas, J-J. (1996) *La Bretagne électorale* Rennes: Apogée.

Van Deth, J. (ed.) (1998) *Comparative Politics: The Problem of Equivalence* London: Routledge.

Van Zanten, A. (2004) *Les Politiques de l'éducation* Paris: PUF.

Vion, A. (1996) 'Retour sur le terrain: la préparation des élections municipales de 1995 par l'équipe d'Edmond Hervé, maire de Rennes' *Sociétés Contemporaines* 24, 95–122.

Welsh Assembly Government (2003) *Iaith Pawb* Cardiff: Welsh Assembly Government.

Welsh Language Board (1999) 'A Strategy for the Welsh Language' Cardiff: Welsh Language Board.

Wieviorka, M. (ed.) (1997) *Une société fragmentée? Le multiculturalisme en débat* Paris: La Découverte.

Williams, C. H. (ed.) (2000) *Language Revitalization: Policy and Planning in Wales* Cardiff: University of Wales Press.

Williams, C. H. (2003) 'The National Assembly for Wales and Welsh Language planning'. Paper presented to the ESRC Conference on Regional Governance in Wales and Brittany, Cardiff University, Cardiff, 14 March.

Williams, D. (1961) *A Short History of Modern Wales* London: John Murray.

Worms, J-P. (1966) 'Le préfet et ses notables' *Sociologie de Travail* 3, 249–275.

Wright, V. (1996) 'The National Co-ordination of European Policy-making: Negotiating the Quagmire'. In J. Richardson (ed.) (1996) *European Union: Power and Policy-making* London: Routledge.

Wunder, B. (1995) 'Les influences du modèle napoléonien d'administration sur l'organisation administrative des autres pays' *Cahiers d'Histoire de l'Administration* Brussels: International Institute of Administrative Sciences, 9–24.

Wyn Jones, R. and Scully, R. (2004) 'Devolution in Wales: What does the Public Think?' ESRC Devolution and Constitutional Change Programme briefing no. 7, June, 4 pp.

Zeller, A. and Stussi, P. (2002) *La France enfin forte de ses régions* Paris: Gualino.